THE McKINLEY AND ROOSEVELT
ADMINISTRATIONS

THE MACMILLAN COMPANY
NEW YORK · BOSTON · CHICAGO · DALLAS
ATLANTA · SAN FRANCISCO

MACMILLAN & CO., LIMITED
LONDON · BOMBAY · CALCUTTA
MELBOURNE

THE MACMILLAN CO. OF CANADA, LTD.
TORONTO

THE
McKINLEY AND ROOSEVELT
ADMINISTRATIONS

1897–1909

BY

JAMES FORD RHODES, LL.D., D.Litt.

AUTHOR OF THE HISTORY OF THE UNITED STATES FROM THE
COMPROMISE OF 1850 TO THE FINAL RESTORATION OF HOME
RULE AT THE SOUTH IN 1877; HISTORICAL ESSAYS;
LECTURES ON THE AMERICAN CIVIL WAR
DELIVERED AT OXFORD; HISTORY
OF THE CIVIL WAR; FROM
HAYES TO McKINLEY

New York

THE MACMILLAN COMPANY

1922

All rights reserved

Norwood Press
J. S. Cushing Co. — Berwick & Smith Co.
Norwood, Mass., U.S.A.

22-22730

CONTENTS

CHAPTER I

CHAPTER II

CHAPTER III

THE McKINLEY AND ROOSEVELT
ADMINISTRATIONS

THE McKINLEY AND ROOSEVELT ADMINISTRATIONS

1897–1909

CHAPTER I

THIS volume naturally begins with the political campaign of 1896 during which three men absorbed public attention — McKinley, Bryan and Marcus Alonzo Hanna, or, as he was familiarly called and will be known in this book, Mark Hanna. Of McKinley and Bryan, up to 1896, the student of affairs will have had some idea, but Mark Hanna deserves an introductory notice before the last eight years of his crowded life are related. Called an enigma in New York City, he was no enigma whatever to his intimates, except that they failed to gauge his towering ability. They knew him for a shrewd money-getter, able and diligent in business, but they could not believe that he would reach a high position in public affairs — that during one administration he would be known as the "king maker" and during another the champion of the financial magnates against Theodore Roosevelt — that he would at least divide with Roose-

1

velt the allegiance of the Labor Unions. In all essentials except political ability he was no enigma to his friends, for he wore his heart upon his sleeve.

New York City is a good point of survey and from this point Hanna's appearance in public life was like that of a comet in the sky. Although fifty-nine years old in 1896, he had gradually, but with steady ambition, been working up to the place from which he was now to begin his most important achievements. His restless mind had always cast about for a new enterprise and, not being a student or reader of books, and having no sympathy with a man who devoted his whole ability to the acquirement of money, he entered the field of politics. Before he was thirty-two he made an informal alliance with an enterprising young man of Cleveland to break up the Republican machine that dominated city politics. Both were good Republicans but objected to the manner in which city affairs were conducted. Somewhat later when the Republican machine nominated one of their representative men for mayor, Hanna led a revolt against the machine and, with the aid of a number of independent associates, nominated a Democrat of excellent business ability and elected him[1] although the rest of the Republican ticket was chosen. In city and ward politics, he was always noted for his independent action and often showed no hesitation in supporting Democrats when they were better men than the Republican nominees.

At the age of forty-three he was recognized as one of the prominent business men of Cleveland. His business was coal, iron ore and pig iron; in 1867 he had been started in it by his father-in-law, an iconoclast in society and

---

[1] In 1873.

trade and an uncompromising Democrat in politics. Hanna's independence however did not come from any family association; it was inherent in himself and gained for him the dislike of the solid financial men of Cleveland, who had built up the city and were naturally the dominant figures in its financial circles. In spite of the dislike of these magnates, Hanna pushed ahead until in 1880, the year of the Garfield campaign, he was known as a reliable Republican and had acquired a very considerable local prominence. He was head and front of the business men's meetings in Cleveland and fully favored making the campaign on the tariff and business issue rather than on the "bloody shirt." Closely connected with the Pennsylvania railroad through business relations, he formed a link between that great organization and the candidate of his party, afterwards president-elect. From that time on he never lost an opportunity to identify himself with any Republican movement. Although he had never read Cicero, he shared the Roman's belief that he must keep himself constantly before the public.

Hanna was attracted to the Civil Service Reform movement and attended the meeting of local organization in Cleveland.[1] He had no hope of being the president of the Cleveland association, but he did aspire to the chairmanship of the Executive Committee. The organization was controlled by men who did not like Hanna and who entirely ignored him in their dispositions, not even awarding him the consolation of membership on the Executive Committee, of which he would have liked to be the directing head. From that night, Hanna must have argued, there is a ring of reformers as well as a ring

---

[1] Either in January or February, 1882.

of politicians. I think the politicians will suit me better.

His failure to secure election as district delegate to the Republican National Convention of 1884 and his subsequent success in being chosen delegate at large gave him an inkling of what was needed for political success. At the Convention he was an avowed supporter of John Sherman, whose candidacy met with little favor. He opposed Blaine, yet when the Convention named him as its candidate Hanna gained prominence in his party by his earnest and sincere efforts for Blaine's election; but no sooner was Blaine defeated than Hanna began to work for Sherman's nomination in 1888. Securing the unanimous support of Ohio, a portion of Pennsylvania and many delegates from the Southern States, he went to the Convention as a delegate confident of success. In my last volume I have told how Harrison's nomination came to be made but, soon after Sherman's defeat, Hanna realized that under certain circumstances McKinley might have been the man; accordingly he decided no longer to put his money upon the wrong horse and became an open advocate of McKinley's nomination for the next presidency. Between 1890 and 1892 Hanna had serious business troubles which, to a certain extent, distracted his attention from politics and he was not as powerful a factor in the Convention of 1892 as he had been four years before; he might have been thought to be losing his grip on politics but he was simply biding his time. After the astounding Republican victory in the election of 1894, he went to his younger brother, then a business partner, and told him that, for the future, he purposed giving more time to politics and less to business. Arrangements were

made with this end in view and thenceforward he gave
nearly his entire attention to securing the nomination of
McKinley in 1896.

Boston, apart from a few men in State Street, did not
like Hanna. His brusque manner, unconventional talk,
ignorance of literature and art alienated many, and he
did not always live up to the moral ideals in politics that
were professed in this city. The general opinion was
afterwards well stated by Henry S. Pritchett, a true West-
erner, although at that time living in Boston, the efficient
President of the Massachusetts Institute of Technology.
"The papers to-day," he said in a speech to the Bowdoin
Alumni Association on February 16, 1904, "have been full
of the life of an interesting man, who now lies dead in
Washington. He was a strong man, a man of noble parts,
of splendid personal power and of high ability for service
and he has played a great part as a leader in this country.
He deserves for all that high praise. And yet we can
never forget in estimating him as a public man that he
must be judged, not only for his high personal qualities
but also for the quality of his public service. One cannot
fail to regret in looking back over that life that it should
have carried with it the noble qualities of devotion, of
energy, of ability and of loyalty to a friend and yet have
not had with it also a higher level of what public service
means . . . and a higher estimate of moral and intellectual force rather than pecuniary force in politics." [1]

New York City and other communities may have had
their opinions influenced by the prevalent caricatures
which always have something to do with the formation
of public sentiment. Hanna once said that, although

---

[1] Boston *Herald*, Feb. 17, 1904.

his ancestry was Scotch-Irish there was more Irish than Scotch in his composition; thus with a plausible exaggeration of his features he was often portrayed as a bloated whiskey-drinking Irishman. A much-repeated cartoon showed him and McKinley sitting over a bottle of whiskey in earnest confabulation. These caricatures caused his friends no little amusement, so entirely were they unfounded in fact. Hanna drank no wine until he was past middle life, did not care for it, and used stronger liquors only for medicinal purposes. McKinley preferred water to wine at a banquet or dinner or any other occasion. Indeed, if the cartoonist had shown McKinley and Hanna, sitting calmly together over a bottle of Waukesha or Poland water drinking to the toast "Here's to honest water which ne'er left man i' the mire," he would have been much nearer the truth.

"I shall never forget," said Senator Scott of West Virginia, "one morning during the campaign of 1896 when Hanna handed me a New York paper containing a cartoon of himself pictured as a huge monster, clad in a suit covered over with dollar marks, smoking an immense cigar, and trampling under foot women and children until their eyes protruded from the sockets and their skeleton forms writhed in agony. After I had looked at it for a moment he said to me, 'That hurts.' " [1]

This was a favorite caricature, Hanna covered all over with the dollar mark, the implication being that he believed money could buy anything. The Nation wrote during the heated political campaign of 1908: "The frankly commercial spirit in which Mark Hanna managed the two campaigns in which he was chairman is no-

[1] Address, April 7, 1904, 39.

torious. A prominent and honored Ohio Republican has
said of Mr. Hanna that his only notion of political activity was 'to go out and buy somebody.' " [1] This remark,
born probably of factional hostility, was unjust. Hanna
paid the penalty of talking too frankly about the use of
money, but no one knew better than he that money would
not accomplish everything and, after he had gained power
and influence, nothing perturbed him more than to be
looked upon simply as an office-broker.

Collecting money for a political party must be regarded
differently from getting means for the support of a church,
a university or a charitable institution and, according
to the cynical view of politics that obtains in certain
quarters, the corruption of voters seems to inhere in the
use of the party chest. But many voters looked upon
the Republican party as something sacred, whose control
was necessary to the well-being and perpetuity of the
Republic. The man who raised money in order to insure
its continuance in power was looked upon by them as
doing holy work. Some such idea must have passed
through Hanna's mind when, without concealment, he
continually preached the use of money to save the party.

His outspoken scorn of bookish men and respect for
those who had money to contribute lent color to *The Nation's* criticism, but in this matter and in others Hanna
stood in need of a certain hypocrisy which was lacking
in his nature. Making no bones of confessing his ignorance of Shelley and Pasteur, he loved Shakespeare as he
saw his plays acted on the stage and took delight in a
good performance of "School for Scandal," in Joseph
Jefferson's "Rip Van Winkle," "Rivals" and "Cricket

---

[1] Oct. 8, p. 328.

on the Hearth." During the fifties when the Lyceum system was at its height, he was a constant attendant and liked above all the lectures of Ralph Waldo Emerson.

It is ordinarily thought that men in active life are apt to become victims of wine, woman or play. Judged by this standard, Hanna was a severely moral man who needed no refuge in the dictum of the preacher, "The moral man is he who is not found out." A generous giver of dinners, he was a spare eater except for an insatiable fondness for sweets to which his corpulence and rheumatism in later life were due. Loving the society of refined and well-bred women, he might be looked upon as a model of chastity. Passionately fond of cards, he preferred whist or bridge without a money stake; he never played draw poker except when a party for his favorite whist was unavailable and then only in what was known as a "small game." He had a pure mind, rarely told a smutty story and did not relish hearing one unless there was something in it that he thought clever. He was nevertheless rather undiscriminating in his response to humorous fancies and, though some of his intimates found in him an amusing companion, it was mainly his whole-hearted audacity that made them laugh. He gravitated toward the society of the best men. Amongst those one met at his dinner table in Washington were Root, Justice White, Taft, Long, O. H. Platt, Hobart, Allison, Aldrich and occasionally Secretary Hay and Senator Lodge.

Popular knowledge of a man of action who left few letters, did not keep a diary nor write a book depends largely upon his biographer and, in this respect, Hanna was exceptionally happy. His son selected Herbert Croly,

who made the work a labor of love and has presented the
real Mark Hanna with remarkable perspicacity and skill.
Some of Hanna's friends, on hearing of the selection, may
have shuddered at the thought of an author with socialistic proclivities undertaking the biography of a strong
individualist; yet the accomplished editor of the American Statesmen series had chosen Carl Schurz, an avowed
tariff reformer, to write the life of Henry Clay and the
wisdom of this selection had been fully demonstrated.
Even so was the choice of Herbert Croly to write the life
of Mark Hanna.   One may learn from that book what
manner of man was Hanna when he determined to bend
all his energies to the nomination of McKinley in 1896.

Hanna and McKinley were warm personal friends.
They had first met in 1876 in the Court House at Canton,
Ohio, where were being tried one miner for assault with
intent to kill and a number of others for being engaged
in a riot.   Hanna as head of his Coal Company was active
in prosecution and McKinley was one of the attorneys
of the Stark County bar who had volunteered for the
defence.   It was a trial in which bitterness developed on
both sides and McKinley won attention from the prosecution by his personal resemblance to Daniel Webster,
and by his gentle consideration for the men who had
deemed it their duty to prosecute the offending miners.
In the same autumn McKinley was elected to Congress
and by degrees he and Hanna became intimate acquaintances.   At the National Convention of 1884, they shared
an apartment at a hotel; their relations were cordial
although McKinley was for Blaine and Hanna for Sherman.   The Convention of 1888, when they both supported
Sherman, increased the mutual attachment.   Each saw

qualities in the other that drew them together and, as both were working for the same end, they were now in complete sympathy.

Hanna's admiration for McKinley was profound. He shared his belief in the protective tariff as something sacred and not to be touched by profane hands. A man put forward for the presidential nomination should lose no opportunity of seeing influential men in the several States and commending himself to them by his personal bearing. Once when Hanna had with some difficulty secured an assemblage of men to meet the prospective candidate in an Eastern city, McKinley sent regrets on account of the illness of an invalid wife. This, for the moment, irritated Hanna as he thought that the wife might in her chronic condition have been left to the care of a doctor and nurse, as she was by no means dangerously ill and that McKinley might have kept the engagement which would have been a signal aid to his candidacy. This misfortune seemed to Hanna a considerable obstacle in the path of McKinley's advancement yet he was so struck with the man's sublime devotion to his invalid wife that he could not help exclaiming, "McKinley is a saint."

Hanna "had not a single small trait in his nature," declared Roosevelt. " I never needed to be in doubt as to whether he would carry through a fight or in any way go back on his word."[1]

Hanna's friendship with Ben Butterworth embodied a rare unselfishness that dignified his strenuous and successful career. Croly prints some letters from Butterworth to Hanna that are charming in the devotion shown by

---

[1] Croly, 361.

him who stuck to the lesser man through thick and thin. Butterworth was of too independent and impulsive a nature to be successful in politics but his honest appearance and conduct gave him a standing with leaders that he seemed unable to acquire with the mass. When he was unsuccessful in politics Hanna redoubled his assistance and when at last he fell fatally ill Hanna watched by his bedside in a Cleveland hotel with the same devotion that he would pay to a brother.

The campaign for the nomination was proceeding apace when McKinley gave it a set-back through his own financial failure. He made himself liable by endorsements to help a friend for one hundred and thirty thousand dollars, a large sum in 1893 and an enormous one for the Governor of Ohio. He had no other idea than that the debt must be paid in full and it seemed to him as if the labor necessary to this end meant the close of his political career. But Hanna, Myron T. Herrick, H. H. Kohlsaat and many others came to his aid and saved him from bankruptcy. These facts were more or less publicly known and McKinley was reproached with having put himself in the power of these men by accepting financial favors for which they would expect repayment in some way. But it does not appear that any of them asked for consideration nor that anything was done for the raisers of the fund except for Hanna and Herrick who received McKinley's support on entirely different grounds.[1]

---

[1] In this characterization I have been helped by Life of Hanna, Herbert Croly; Mark Hanna, Solon Lauer, Cleveland, 1901; William Allen White's article, *McClure's Magazine*, Nov. 1900; Murat Halstead, *Review of Reviews*, Oct. 1896; the contemporary cartoons; many newspaper notices of Hanna's death in Feb. 1904. My son, Daniel P. Rhodes, was private secretary of Mark Hanna for a year and a half covering 1897 and a part of 1898; to him I owe a careful revision of this whole chapter.

Croly has related in sufficient detail Hanna's labor in securing the nomination of McKinley. From January 1, 1895, his whole attention was devoted to the work and everything that energy, social entertainment, political blandishment and the judicious use of money could accomplish was forthcoming in full measure. He spent, said Croly, "something over $100,000" (which would not now [1] be considered a large amount) obtaining almost no assistance from his friends. "Corrupt methods were always expressly and absolutely forbidden," wrote Croly, but when Hanna put in his own time and energy he could make a dollar go a great way, as he did in this case although he had opposed to him Quay and Thomas C. Platt, adepts in all the arts of political management, as well as a hearty New England backing of Thomas B. Reed who, by common consent, was well fitted for the place. Yet it was not Hanna's work alone that won the prize. McKinley, in capacity and manner, was well fitted for the White House; moreover, since 1893, affairs had been working his way. The panic of 1893 had been followed by a commercial crisis and business was extremely bad. The Republicans ascribed the evil condition to Democratic success and to the avowed promise of a reduction of the tariff. The tariff was reduced during the summer of 1894 and the autumn elections for Congressmen showed a complete change in public sentiment. It was natural that a distracted public should turn to the arch-protectionist for relief. McKinley was reëlected Governor of Ohio in 1893 by an increased majority [2] and in geographical and all other respects was an available candidate.

---

[1] 1919.   [2] For McKinley's first election see my vol. viii. 374.

Henry Clay said in the bitterness of his disappointment at failing to receive the Whig nomination in 1840,
"If there were two Henry Clays, one of them would make
the other President of the United States." [1]   But
McKinley's and Hanna's relations were so intimate that
Hanna might be called an alter-ego. What one could
not do, the other could. McKinley knew the men in
public life through and through, and Hanna learned how
to manipulate conventions and secure delegates; and he
thought that he was serving party and country well in
putting to the fore an arch-protectionist. By May 1,
1896, if not before, Hanna felt that McKinley's nomination was assured, but before the Convention met on
June 16 in St. Louis the question of platform was the
most important one, and the only portion on which there
was a marked divergence of opinion related to silver;
this difference grew as the time for the assembling of the
Convention approached. When the delegates began to
come together, the Committee on Resolutions, of which
Foraker was the chairman and Senator Lodge the Massachusetts member, had many declarations to consider but,
out of the confusion and heat of convention days, only
two resolutions are important for the historian; these
are the McKinley-Hanna resolution, which Hanna brought
with him to Chicago, and the resolution finally adopted
by the Convention, on which the canvass of 1896 was
made.

Both McKinley and Hanna were bimetallists. While
in Congress, McKinley had in 1877 and 1878 voted for
free silver, for the Bland-Allison bill and for its passage
over President Hayes's veto; but in his support of silver

[1] Schurz's Clay, ii. 181.

he was backed by both senators from Ohio and all the representatives except James A. Garfield. In the discussions of Garfield's course, which were of daily occurrence among business men in Cleveland, his dissenting voice was generally approved, but Hanna vigorously opposed his position and endorsed that of the other members, especially of the representative from Cleveland, who was a personal and political friend. Thus McKinley and Hanna had been favorable to silver for eighteen years when it fell to them to decide the issue on which the campaign of 1896 should be made. And they both, for obvious reasons to anyone who understands their political careers, desired to have the paramount issue the tariff, while silver should be relegated to a subsidiary place.

In 1896 in Ohio it was no disgrace to be a bimetallist. It was much easier to favor a single gold standard in New York or Boston; yet in Boston some of the most eminent statesmen, authors, business men and politicians, under the brilliant leadership of General Walker, had embraced the doctrine of silver and, though opposing the free coinage of the metal, were eager for its adoption as a money standard by international agreement. Between 1894 and 1896 many of these Bostonians were converted to a single gold standard although they still held to the fiction of international agreement which, as the wisest of them knew, was out of the question. This conversion was undoubtedly due to the great work of Grover Cleveland and while most Republicans would have spurned the idea of having been so influenced yet to the historian it appears that they were thus unconsciously swayed.

In the pre-Convention days in St. Louis the Eastern

men, whose leader may be said to have been Senator
Lodge, were eager for the mention of gold; many from
the Middle West desired a plank which could be interpreted as favoring gold in the East and yet not condemn-
ing silver in the West. The McKinley-Hanna resolution read: The Republican party "would welcome
bimetallism based upon an international ratio, but, until
that can be secured, it is the plain duty of the United
States to maintain our present standard, and we are therefore opposed under existing conditions to the free and
unlimited coinage of silver at sixteen to one." Before
these words, it spoke of "maintaining all the money of
the United States whether gold, silver or paper at par
with the best money in the world and up to the standard
of the most enlightened governments." The resolution
adopted by the Convention, which was agreed to by Senator Lodge and his associates, read: "We are opposed
to the free coinage of silver except by international agreement with the leading commercial nations of the world,
which we pledge ourselves to promote, and until such
agreement can be obtained the existing *gold* standard
must be preserved. All our silver and paper currency
must be maintained at parity with gold and we favor all
measures designed to maintain inviolably the obligations
of the United States and all our money, whether coin or
paper at the present standard, the standard of the most
enlightened nations of the earth." It is easy to see that
the controversy turned on a few words. Should the Republican party "maintain our present standard" or preserve "the existing *gold* standard"? To the historian
conversant with the action of Grover Cleveland, the difference does not seem great, but to the framer of platforms

and the campaigner it was immense. One resolution declared in favor of gold by name, the other did not; hence it turned out that the Republicans were known throughout the campaign as the party of gold, the Democrats as the party of silver. It is no wonder, then, that the adoption of this resolution is considered so important an episode in the history of the Republican party and of the country, and that so many lay claim to a paramount influence in securing its insertion.

When Hanna saw that, owing to the sentiment developed among the delegates, his own view could not prevail, he accepted the result gracefully and persuaded McKinley to do likewise. The Committee agreed on the financial plank and reported it to the Convention, which adopted it by a vote of 812½ to 110½. Before the adoption of this plank, Senator Teller of Colorado offered a substitute demanding the free coinage of silver but obtained only 105½ votes against 818½; this vote foreshadowed the adoption of the financial plank by nearly the same majority. After making some pathetic remarks, he, with thirty-three others, seceded from the Convention. The rest of the platform was then adopted by acclamation.[1]

McKinley was then nominated by 661½ votes, his leading opponent, Thomas B. Reed, receiving 84½. Garret A. Hobart of New Jersey was named for Vice President.

---

[1] Life of Hanna, Croly; Foraker, Notes of a Busy Life, i.; Charles Emory Smith, *Philadelphia Press*, June 24, 1896, cited by *Boston Daily Advertiser;* The Autobiography of T. C. Platt; MS. statement of Eben S. Draper, Chairman of the Mass. delegation, Jan. 9, 1900; H. H. Kohlsaat's story, *N. Y. Eve. Post*, April 30, 1910; Letter of Frank S. Witherbee, *N. Y. Eve. Post*, April 13, 1910; W. A. White, *McClure's*, Nov. 1900; Halstead in *Review of Reviews*, Oct. 1896; Lodge, Speeches and Addresses, 1900; Stanwood, Hist. of the Presidency.

On June 18 when McKinley was nominated, Republican success was deemed more than probable. Mark Hanna was made Chairman of the Republican National Committee but thought of taking a yacht cruise along the New England Coast to obtain a needed rest after "the great strain" imposed by the work resulting in McKinley's nomination. "I would have been glad," he wrote in a private letter, "to have escaped the responsibility of managing the campaign, but there was no way out of it and I feel that I am 'enlisted for the war' and *must* win." This letter was written on July 3 when Hanna had no idea that he had an easy victory before him; as between June 18 and July 3 public sentiment showed that the Republican party in identifying itself with gold had run the risk of losing some of the Western States. "I must get the work of education started," he said, " before I can take my necessary recreation." "The fight will be in the Mississippi Valley States," he added. "The 'gold' basis is giving us lots of work." [1]

The Democratic Convention in Chicago, meeting on July 7, defined the issue plainly between gold and silver and changed the hoped-for victory of the Republicans into a premonition of defeat. There were many indications that the Democrats would espouse the cause of free silver. Richard P. Bland of Missouri was their idol, leader and probable candidate for the presidency and he had publicly said that the Democracy of the West was convinced that "the gold standard meant bankruptcy" and that the Convention would declare for the "free coinage of silver at 16 to 1." [2] The delegates who were

---

[1] Letter from Cleveland.
[2] Twenty Years of the Republic, Peck, 492.

known as Cleveland men made a valiant fight, but their
financial plank was rejected by 303 to 626 and their endorsement of Cleveland's administration by 357 : 564.
During the discussion of the financial resolution, William
J. Bryan leaped into prominence through a speech that
carried the Convention. "Upon which side will the Democratic party fight," he asked, "upon the side of the idle
holders of idle capital or upon the side of the struggling
masses? . . . Having behind us the producing masses
of this nation and the world, supported by the commercial interests, the laboring interests and the toilers everywhere, we will answer their demand for a gold standard
by saying to them : 'You shall not press down upon the
brow of labor this crown of thorns, you shall not crucify
mankind upon a cross of gold.' " [1] The platform as reported by the Committee on Resolutions was adopted
by 628 to 301. It declared that, "Gold monometallism
is a British policy and its adoption has brought other
nations into financial servitude to London. . . . We
demand the free and unlimited coinage of both silver and
gold at the present legal ratio of sixteen to one without
waiting for the aid or consent of any other nation." [2]
Some of the other resolutions were judged to be "anarchistic"; they were certainly extremely radical for 1896.

Bryan's speech, especially the last clause of the last
sentence cited above, made him the Democratic candidate for the presidency.

"The Chicago convention has changed everything,"
wrote Hanna in a private letter on July 16. It has
knocked out my holiday and cruise along the New England coast. The campaign "will be work and hard work

---

[1] Bryan, The First Battle, 206.   [2] Stanwood, 542.

from the start. I consider the situation in the West quite alarming as business is all going to pieces and idle men will multiply rapidly. With this communistic spirit abroad the cry of 'free silver' will be catching." Both Hanna and McKinley felt that the Republican party was united on the tariff but divided on the silver question. During a conference, probably before Bryan's nomination, McKinley said, "I am a Tariff man standing on a Tariff platform. This money matter is unduly prominent. In thirty days you won't hear anything about it," when William R. Day [1] remarked, "In my opinion in thirty days you won't hear of anything else." [2] Even after the Chicago Convention, Hanna expressed himself as not wishing to allow the tariff issue to be overshadowed by the financial. [3] But the logic of events taught both McKinley and Hanna that a determined fight must be put up against free silver in the Western States; and in point of fact their belief in bimetallism, but only on an international basis, proved as effective in the conduct of the campaign as if they had been uncompromising advocates of the single gold standard.

The Republican secession affected the vote in some of the Western States but the Democratic "bolt" was more significant. It took two forms: one, the nomination of separate candidates for President and Vice President known as gold Democrats, and the other votes given directly to McKinley as the surest means of beating Bryan.

There is no question that business was much depressed and that many men were out of employment. The Republicans had hoped to charge this condition to the Dem-

---

[1] Now Justice of the United States Supreme Court (1919).
[2] Life of McKinley, Olcott, 321.   [3] Life of Foraker, i. 492.

ocratic administration and to the Tariff bill of 1894, and therefore McKinley, who represented protection more than any other man in the country, was the logical candidate. He was the "advance agent of prosperity" and promised the "full dinner pail"; prosperity was to be secured by a return to the protective tariff of the Republican party. On the other hand, the Bryan Democrats, though agreeing to the Republican estimate of present conditions, promised an entirely different remedy for the hard times, and proposed a different policy for reducing the army of the unemployed. Remonetize silver, coin it at the ratio of 16 to 1, stop measuring money by the English standard but increase its volume, they averred, and the distress of men in legitimate business and of honest laborers out of employment will disappear. The demonetization of silver enhanced the value of the circulating medium and was in the interest of the creditor; restore it to its proper place, they argued, and the augmented circulation will enable the debtor to pay his debts and start all the wheels of industry going.

Bryan proved an effective campaigner, although his first move was not successful. Determined to open the campaign in "the enemy's country" he formally accepted the nomination in a speech in Madison Square Garden, New York City. But he committed an error in reading the speech which he had carefully written out. For Bryan, though an orator, was a poor reader. Other conditions were against him. The weather, even for the second week of August, was extremely hot and the notification speech unduly long. The large audience who had expected to laugh at "his free Western sallies and audacities" found him "transformed into a Professor

Dryasdust prosing through two mortal hours. . . . No wonder that they fled before his portentous pile of manuscript with cries of 'Good-night, Billy.'" [1]

New York and other Eastern financial centres breathed a sigh of relief. They had been greatly alarmed at Bryan's stirring speech before his nomination and his short addresses on the way from Lincoln to New York City, but now they heard or read a dull economic argument, which could not carry conviction to thinking men and which utterly failed to rouse the proletariat. Depression at the fear that Bryan and his financial fallacies would carry the country was succeeded by a momentary and undue elation of the conservative forces.

But when Bryan began his trip through the country, his native ability as an orator and his sincere belief in the fallacies that he advocated gained him large audiences and shaped convictions. Farmers, obliged to accept a low price for their products, and laborers, who desired work but could not get it, were glad to learn that free silver was the one simple remedy for their trouble. The distress was indeed grave. If we subtract from Dr. Talmage's remarks what they contained of rhetorical exaggeration, an extract from his non-partisan sermon will give us an excellent idea. "Never within my memory," he said, "have so many people literally starved to death as in the past few months. Have you noticed in the newspapers how many men and women here and there have been found dead, the post-mortem examination stating that the cause of death was hunger? There is not a day when we do not hear the crash of some great

---

[1] *The Nation*, Aug. 20, 134.

commercial establishment and as a consequence many
people are thrown out of employment. Among what we
considered comfortable homes have come privation and
close calculation and an economy that kills. Millions
of people who say nothing about it are at this moment
at their wits' end. There are millions of people who do
not want charity but want work." [1]

Goldwin Smith, a keen observer, felt Bryan's "pre-
ternatural power of clap-trap declamation." [2] The Democratic National Committee coöperated skilfully with
their candidate and made their appeal for funds in an
attractive manner. Their pressing need was the hiring
of speakers and the distribution of documents "for the
dissemination of the truth." One hundred and twenty-
five thousand of "Coin's Financial School" were circulated, a device that showed how clever they were. This
little book was made up of addresses purporting to be
delivered daily to large Chicago audiences, that were
hereby instructed in the science of money by Coin, a
"smooth little financier." The fascination of his manner,
his ready argument, apparent fairness, cannot fail to
charm even the reader of to-day who knows that the
school was a fiction designed to serve as the subject of an
attractive book in which fallacious arguments might be
presented that would otherwise remain unheard. So this
amiable-looking little man was supposed to deliver six lectures from the platform of a large hall of the Art Institute; and these were attended fictitiously by men prominent in business and finance, who were argued with and
either convinced or refuted. This was not a difficult

---

[1] Sept. 27. The First Battle, Bryan, 474.
[2] *Sat. Rev.*, Oct. 31, 462.

task as the opponents were men of straw, and the sympathetic reader of the book was quite ready to believe that "the little financier could not be cornered."

England cannot always be defended, but it was unmerited ill-luck that her work in the cause of sound finance should be bandied about in the course of an excited political campaign. "Coin's Financial School" is illustrated with rude but effective wood-cuts and, when Cleveland or Sherman is lampooned, such illustrations can be considered only proper game; but the comity of nations is transcended when Uncle Sam is pictured firing a cannon to the utter discomfiture of England with the amiable little Coin standing by, doffing his silk hat to the hurrah, "What our answer to England should be." This sentiment he elaborated in his last lecture: "A war with England," he said, "would be the most popular war ever waged on the face of the earth. If it is true that she can dictate the money of the world and thereby create world-wide misery, it would be the most just war ever waged by man." [1]

To no better team could the defence of the financial honor of the country have been confided than to McKinley and Hanna. When they came to appreciate that the fight must be against free silver, they wrought like veterans in the cause. Hanna exerted his wonderful talent of organization and threw himself into the contest with unstinted energy. He raised the necessary funds. Soon gaining the confidence of New York City financial men, he obtained from them important contributions to his campaign. Some concerns were assessed by Hanna ac-

---

[1] Coin's Financial School, by W. H. Harvey, 150 pages and 64 illustrations. Popular edition, 25 cents; Cloth, $1.00. This book sold well.

cording to what he conceived to be their financial interest in the canvass, a uniform assessment of one quarter of one per cent being levied on the banks. He systematized the expenditure and had the books kept on true business principles. The Republican National Committee spent between three and three and a half millions and had also in reserve a guarantee fund which was not called upon.

Hanna early perceived that this was to be a campaign of education. Six hundred thousand dollars were spent for documents that were printed in German, French, Spanish, Italian, Swedish, Norwegian, Danish, Dutch and Hebrew, as well as English; among those which were carefully distributed were Sherman's, Carlisle's and McKinley's speeches. The *New York Evening Post's* Free Coinage Catechism was much in demand and gladly supplied. It was written by Alexander D. Noyes, the *Post's* financial editor, and two million copies of it were circulated. Carl Schurz was induced to enter the canvass on behalf of McKinley, and one million and a half copies of a clear and convincing speech of his were scattered abroad. This speech lent itself to sententious quotations; hence the leaflets called Schurz nuggets that were placed before many readers. Innumerable speakers of lesser note presented the case against free silver. Men in every county of the pivotal Western States were supplied with sound money literature; and, as they could not give their time for nothing, they were hired to read and explain the pamphlets and talk to the few or many who might gather at the school-houses or other places of resort to hear expounded the political issue of the day. Probably the most effective speaker in gaining votes was McKinley himself. Declining to emulate Bryan in his "whirlwind tour," he spoke from the front veranda of his house in Canton to many deputations, some of them spontaneous, others arranged for, discussing mainly the financial question.   He almost always knew what the visiting spokesman was going to say so that he was often able to revise his own address beforehand.   These speeches of McKinley's were carefully prepared, as he well knew that he was addressing the newspaper-reading public of the whole country as well as the men who had travelled some distance to greet their candidate in person.   Close students of the art of guiding public sentiment assert that people will often read in the newspaper a speech that has been orally delivered while they pass by an essay or letter in the same type and given the same prominence.   McKinley's efforts were called his "front porch"[1] speeches and, in their general tenor were of a piece with the formal letter of acceptance that was given to the public on August 26. Acknowledging that the money question was the chief issue of the campaign he gave it the first and most prominent place in his letter.   "The meaning of the coinage plank adopted at Chicago," he wrote, "is that anyone may take a quantity of silver bullion, now worth fifty-

---

[1] John Hay said in his Memorial Address on McKinley delivered in the Capitol at Washington on Feb. 27, 1902: "From the front porch of his modest house in Canton he daily addressed the delegations which came from every part of the country to greet him in a series of speeches so strong, so varied, so pertinent, so full of facts briefly set forth, of theories embodied in a single phrase, that they formed the hourly text for the other speakers of his party and give probably the most convincing proof we have of his surprising fertility of resource and flexibility of mind. All this was done without anxiety or strain. I remember a day spent with him during that busy summer. He had made nineteen speeches the day before; that day he made many. But in the intervals of these addresses he sat in his study and talked, with nerves as quiet and free from care as if we had been spending a holiday at the seaside or among the hills."

three cents, to the mints of the United States, have it coined at the expense of the Government and receive for it a silver dollar which shall be legal tender for the payment of all debts, public and private. . . . Until international agreement is had, it is the plain duty of the United States to maintain the gold standard. It is the recognized and sole standard of the great commercial nations of the world with which we trade more largely than with any other. Eighty-four per cent of our foreign trade for the fiscal year 1895 was with gold standard countries and our trade with other countries was settled on a gold basis." Addressing himself to the argument that the "present industrial and financial depression was the result of the gold standard," he declared, "Good money never made times hard."

Hanna had a high opinion of the influence of the Fourth Estate and knew the hold that the weekly county journals had on their readers. He sent them specially prepared matter, plates and ready prints. It was fortunate that nearly all of the large daily newspapers, whether Democratic or Republican, were ardent advocates of the cause of sound money; copies of these were industriously distributed. "Of course," wrote Croly, "cartoons, posters, inscriptions and buttons were manufactured by the carload — the most popular poster being the five-colored, single-sheet lithograph, bearing a portrait of McKinley with the inscription underneath, 'The Advance Agent of Prosperity.'" [1]

During August Hanna was somewhat staggered by the poll of Iowa which indicated that this sure Republican State would cast her electoral vote for Bryan. Yet ad-

---

[1] P. 218.

mitting, for the moment, that Iowa must be placed in the doubtful column, he was still confident of McKinley's election, believing that at the worst it would be a close shave, while he really hoped for a stampéde. At any rate, the campaign was to him too serious a matter for any phase of it to be left to chance; indeed, he and McKinley had decided that, if matters got desperate, McKinley should take the stump in Illinois, Indiana, Michigan, Iowa and Kansas.

The Methodist, the Roman Catholic and the other churches were mainly on the side of sound money and many preachers did not hesitate to bring politics into the pulpit during their Sunday exhortations. Nature gave a welcome help to Hanna in an advance in the price of wheat. Now do something for corn came a witty demand from the Indian corn-growing States.

To Bryan's oratory more than to any other one cause was due the impression that the campaign was one of the masses against the classes. Some of the resolutions of the Chicago platform were deemed anarchistic [1] and influenced votes against Bryan who thought it wise to deny the imputation. "We have been called anarchists," he said. "I am not an anarchist. There is not beneath the flag a truer friend of government or a greater lover of law and order than the nominee of the Chicago convention." [2] It is difficult to describe with strict impartiality a heated political campaign in one's own country and one's own time, but a keen observer from England should have been able to view the events of 1896 with a comparative lack of bias. "I have never thought the Republic in [such] serious peril as I do now," wrote Gold-

---

[1] *Ante.*   [2] Speech in Baltimore during September, 463.

win Smith, "when I see the organization of the Democratic party captured by Anarchism and Repudiation. Bimetallism, you will understand, is the least part of the matter; even Repudiation is not the greatest. The greatest is the uprising of disorder, in all its forms and grades against the institutions of the American Republic. . . . Bryanism is a vast cave of Adullam, in which are combined all the distressed, all the discontented, all who have nothing to lose and may hope to gain by a general overturn. . . . In November the Republic of the Fathers will be fighting for its life." [1]

During October the stampede to McKinley took place. General J. D. Cox, who was then living in Cincinnati, Ohio, wrote on October 26 in a private letter: "When I went East in June I am sure nine-tenths of the Ohio Republicans were ardent bimetallists, with more leaning to free silver than to gold monometallism. Now nearly every man seems to rival his neighbor in putting gold forward as the single standard. . . . The claim of Republican managers that there is a 'landslide' going on in McKinley's favor, I assume to be sufficiently true to warrant a confident expectation of his election."

Bryan made a wonderful canvass, travelling 18,000 miles and addressing audiences almost every day. The mere fact of his bearing the physical strain he was undergoing and the eagerness of people to see and hear this famous orator must have counted in his favor. [2]

---

[1] *Saturday Review*, Aug. 1, Sept. 5, Oct. 31.

[2] In this account of the campaign of 1896, I have been assisted by Croly's Life of Hanna; Olcott's Life of McKinley; Bryan, The First Battle; Peck; Stanwood, Hist. of the Presidency; *The Nation, passim;* Goldwin Smith's articles in the *Saturday Review;* Foraker, Notes of a Busy Life, i.; Conversations with Mark Hanna, Aug. 23, Dec. 20.

On Tuesday, November 3, nearly fourteen millions voted. McKinley was triumphantly elected. He was to receive 271 electoral votes to Bryan's 176, a majority of 95. His plurality in the popular vote was somewhat over six hundred thousand. "No President since U. S. Grant," wrote Croly, "entered office supported by so large a proportion of the American people as did William McKinley." [1] Bryan congratulated McKinley on his election and the successful candidate made a graceful reply.

McKinley carried the New England States, New York, New Jersey and Pennsylvania by large majorities. The Middle Western States gave him their electoral votes. He invaded the solid South, carrying Delaware, Kentucky, West Virginia and Maryland, Maryland by an imposing plurality. Bryan carried Kansas and Nebraska, all the mining States except California, and also Washington, while Oregon voted for McKinley. North Dakota did likewise, while South Dakota gave her electoral vote to Bryan by a small plurality. Ohio, the State of McKinley and Hanna, was a disappointment to the Republicans. While they never regarded seriously the boasts of the Bryanites that they would carry the State, yet her plurality, being less than that of Michigan and about one third that of Illinois, showed that Ohio was somewhat uncertain. For, in the August forecast, Michigan was set down as very doubtful and, while Illinois was considered less doubtful, she was not regarded, like Ohio, as safe beyond peradventure for McKinley.

---

[1] P. 227.

CHAPTER II

AFTER the election of McKinley, Mark Hanna occupied an enviable position. Had it been usual, the freedom of Cleveland would have been conferred upon him. "He can own this city," said an enthusiastic financial adherent. "What a glorious record Mark Hanna has made this year!" wrote John Hay in a private letter. "I never knew him intimately until we went into this fight together, but my esteem and admiration for him have grown every hour. He is a born general in politics, perfectly square, honest and courageous with a *coup d'œil* for the battle-field, and a knowledge of the enemy's weak points which is very remarkable. I do not know whether he will take a share in the government, but I hope he will." [1] McKinley desired him to accept a Cabinet position and for a while he revolved in his mind whether he would not take the post of Secretary of the Treasury, a place which he was entitled to and which he would have admirably filled. On looking into the matter, however, he found the routine and confinement of the office objectionable ; more-over, he aspired after the senatorship from his State — an office that would give him the influence he desired to exert, and yet effectually preserve his independence. Therefore he made public the declaration that he would accept no office from the McKinley administration.

---

[1] Croly, 228.

Hanna did not appreciate that this statement would rise up to plague him. For he had conceived the idea of inducing the President to appoint Senator John Sherman Secretary of State and of being appointed by the Governor of Ohio to succeed him for his unexpired term in the Senate [March 4, 1899]. During his many interviews and conferences with McKinley he canvassed the matter, with the result that on January 4, 1897, the President-elect offered to Sherman the position of Secretary of State in his administration, and this was promptly accepted.[1] The course of events gave efficient support to those who wished to attack McKinley and Hanna, as it demonstrated that the appointment was utterly unfit owing to mental failure on the part of the Secretary of State. The critics averred that Sherman had given way to unusual excitement, both on the floor of the Senate and in a newspaper interview, that his memory had been failing for two or three years, that this fact was so presented to Hanna and McKinley that they ought to have recognized it, staying their hands from such procedure; that it was in short, a case of an aged statesman being "kicked upstairs" to make a place for Mark Hanna. Sherman himself, after the resignation of the office of Secretary of State [April 25, 1898] by newspaper interview and private letter, confirmed this criticism. "No doubt," he wrote confidentially on November 8, 1898, "I ought to have remained in the Senate during my term, which would not have expired until the 4th of March next. At that time I regarded McKinley as a sincere and ardent friend, whom I had assisted and whose election I had promoted. When

---

[1] Life of McKinley, Olcott, 329.

he urged me to accept the position of Secretary of State, I accepted with some reluctance and largely to promote the wishes of Mark Hanna. The result was that I lost the position both of Senator and Secretary. . . . They deprived me of the high office of Senator by the temporary appointment as Secretary of State." [1]

Wisdom after the event is the source of much criticism, and so it is in this case when the well-meant plan of Hanna and McKinley turned out badly. Hanna had twice supported Sherman for the presidential nomination, and had a high idea of his wisdom, not only in finance but in foreign affairs; seeing something of his work as chairman of the Committee on Foreign Relations in the Senate, he admired his clear comprehension and effective statement, and as he felt in a measure responsible for the success of the McKinley administration, he really thought that he was contributing to it by helping Sherman to the leading place in the Cabinet. His attitude to the stories that came to him regarding Sherman's mental failure was characteristic; he had such confidence in Sherman's ability and so desired the succession to the Senate that he did not believe the stories, even though some of them must have been endorsed by his New York financial friends to whom he had been drawn closely by the exigencies of the political campaign. He knew Sherman well socially; was aware that he had always been temperate in eating and drinking, moderate in all of his pleasures and, although nearly 74, could not see that there

---

[1] Notes of a Busy Life, Foraker, i. 508. Sherman died in 1900. This letter was handed to Foraker by General Miles, March 1, 1902, but was not printed until the first edition of this book, which was published in February, 1916.

was any reason for thinking, apart from the stories that were afloat, that he might not be physically and mentally fit for six years to come. *The Nation*, which became a severe critic of the appointment, said in an editorial on August 20, 1896: "Senator Sherman can make a good speech when he tries to do so. His speech at Columbus on Saturday was one of the best he has ever made." [1]

McKinley's first impression against Sherman's appointment was entirely different from the result. The Senator was generally considered as the leader of his party in his State and McKinley feared that on account of his masterfulness he would wish to dominate the administration. It is not surprising, therefore, that with this idea fixed in his mind McKinley should have made little account of the reports that he heard of Sherman's mental failure and should write to Joseph Medill on February 8, 1897: "I concur in your opinion that the stories regarding Senator Sherman's 'mental decay' are without foundation and the cheap inventions of sensational writers or other evil-disposed or mistaken people. When I saw him last [this was January 15, 1897] I was convinced both of his perfect health physically and mentally, and that his prospects of life were remarkably good." [2]

Sherman was glad to accept the Secretaryship of State. He exchanged two years in the Senate with a doubtful succession for apparently a four years' tenure of the Cabinet head of the new Republican administration, which was undoubtedly a promotion. It was not unusual, however, for Senators to decline Cabinet appoint-

---

[1] P. 134; see also June 24, 1897.
[2] Life of McKinley, Olcott, i. 334.

ments, and it was open to Sherman to do so, but as matter of fact the prospect was attractive. He had enjoyed himself in the Treasury Department under Hayes, having great influence with the President and he might well have thought that a similar experience now awaited him.

The important question was, would Governor Asa Bushnell appoint Hanna? The two belonged to different factions in the Republican party in Ohio and there was no love lost between them. Sherman used his influence to get the Governor to name Hanna as his successor, and the President-elect wrought powerfully in his friend's behalf. Nevertheless the Governor did not want to appoint a factional enemy and he authorized his personal and political friend, Joseph B. Foraker, to offer the place to Theodore E. Burton of Cleveland, then a Representative in Congress who, however, declined it. During the first part of February, McKinley must have despaired of the carrying out of this part of the program, as he still urged Hanna to accept a Cabinet position, writing to him on February 18, 1897, "I have hoped, and so stated to you at every convenient opportunity, that you would yet conclude to accept the Postmaster-Generalship." The Treasury was no longer at the President-elect's disposal, as on January 28 he had authorized the announcement that he had selected for that post Lyman J. Gage of Chicago.[1] "You have as often declined," McKinley continued in this letter to Hanna, "and since our conversation on Tuesday last (February 16) I have reluctantly concluded that I cannot induce you to take this or any other

---

[1] *The Nation*, Feb. 4.

Cabinet position. You know how deeply I regret this determination and how highly I appreciate your life-long devotion to me. You have said that if you could not enter the Senate you would not enter public life at all."

Those who like to consider the "might have been" may conjecture whether, if Hanna had even now decided to go into the Cabinet, McKinley would have induced Sherman to withdraw his acceptance of the office of Secretary of State on the ground that he would prefer not to have two men from Ohio in his Cabinet? In which event he would have appointed as Secretary of State a man flatly opposed to a warlike intervention in favor of Cuba, as at that time McKinley was himself.

Hanna, more persistent than McKinley, had no idea of giving up the game. Bushnell was a candidate for the Republican nomination for Governor who would be elected in the autumn of 1897, and, if he failed to appoint Hanna Senator, he would jeopardize materially his chance of nomination. Finally, through fear of failing to receive the renomination he desired, and from the unmistakable sentiment in the Republican party in Ohio that Hanna should have the place, he determined to appoint his ancient enemy, and wrote to him on February 21, "I wish to communicate to you my conclusion to appoint you as the successor of Senator Sherman when his resignation shall have been received." [1]

William McKinley was inaugurated on March 4, 1897, and in his address made clear the immediate policy of the

[1] Life of Hanna, Croly, 240. This book has been used freely in this account. Also Foraker, Notes of a Busy Life, i.; Life of McKinley, Olcott; John Sherman, Theodore E. Burton; do. W. S. Kerr, ii.; The Nation, passim.

government.[1] There were "depression in business, distress among the people." The government needed more revenue and ought to get it by an increase in tariff taxation. On this point he spoke to a united party and had Congress and Republicans with him; to carry out this purpose he summoned an extra session for March 15.

The position which McKinley took need not have surprised anyone; nevertheless, the gold Democrats who had supported him were disappointed that he did not put the money question to the fore and advocate legislation which should fix by law permanently the gold standard; this development received fit expression in the speeches of ex-President Cleveland and ex-Secretary Carlisle at the New York City Reform Club dinner of April 24. Cleveland could speak with authority, as he was the hero of the gold standard even as McKinley was the apotheosis of a protective tariff. And Cleveland and his Cabinet had given McKinley a hearty welcome, unusual in a change of one party administration to its opponent. But McKinley was wiser than his critics in declaring that the securing of adequate revenue must precede financial legislation. So far as finance was concerned he must endeavor to effect international bimetallism; until that was decided, the existing gold standard would be maintained. The President knew that no act such as he desired could pass the existing Senate, and his foresight was confirmed by that body adopting, within less than a year, a resolution which declared that the principal and interest of the government bonds were payable in silver dollars at the option

---

[1] The Inaugural Address is printed in Cong. Record, xxx. Pt. 1. For McKinley's Cabinet, see Peck, 521.

of the administration.[1] McKinley made a sincere attempt to obtain international bimetallism but, when Great Britain blocked the way,[2] he appreciated that business in the United States must be conducted on the single gold standard. In the attempt to secure this by proper legislation, he said, in a confidential talk with Senator Hanna and Secretary Alger on one of the last evenings of August, 1897, the Republican party may go down and I may go down with it but, after that temporary sacrifice, the Republican party devoted to such a noble cause will rise again.

Everything was in proper shape to enact a protective tariff to take the place of the Democratic Act of 1894. It had been tacitly agreed that Thomas B. Reed should be reëlected Speaker of the new House, and Nelson Dingley, also of Maine, should be chairman of the Committee on Ways and Means; this tacit agreement was at once carried into effect. This Committee, which was substantially the same as that of the preceding Congress, had at that session, after hearing abundant testimony, prepared a tariff bill which was now introduced into the House and passed on March 31. The Senate offered many amendments and did not pass their bill until July 7, when it went to a Committee of conference whose report was adopted by the House on July 19 by yeas 187, nays 116, and by the Senate on July 24 by yeas 40, nays 30 ; on this day the President signed it and it became a law.

"We expect," Dingley had written in a private letter, "to cut nearly all our duties considerably below those of

---

[1] Life of McKinley, Olcott, i. 358. It was a concurrent resolution. It passed the Senate by a vote of 47 : 32 on Jan. 28, 1898, and was rejected by the House on Jan. 31, the vote standing 133 : 181.   [2] Ibid., 355.

the Act of 1890." [1] To no better man could the tariff bill have been confided. No one in public life, except McKinley and Senator Aldrich, understood the subject better. For Dingley, it was a labor of love, and with the assistance especially of Sereno E. Payne of New York and John Dalzell of Pennsylvania, fellow members of the Committee, he presented to the House "a fairly good protectionist measure." [2] As showing the confidence felt in him by the President, he had been offered the Treasury Department which, on account of a question of health, he had declined, but saying at the same time that he could do more for the success of the administration as chairman of the Committee on Ways and Means than he could in the Treasury. [3] The measure is quite properly called the Dingley Act and is so known in history.

When Nelson W. Aldrich of Rhode Island reported the bill from the Senate Committee on Finance, he said that it was "thoroughly understood throughout the country in the last political campaign, that if the Republican party should be again entrusted with power, no extreme tariff legislation would follow." [4] Dingley and Aldrich expressed the idea of the Republican leaders and, while the House was readily controlled by the power of the Speaker Thomas B. Reed, it was quite different when the tariff question was opened up in the Senate. It was as John Sherman had previously said, "When Republicans and Democrats together are framing a tariff, each Member or Senator consults the interest of his 'district' or State." [5]

---

[1] Tarbell, Tariff in Our Time, 242.   [2] Ibid., 243.
[3] Life and Times of Nelson Dingley, 413.
[4] Stanwood, American Tariff Controversies, ii. 384.
[5] Recollections, ii. 1085.

Copyright by Courtney.

A feature of the case in hand is told by Edward Stanwood, "The plans of the Republican leaders were overturned . . . by senators who were more in favor of silver than of a protective tariff." [1] The Dingley Act, when it became a law, had rates of duty higher than they had been under any preceding tariff.[2] The McKinley Act was a $49\frac{1}{2}$ per cent tariff, the Wilson, 40 to $41\frac{3}{4}$, while the percentage of the Dingley Act ran from $49\frac{7}{8}$ to 52.[3]

McKinley enjoyed the first few months of his presidential life more than the later ones. As he did the honors of the White House, he appeared to have lived there always, so well did he fit into the place. He had a genuine liking for his predecessor. "Fine old fellow, wasn't he?" was a not uncommon remark to his Secretary. Alive to the power and influence of the presidential office, he said to Cleveland as they drove together to the Capitol on Inauguration Day, "What an impressive thing it is to assume tremendous responsibilities!" [4] And Cleve-

---

[1] Stanwood, ii. 386.   [2] Ibid., 391.

[3] Noyes, Amer. Finance, 269.

The Dingley Act reimposed the duties on wool; brought about a duty on hides that had been on the free list since 1872; imposed lower duties on cotton goods than those of 1890 but higher on silks and linens; restored the rates on chinaware of 1890. Iron ore was dutiable at 40¢, pig iron at $4, steel rails $7.84 per ton, the same as in 1894. Tin plate under the Act of 1890 paid 2¼¢, in 1894, 1¼¢, and in 1897, 1½¢ per pound. On sugar the differential was the same as under the act of 1894. "But the moral effect was very different. The House in 1897 had adopted the plan of leaving things as they were and had successfully resisted the effort of the refining monopoly to secure more." — Taussig. Tariff History, 5th ed., 328, 332, 335, 336, 342, 347, 352. See also correspondence in Life and Times of Dingley, 424 et seq.

"The Dingley Act restored the duty on works of art, free under the Tariff of 1894." — Tarbell, 243. "European travellers could bring in free only one hundred dollars worth of goods bought abroad." — Dingley, 443. "The tariff of 1897 like that of 1890 was the outcome of an aggressive spirit of protection." — Taussig, 358.

[4] Olcott, ii. 367.

land returned the liking and respect. "McKinley was distinguished, great and useful," he declared in his Memorial address at Princeton, "patriotic and faithful as a soldier, honest and upright as a citizen, tender and devoted as a husband and truthful, generous, unselfish, moral and clean in every relation of life."[1]

Cleveland and Olney had negotiated "a treaty for the arbitration of all matters in difference between the United States and Great Britain" which Cleveland had transmitted to the Senate during January, 1897, where it was pending when McKinley took the oath of office. Believing that politics should cease at the water's edge, he took the rather unusual course of approving emphatically a treaty negotiated by a preceding administration, which was that of a partisan opponent. "We want no wars of conquest," McKinley said in his inaugural address; "we must avoid the temptation of territorial aggression. War should never be entered upon until every agency of peace has failed; peace is preferable to war in almost every contingency. Arbitration is the true method of settlement of international as well as local or individual differences. . . . Since this treaty [the Olney-Pauncefote treaty of Jan. 11, 1897] is clearly the result of our own initiative, since it has been recognized as the leading feature of our foreign policy throughout our entire national history — the adjustment of difficulties by judicial methods rather than by force of arms — and since it presents to the world the glorious example of reason and peace, not passion and war, controlling the relations between two of the greatest nations of the world, an example certainly to be followed

---

[1] This address was delivered on Sept. 19, 1901, Andrew F. West, *Century Magazine*, Jan., 1909.

by others, I respectfully urge the early action of the Senate thereon, not merely as a matter of policy but as a duty to mankind. The importance and moral influence of the ratification of such a treaty can hardly be overestimated in the cause of advancing civilization." [1] The Senate acted on the treaty but failed to ratify it, the vote on May 5, 1897, standing 43, to 26, less than the necessary two thirds. The result was a disappointment to the President and his intimate friends.

McKinley felt fully competent to deal with the tariff, which was one of the absorbing questions during his first months in the White House, and he gave efficient aid to the supporters of the Dingley Act. The Cuban question troubled him from the first. With Cleveland at the White House on the evening before his inauguration, he manifested the subject uppermost in his mind — the threatened conflict with Spain and the horrors of war. "Mr. President," he said, "if I can only go out of office at the end of my term, with the knowledge that I have done what lay in my power to avert this terrible calamity, with the success that has crowned your patience and persistence, I shall be the happiest man in the world." [2] Sherman's failure disturbed him, but during April [3] he called to his aid William R. Day as Assistant Secretary of State. Day had inherited his essential qualities from his father who was of fine subtle fibre all through and a retiring nature. [4] William R. Day was a fellow practitioner

---

[1] Moore, International Law Digest, vii. 75 et seq.
[2] Parker's Rec., 249.
[3] 1897. Day was nominated April 24. The nomination was not received in the Senate until May 3. He was confirmed on the same day.
[4] Riddle, Rec., 234.

of McKinley at the Canton, Ohio, bar, and was known by the President as one comes to know one's daily associates and competitors. The two now wrought together in entire harmony and, so far as one may judge by the diplomatic correspondence, foreign relations did not suffer from the defection of Sherman. Sherman, however, could not brook his relegation to an inferior place and he therefore resigned on April 25, 1898, leaving Day the nominal as well as the real Secretary of State.[1] For a long while McKinley thought that he could settle the Cuban question without war and that he would have the country at his back, but he was hampered in the choice of a minister to Spain. He wanted Seth Low, and he thought that he might have persuaded him to undertake the difficult job could he have induced him to visit Washington. His next choice fell upon General J. D. Cox, an admirable appointment, who for personal reasons was obliged to decline it. McKinley would have liked John W. Foster, but finally he named Stewart L. Woodford[2] whose work turned out much better than might have been expected.

From his inauguration to the assembling of Congress at its regular session in December, 1897, McKinley tasted the sweets of office. After the adjournment of Congress on July 24, he took a trip East, stopping at a hotel on the New York side of Lake Champlain. One day he crossed over into Vermont and was struck with the sturdy patriotism of the men of the Green Mountain State and their devotion to Republican party ideals. Returning to his own State, he paid a memorable visit to Mark Hanna,

---

[1] Day was nominated as Secretary of State and confirmed on April 26, 1898.

[2] Woodford was nominated on June 16, 1897.

whose hospitality he enjoyed for a number of days, meeting men connected with his administration and Republicans whom he looked to for countenance and support. Of a genial nature and possessing attractive manners, he commended himself to all sorts and conditions of men and, at this time, might sincerely have felt that his influence was second to that of no other man in the country.

CHAPTER III

McKINLEY's opinion expressed to Cleveland regarding his treatment of Cuban affairs was thoroughly sincere, and at this distance may be justified. "Patience and persistence" were well applied to Cleveland's and Olney's management. The Cuban insurrection began in February, 1895, and failed to be suppressed by a humane governor-general who conducted the war in accordance with civilized usage. He was succeeded less than a year later by Weyler, who adopted at once drastic methods, the most important of which was his proclamation requiring a concentration of inhabitants at military headquarters in the provinces still under his control. To require people to quit their plantations and villages where they might secure a living and herd together in towns subject to starvation and disease was extreme cruelty and deserved McKinley's statement that "it was not civilized warfare" but "extermination." [1]

During the spring of 1896, both Houses of Congress adopted a concurrent resolution declaring that in their opinion the United States should accord to the insurgents belligerent rights [2] but Cleveland and his Secretary

[1] Annual Message, Dec. 6, 1897. "The cruel policy of concentration was initiated February 16, 1896" — ibid. See The Relations of the United States and Spain, Diplomacy, Chadwick, 431. This valuable book will be referred to as Chadwick.

[2] The Resolution as finally passed, April 6, 1896, declared that the United States should be strictly neutral granting belligerent rights to both parties and that the president should offer the friendly offices of the United States to Spain for the recognition of the independence of Cuba. The resolution as passed was the Senate one. The milder one of the House was rejected by the Senate and the House receded.

44

of State Olney declined to act in accordance with this advice, not deeming that the insurgents had acquired a condition of proper belligerency. In his last Message to Congress, Cleveland told clearly the actual state of affairs. While Spain held "Havana and the seaports and all the considerable towns, the insurgents still roam at will over at least two thirds of the inland country. . . . If Spain has not yet reëstablished her authority, neither have the insurgents yet made good their title to be regarded as an independent state. . . . The excesses on both sides have become more frequent and more deplorable. . . . The rural population is required to concentrate itself in the towns." The industrial value of the island, consisting very largely in its capacity to produce sugar, was fast diminishing. In most of Cuba a state of anarchy existed, where property was no longer protected and life was unsafe. Despite the avowed sympathy of the inhabitants of the United States, the number of resident Cubans ready to help their brother insurgents, and the utter ruin threatening a neighboring and fertile country, our obligations to Spain, so Cleveland asserted, had been duly observed. But he uttered a note of warning when he said that a situation may be presented "in which our obligations to the sovereignty of Spain will be superseded by higher obligations." [1]

Reviewing carefully the last two years of Cleveland's administration, his conduct and that of his Secretary of State Olney in regard to Cuba merit commendation; they might easily have brought on a war with Spain.

The Cuban question was inherited by McKinley. The

---

[1] Message of Dec. 7, 1896.

Senate at the special session called in March, 1897, passed a resolution in favor of recognizing the belligerency of the Cuban insurgents, but it was never acted upon by the House, as Speaker Reed had not appointed a Committee on Foreign Affairs to which it should properly be referred. Anarchy in Cuba continued. In the destruction of property and disregard of life, the insurgents were equally to blame with the Spaniards. "The deliberate destruction of the support of a people," wrote Chadwick, "shown in the orders of Gomez [the insurgent leader] are deep stains upon the conduct of the Cuban cause." A large number of sugar mills were wrecked and this wreckage involved deprivation of work, and consequent suffering and death to vast numbers of working people. "Historic truth," Chadwick added, "demands the setting forth of the fact that Cuban and Spaniard were alike regardless of the misery caused by their methods and of its extent." [1]

During the summer and autumn of 1897, McKinley gave the subject much anxious thought which was apparent in his first annual Message to Congress. He referred with elation to the performance of its full duty according to the law of nations by the United States. The Government had "successfully prevented the departure of a single military expedition or armed vessel from our shores in violation of our laws." He argued against the recognition of the belligerency or the independence of Cuba and did not deem it wise to intervene for the present in the contest. Rather should we await the result of the entire change of policy promised by the new ministry in Spain.[2] The reactionary premier had been assassi-

---

[1] P. 524.   [2] Message of Dec. 6, 1897.

nated and Sagasta, a Liberal, had succeeded to the head of the new ministry which was in sympathy with his aims. When John Hay was first Secretary of Legation to Spain, he wrote in his Diary during 1869 : "Sagasta is the hardest hitter in the Cortes. Everybody calls him a scamp and everybody seems to admire him nevertheless. He is a sort of Disraeli — lithe, active, full of energy and hate." [1] A writer in the Encyclopædia Britannica said that Sagasta was a "leader, skilful in debate, a trimmer *par excellence*." He now appreciated in some degree, if not fully, the pressure from the United States. His ministry "recalled the commander whose brutal orders inflamed the American mind and shocked the civilized world; it modified the horrible order of concentration and has undertaken to care for the helpless and permit those who desire to resume the cultivation of their fields to do so." It also proclaimed by decree a scheme of autonomy to become effective upon ratification by the Cortes.[2] It was extremely doubtful whether the Spanish mind understood autonomy as did the British and American, and a self-governing colony as was Canada could hardly be expected, but Sagasta was sincere in offering autonomy as he understood it.

It is easy to see that the President hoped for a peaceful solution despite the fact that the Sagasta scheme was not satisfactory to the extremists on either side. Riots occurred in Havana, which was loyal to Spanish interest, directed against the governor-general and autonomy; owing to the prevailing excitement the United States Consul-General in Havana thought that it might be neces-

---

[1] Life of Hay, W. R. Thayer, i, 321.
[2] McKinley Message, Dec. 6, 1897.

sary to send a war-ship thither for the protection of the American residents. The President considered the matter and determined to send the battleship *Maine* to Havana, but the statement was made to the Spanish minister that it was "an act of friendly courtesy" and it was so given out to the press. Spain looked upon "the proposed visit of the *Maine*" as a proof of "cordial friendship," and replied that "wishing to reciprocate such friendly and courteous demonstrations we shall arrange, also, that vessels of our squadron may visit the ports of the United States in passing to and from the island of Cuba." [1] While the President feared that the scheme of autonomy had come to nothing, he nevertheless exhibited his continued friendship to Spain. At the diplomatic dinner of January 27, 1898, he showed marked attention to the Spanish minister and congratulated him on the fact that "we have only good news." [2]

These friendly relations were interrupted by an indiscretion on the part of the Spanish minister in Washington, de Lôme. A confidential letter written by him during the previous December to a friend sojourning in Cuba was "surreptitiously, if not criminally obtained" [3] and, on February 9, published by a New York newspaper. De Lôme said: "The message [the President's of December 6, 1897] has been a disillusionment to the insurgents who expected something different; but I regard it as bad [for us]. Besides the ingrained and inevitable ill-breeding with which is repeated all that the press and public opinion in Spain have said about Weyler, it once more shows what McKinley is, weak and a bidder for the

---

[1] Spanish Corr. and Docs., 68, 69.   [2] Ibid., 71.
[3] Day, Foreign Relations, 680.

admiration of the crowd, besides being a would-be politician who tries to leave a door open behind himself while keeping on good terms with the jingoes of his party." [1] De Lôme's folly was astounding. It was well known in Spain that while Congress was for war, the President was earnest for peace and no one could be in daily relations with him without feeling the sincerity of his purpose. The aim, therefore, of a Spanish diplomatist should have been to humor the President, not to impugn his motives. So far, however, as McKinley was concerned, he found most objectionable the intimation further on in the letter that the negotiations for commercial reciprocity with the autonomous government of Cuba might be "for effect" only. But as Assistant-Secretary of State Day wrote, "The publication of the letter created a good deal of feeling among Americans." [2] De Lôme at once cabled to Madrid his resignation which was promptly accepted. Day conducted the affair with discretion and on March 3 was glad to tell Stewart L. Woodford, our minister to Spain that the de Lôme incident was "fortunately closed." [3]

Meanwhile an occurrence took place in Havana which prevented the peaceful solution that the President sought. At forty minutes past nine on the evening of February 15, the *Maine*, lying peacefully at anchor in the harbor, was destroyed by an explosion with a loss of two officers and 258 men. The Spanish Government and the Cuban authorities expressed at once their sympathy with the United States on account of this dreadful occurrence, and their immediate action was all that could be desired.

---

[1] Foreign Relations, 1007.
[2] March 3. Foreign Relations, 680.   [3] Ibid.

The Court of Inquiry into the disaster was composed of three members and a judge advocate of the American Navy. Captain William E. Sampson was at its head and another member was Captain French E. Chadwick, whose excellent book on "The Relations of the United States and Spain, Diplomacy," gives an account of the transaction. "The situation," wrote Chadwick, "precluded any haste, and the inquiry was carried on deliberately, carefully, and searchingly for twenty-three days and with every effort to reach a fair and just finding."[1] The question in the official and public mind was, did the destruction take place from an external or an internal explosion? Chadwick was one of the two members of the Court who had thought the explosion was internal, and he and his colleague were convinced against their prepossessions.[2]

On March 28, 1898, Congress and the public were informed of the finding of the Court by a special message of the President to Congress. The Court determined that the disaster was not in any respect due to the fault or negligence of officers or crew. "In the opinion of the Court the *Maine* was destroyed by the explosion of a submarine mine which caused the partial explosion of two or more of the forward magazines. The Court has been unable to obtain evidence fixing the responsibility for the destruction of the *Maine* upon any person or persons."[3]

John D. Long, who at this time was Secretary of the Navy, in his book published in 1903, wrote: "The mystery of the loss of the *Maine* remains yet to be solved."[4] Chadwick, however, had keener insight, writing in his

---

[1] P. 543.   [2] Chadwick, 562 *n.*
[3] Senate Doc. Destruction of Battleship *Maine.*
[4] The New American Navy, i. 144.

book published in 1909 that he "would welcome an examination of the wreck by a complete exposure of it as it lies.   It could only result in substantiating the description of the injuries by the Court whose examination was too complete to leave chance of serious error." [1]   Chadwick's expressed wish was gratified. In 1911, by a fine piece of engineering, the wreck was exposed and a board of one army and four navy officers made an examination of it, reporting on December 1, 1911, that the destruction was due to "the explosion of a charge of a low form of explosive exterior to the ship. . . .   This resulted in igniting and exploding the contents of the 6-inch reserve magazine, said contents including a large quantity of black powder. The more or less complete explosion of the contents of the remaining forward magazines followed. The magazine explosions resulted in the destruction of the vessel." [2]

Contemporaneous material and many later books attribute much influence to Senator Redfield Proctor's speech in the Senate on March 17, which, owing to the confidence reposed in him by the country, held their attention. "My trip," he said, "was entirely unofficial and of my own motion." Of the six provinces in Cuba, "my observations were confined to the four western provinces which constitute about one half of the island. The two eastern ones are practically in the hands of the insurgents, except the few fortified towns. . . . All the country people in the four western provinces, about 400,000 in number, remaining outside the fortified towns

---

[1] Chadwick, 563 *n.*
[2] House Docs. 62d Cong. 2d Sess. No. 310.

when Weyler's order was made, were driven into these towns, and these are the *reconcentrados*. They were the peasantry, many of them farmers, some landowners, others renting lands and owning more or less stock, others working on estates and cultivating small patches; and even a small patch in that fruitful clime will support a family. . . . General Blanco's [the governor-general succeeding Weyler] order of November 13 last somewhat modifies the Weyler order but is of little or no practical benefit. . . . In fact though the order was issued four months ago I saw no beneficent results from it worth mentioning." "I am not in favor of annexation," he declared; and while Senator Proctor suggested no plan it is easy to see that intervention would have from him powerful support. "To me," he said, "the strongest appeal is not the barbarity practised by Weyler, nor the loss of the *Maine* . . . terrible as are both these incidents, but the spectacle of a million and a half of people, the entire native population of Cuba, struggling for freedom and deliverance from the worst misgovernment of which I ever had knowledge." [1]

The Spanish minister [2] in Washington was much impressed, telegraphing to the home government that Senator Proctor's speech had "produced great effect because of his temperate stand. He set forth in black colors the situation of the *reconcentrados*, declared that the country was opposed to autonomy and favorable to independence. . . . Before making the speech he had seen the President

---

[1] Cong. Record, 2916 *et seq*. Senator Proctor gave also the estimated population of Cuba with its racial divisions. He also discussed the military and political situations. Proctor had been Secretary of War under Harrison.

[2] Polo, who succeeded de Lôme.

and Day, for which reason more importance is attached
to his words. My impression is that the President will
try to withstand the powerful public sentiment in favor
of the insurrection." [1]

As early as March 20 the President learned confidentially that the naval board would make a "unanimous report that the *Maine* was blown up by a submarine
mine." [2] This knowledge and Proctor's account dictated
Day's midnight telegram of March 25 to Woodford at
Madrid: "The concentration of men, women and children in the fortified towns and permitting them to starve
is unbearable to a Christian nation geographically so
close as ours to Cuba. . . . It was represented to the
President in November that the Blanco government would
at once relieve the suffering and so modify the Weyler
order as to permit those who were able to return to their
homes and till the fields from which they had been driven.
. . . The reconcentration order has not been practically superseded. There is no hope of peace through
Spanish arms. . . . The Spanish government seems unable to conquer the insurgents. . . . We do not want
the island. . . . Peace is the desired end." [3] Be it remembered that Congress, the country and Spain had the
report of the Naval Board concerning the destruction of
the *Maine* on Monday, March 28. Next day was submitted to the Spanish ministry what turned out to be the
President's ultimatum. Premising that "the President
instructs me to say that we do not want Cuba," Woodford said in conversation with Sagasta, with the Minister
for Foreign Affairs and the Minister for the Colonies, who,

---

[1] Spanish Corr. and Docs., 95.
[2] Foreign Relations, 692.   [3] Ibid., 704, 712.

being well acquainted with English, acted as interpreter, "we do wish immediate peace in Cuba." The President "suggests an immediate armistice lasting until October 1, negotiations in the meantime being had looking to peace between Spain and the insurgents through the friendly offices of the President of the United States. He wishes the immediate revocation of the reconcentration order."

With effect, does Chadwick, in recounting the history of the diplomacy of these days, speak of Spain's "fatal habit of procrastination."[1] On March 31, two days after Woodford's conversation, she showed this in her answer to the President's reasonable request. Far from acceptance of the suggestion relating to the Armistice and consequent negotiations, it laid down propositions utterly inadmissible. Well did Woodford write to McKinley on April 1, "Yesterday's conference was a sorrow to me, for I have worked hard for peace."[2]

On March 30, the day between the President's request and Spain's answer, Day apprised Woodford of the state of affairs in Washington. "You should know and fully appreciate," he telegraphed, "that there is profound feeling in Congress and the greatest apprehension on the part of most conservative members that a resolution for intervention may pass both branches in spite of any effort which can be made. Only assurance from the President that, if he fails in peaceful negotiations he will submit all the facts to Congress at a very early day, will prevent immediate action on the part of Congress."[3]

It was evident that submission of the question to Congress meant a declaration of war against Spain. Public

---

[1] P. 554.   [2] Foreign Relations, 727.   [3] Ibid., 721.

sentiment had been worked up by the sensational press, frequently called the "yellow press"; it had manipulated the real news, spread unfounded reports, putting all before their readers with scare headlines. Newspaper editors and their assistants differed from those between 1850 and 1860, who made their appeals to the electorate by cogent editorials directed against the slave power. Now recourse was had to the news columns in which Spain was painted as perfidious and untrustworthy. After the Naval Board had made its report in regard to the *Maine*, it was impossible to convince the multitude that Spain had not, in some way or other, touched off the submarine mine which caused the explosion. "Remember the *Maine*" became the watchword. Appeal was made to what England would have done under like circumstances, whose "commonest phrase" was, "I wish you would take Cuba at once. We wouldn't have stood it this long." [1] Public sentiment acted effectually upon Congress, a dominant majority of which wanted war with Spain. "Every Congressman," said Boutelle of Maine, "had two or three newspapers in his district — most of them printed in red ink . . . and shouting for blood." [2]

It may be affirmed that if a referendum had been taken on April 1, 1898, a majority would have voted for war with Spain in order to expel her from Cuba. But the financial and business interests of the country were opposed to the war, as they deemed it needless and they shrunk from its horrors and expense. The Jingoes taunted men who held this view with being influenced by Wall Street, and it proved an effective taunt, but really Wall

---

[1] Life of Hay, Thayer, ii. 166.
[2] Oct. 22, 1898. Boston *Herald*, Oct. 23.

Street was only one part of this sentiment which was shared by business men throughout the country whose fit representative was Mark Hanna. "I am not," he declared, "in favor of heedlessly precipitating the country into the horrors of war" on account of the *Maine* incident or Spain's attitude to Cuba.[1] As late as April 5, he wrote in a private letter that in his opinion the Senate Committee on Foreign Relations ought to pass a resolution giving the President some discretion; otherwise, he added, "War cannot be avoided, and even under the most favorable circumstances it must come unless Spain backs down, which I believe she will do."

A phase of the reflecting and intelligent part of the community was well represented in the private letters of General J. D. Cox. "The dreadful accident to the *Maine*," he wrote, "ought to make everybody sober and reasonable in thinking of foreign affairs. It ought to be a very good cause that would justify a war in which such things might be happening any day. I don't envy the public man who should have to look back on an unnecessary war as in any part the work of his hands; and to rush into it for mere wantonness, as many seem inclined to, is such unspeakable folly as to make one wonder that it is possible in an enlightened age." Again, on March 2, "It is entirely incredible that a civilized government should have ordered or approved the destruction of a ship in her port in time of peace." And on March 29, "as to intervention, the whole island and everybody on it are not worth the American volunteers who would inevitably die of yellow fever if we sent an army there."

The officers and men who went forth to fight Spain,

---

[1] Interviews, N. Y. *Tribune*, Feb. 24, 27.

obedient to a dominant public sentiment and the fiat of
Congress, might have used the words with a variation
suitable to the time and country, which Philip Gibbs put
into the mouth of British soldiers who suffered and fought
in the trenches during the great World War: "I don't
want to die — I want to live. Why should I be sacrificed to please the politicians of the world — those fools
who are the cause of all this? People at home don't
understand what we have to suffer. They don't care.
Those infuriated old females in England, those compla-
cent old bald-heads in St. James Street Clubs would see
us all smashed to pulp, and die to the last man, without a
question. They think it natural and nice, 'Dulce et de-
corum est,' etc."[1]

A phase of the sentiment of "literary fellows" was reflected by Theodore Roosevelt, Henry Cabot Lodge and
John Hay. "When the *Maine* was blown up in Havana
harbor," wrote Roosevelt in 1913, "war became inevitable."[2] He, in 1898, was impatient that the President did
not act more promptly and wrote in a private letter,
"The blood of women and children, who have perished
by the hundred thousand in hideous misery, lies at our
door; and the blood of the murdered men of the *Maine*
calls not for indemnity but for the full measure of atone-
ment which can only come by driving the Spaniard from
the New World. I have said this to the President before
his Cabinet; I have said it to Judge Day . . . ; and to
my own chief;"[3] and again, "McKinley has no more
backbone than a chocolate éclair!"[4]

---

[1] Boston *Herald*, May 4, 1919. [2] Autobiography, 232.
[3] Letter of March 21 to Brooks Adams, J. B. Bishop. *Scribner's Magazine*, November 1919, 524.   [4] Peck, 642.

Henry Cabot Lodge wrote in 1899: "The outside engine of destruction [of the *Maine*] was a government submarine mine and had been exploded without the authority or knowledge of the Spanish government by men who wore the uniform of Spain. . . . The result had been inevitable since the fatal 15th of February, although men did not understand it at the moment and still thought they could stay the current of events which had been gathering strength for seventy years and broken loose at last." [1]

On May 8, 1898, John Hay, now our Ambassador to England, wrote in a private letter: "I detest war and had hoped I might never see another, but this was as necessary as it was righteous. I have not for two years seen any other issue." [2]

One may wonder if Roosevelt, Lodge and Hay took fully into account the Spanish habit of procrastination. Did Roosevelt with his habit of omnivorous reading come across the reported remark of Lord Clarendon: "Spanish dynasties go and come; Spanish queens go and come, and Spanish ministries go and come; but there is one thing in Spain that is always the same — they never answer letters"? [3]

Senator Lodge of course knew all about Lowell's mission to Spain, and he might have read before the Spanish War his impressions of the people to whom he was accredited. "I like the Spaniards very well so far as I know them," Lowell wrote, "and have an instinctive sympathy with their want of aptitude for business."

---

[1] The War with Spain, 31 *et seq.*
[2] Life of Hay, Thayer, ii. 167.
[3] Life of Lord Granville, Fitzmaurice, 1905, ii. 31.

"They are unenterprising and unchangeable." "Spain is as primitive in some ways as the books of Moses, and as Oriental." "They fancy themselves always in the age of Charles V, and the perfect gravity with which they always assume the airs of a Great Power is not without a kind of pathetic dignity. We all wink at the little shifts of a decayed gentleman, especially when he is Don Quixote, as this one certainly is." [1]

John Hay in Spain, as first Secretary of Legation in 1869–1870, during the earlier insurrection, was impressed with her procrastination. Sagasta was one of the ministry and defended the government "with wonderful vigor and malice." "This government," wrote Hay in 1870, "wants to sell Cuba but dares not, and has no power to put a stop to the atrocities on the island. The only thing left to our government is to do nothing and keep its mouth shut; or interfere to stop the horrors in Cuba on the ground of humanity or the damage resulting to American interests." [2]

The pressure upon the President in 1898 to refer the matter to Congress was great. The Secretary of War, Russell A. Alger, said to a senator: "I want you to advise the President to declare war. He is making a great mistake. He is in danger of ruining himself and the Republican party by standing in the way of the people's wishes. Congress will declare war in spite of him. He'll get run over and the party with him." A bellicose senator said to the Assistant Secretary of State : "Day, don't your President know where the war-declaring power is

---

[1] Dec. 23, 1877, Apr. 14, 1878, May 2, 1879, Dec. 30, 1879. Letters of James Russell Lowell (1894), ii. 205, 213, 241, 246.

[2] Life of Hay, Thayer, i. 324.

lodged? Tell him that if he doesn't do something, Congress will exercise the power." [1] Congressman Boutelle, who was opposed to the war, is authority for the statement that forty or fifty Republican members of Congress held a caucus, sent a committee to the President and told him that unless he sent an aggressive message to Congress, they would introduce a resolution for war and vote with the Democrats to carry it through.[2] Olcott, the biographer of McKinley, is authority for the statement that the Vice President and a number of senators who were opposed to war polled the Senate in order to see if they could sustain a veto should a war resolution be prematurely passed; [3] but this must have been only a momentary thought, as for the President to veto a declaration of war by Congress was hardly to be considered.

McKinley was averse to war. He said to Senator Fairbanks: "It isn't the money that will be spent nor the property that will be destroyed, if war comes, that concerns me; but the thought of human suffering that must come into thousands of homes throughout the country is almost overwhelming." [4] But he was much perturbed at the idea that his action might break up the Republican party. He could not sleep without sleeping powders. During the week when he sent what turned out to be his ultimatum to Spain he was much cast down but, on receiving her rejection of his terms, he determined to go with the war party and to turn the affair over to Congress. "Congress," wrote Senator Lodge, "has no diplomatic functions or attributes. With a foreign nation it has

[1] Life of McKinley, Olcott, ii. 28.
[2] Boston *Herald*, Oct. 23, 1898.   [3] Olcott, ii. 28.
[4] Life of McKinley, Olcott, i. 400.

but one weapon — the war power; and when a President calls in Congress in a controversy with another nation, his action means that Congress, if it sees fit, must exercise its single power and declare war." [1] The President had decided to send his message to Congress on Monday, April 4; he postponed it until the 6th, then until Monday, April 11th, on account of an urgent request from the Consul-General in Havana to delay it in order that he might insure the safe departure of Americans from Cuba. On that day [April 11th] the message went to Congress: this action meant war with Spain.

No one can go through carefully the diplomatic despatches without thinking that up to March 31 McKinley's conduct of the affair had been faultless. The pressure exerted upon the Spanish ministry and people was marked by courtesy, discretion and thorough knowledge of the situation. John D. Long is the excellent authority for the consideration which McKinley and his Cabinet showed for the susceptibilities of the Spaniards. [2] But just about as the President was to succeed completely he abandoned his policy and went over to the war party. "To the people we come sooner or later," wrote James Bryce, [3] and the ministry of the cabinet government of Spain, though eager for peace, could go no further than they could count upon the support of public sentiment. On April 3, Woodford telegraphed to the President: "The Spanish Minister for Foreign Affairs assures me that Spain will go as far and as fast as she can. . . . I know that the Queen and her present ministry sincerely desire peace, and that the Spanish people desire peace, and if you can still give

---

[1] The War with Spain, 36.   [2] American Navy, i. 133.
[3] American Commonwealth, i. 270.

me time and reasonable liberty of action . . . I am sure that before next October I will get peace in Cuba, with justice to Cuba and protection to our great American interests." [1]

For the sake of clearness reference will again be made to the President's ultimatum of March 27–29.[2] He demanded the immediate revocation of the *reconcentrado* order and an armistice until October 1. The revocation of the *reconcentrado* order was at once made. And now the Pope, assisted by Archbishop Ireland of St. Paul, who went to Washington by his order,[3] interfered in the interest of peace. His intervention, supported by that of "six great European powers," induced the Spanish ministry to direct on April 9 the governor-general of Cuba to grant immediately an armistice, leaving the length of time to himself. Having submitted this action to Day, Woodford telegraphed on April 10 to the President that if he could get full authority from Congress he might secure a final settlement "before August 1st on one of the following bases: either such autonomy as the insurgents may agree to accept, or recognition by Spain of the independence of the island, or cession of the island to the United States. I hope that nothing will now be done to humiliate Spain, as I am satisfied that the present government is going, and is loyally ready to go, as fast and as far as it can." [4]

The President and his immediate advisers had been brought by the logic of events to see that no permanent

[1] Foreign Relations, 732.

[2] The despatch of Day to Woodford was Sunday, March 27; the submission of the ultimatum to the Spanish ministry, Tuesday, March 29. The report on the *Maine* went to Congress on Monday, March 28.

[3] Spanish Corr. and Docs., 111, 112.   [4] Foreign Relations, 746, 747.

peace could be secured unless the Spaniards abandoned
Cuba; and in this they agreed with the war party. But
the Jingoes desired to smash Spain and were "spoiling
for a fight"; and the well-informed men of the war party
did not believe that Spain would give up Cuba without
war. But they could not see things as we see them now.
The Spanish ministry feared that a contest with the United
States would be hopeless. Whatever might happen
at first they appreciated that America had the "sinews of
war." The unanimous passage by the House of the bill
placing fifty millions at the President's disposal did not
excite the Spaniards but "stunned them." [1] On March
31, Woodford telegraphed to the President: "I believe
the ministry are ready to go as far and as fast as they can
and still save the dynasty here in Spain. They know
that Cuba is lost. Public opinion in Spain has moved
steadily toward peace." [2] "Speak softly and carry a
big stick," was Theodore Roosevelt's idea of a foreign
policy. Up to March 31 McKinley had spoken softly,
but after that he failed to continue the soft speech and
yet he had strong and what might have been efficient
support. The Speaker of the House, the Vice President,
all of his Cabinet but two, nearly all of the leading Republicans in the Senate were with him.[3] For it seems
clear that the Spaniards might have been led to grant independence to Cuba through negotiation. Jules Cambon, Ambassador from France, representing on the part
of his country financial and personal sympathy with

---

[1] Woodford, March 9. Foreign Relations, 684.   [2] Ibid., 727.
[3] Letters of T. Roosevelt to Captain Cowles, March 29, 30, 1898; to
Douglas Robinson, March 30; to Elihu Root, April 5; to Dr. Henry Jackson, April 6; J. B. Bishop; *Scribner's Magazine*, Nov. 1919, 524.

Spain, could see that she ought not to go to war with America, and labored to bring about a peaceful result. McKinley feared a rupture in his own party, and on account of that fear, had not the nerve and power to resist the pressure for war. We may rest assured that if Mark Hanna had been President there would have been no war with Spain. As much of a partisan as McKinley, he would have had the self-determination to resist the war party and the confident belief that he could secure the end desired without war and without the rupture of the Republican party; at all events he would have taken the risk.[1]

That the President had cast his lot freely with the war party was evident from his reply to the six representatives of Great Britain, Germany, France, Austria-Hungary, Russia and Italy, who hoped that further negotiations would lead to peace. We must end a situation, he said, on Wednesday, April 6, "the indefinite prolongation of which has become insufferable." [2]

---

[1] John W. Foster said at the Conference of the American Society for the Judicial Settlement of International Disputes on Dec. 15, 1910: "It is well known that President McKinley was strongly opposed to the war, and he was ably supported in striving for peace by General Woodford, to whom too much praise cannot be given for his conduct of the negotiations. It is now apparent that had not the President yielded to the war clamor in the country and the demands of Congress, the war might have been averted. . . . In the light of the Woodford despatches, we must conclude that had President McKinley displayed the same firmness as Grant and Cleveland and continued to 'keep hold of the reins of diplomacy' the Spanish War with its long train of consequences might never have come upon us." See the Speeches of General Woodford and Congressman Boutelle before the Massachusetts Club, Oct. 22, 1898; Boston *Herald*, Oct. 23; Chadwick, 575; Remarks in the Senate by Senators Hale and Depew, May 25, 1908; Boyle's statement, Columbus, Ohio, May 25. Boyle was private secretary of McKinley when governor of Ohio, and afterwards his appointee as consul to Liverpool. Boston *Evening Transcript*, May 26, 1908; Boston *Daily Advertiser*, May 19, 1913; Conversations with Mark Hanna and Henry S. Pritchett.   [2] Foreign Relations, 741.

His message to the Congress on Monday, April 11, brought on the war. "With this last overture in the direction of immediate peace" [his ultimatum of March 27–29], he said, "and its disappointing reception by Spain, the Executive is brought to the end of his effort." [1] The disaster to the *Maine* was put in a subsidiary place in his message.[2] The President said toward the end of the message: "The issue is now with Congress. . . . I have exhausted every effort to relieve the intolerable condition of affairs which is at our doors. Prepared to execute every obligation imposed upon me by the Constitution and the law, I await your action." [3]

To the crowning effort of his diplomacy of being able to secure peace and in all probability Cuban independence, he referred in the last two paragraphs of his message in a perfunctory manner. "Yesterday" (Sunday, April 10), he said, "and since the preparation of the foregoing message, official information was received by me that the latest decree of the Queen Regent of Spain directs General Blanco, in order to prepare and facilitate peace, to proclaim a suspension of hostilities, the duration and details of which have not yet been communicated to me." [4]

Congress, the country and Spain knew that this message meant war. Congress immediately addressed itself to the subject and after certain disagreements united in the fol-

---

[1] Foreign Relations, 755.

[2] "In any event the destruction of the *Maine*, by whatever exterior cause, is a patent and impressive proof of a state of things in Cuba that is intolerable. That condition is thus shown to be such that the Spanish government cannot assure safety and security to a vessel of the American Navy in the harbor of Havana on a mission of peace, and rightfully there."

[3] Foreign Relations, 760.

[4] Foreign Relations, 760.

lowing resolutions, which were adopted on April 19, and signed by the President on the next day.[1] They said: "First. That the people of the Island of Cuba are, of right ought to be, free and independent.

"Second. That it is the duty of the United States to demand, and the Government of the United States does hereby demand, that the Government of Spain at once relinquish its authority and government in the Island of Cuba, and withdraw its land and naval forces from Cuba and Cuban waters.

"Third. That the President of the United States be, and he hereby is, directed and empowered to use the entire land and naval forces of the United States and to call into the actual service of the United States the militia of the several States to such extent as may be necessary to carry these resolutions into effect.

"Fourth. That the United States hereby disclaims any disposition or intention to exercise sovereignty, jurisdiction or control over said Island except for the pacification thereof and asserts its determination, when that is accomplished, to leave the government and control of the Island to its people." [2]

President Taft said that the Spanish War was an altruistic war.[3] The ground on which such a statement may be defended lies in the fourth resolution. It was offered by Senator Teller of Colorado and agreed to in the Senate without a division. It is wonderful that the United States, large and powerful, about to make war on

---

[1] The stages which led to these resolutions and the disagreements are well told by Henry Cabot Lodge in the War with Spain, 35 *et seq.;* see also Chadwick, 582.

[2] Foreign Relations, liv.   [3] John W. Foster, *l.c.*

Spain, weak and decadent, should renounce solemnly
any desire to get Cuba.   The fertile island, the Pearl of
the Antilles, Cuba, had long been coveted by America,
and now when the plum was ready to drop into her mouth
she abjured the wish of conquest.   But it seemed impossible to convince the Spaniards that our aim was not the
annexation of Cuba.   This resolution had the sympathetic adhesion of the President and many, if not all, of his
warmest friends.   It lightens up the declaration of this
unnecessary war.

CHAPTER IV

NOTHING excites a nation so much as going to war. The first few days after its declaration, tumult reigns. So it came to pass in 1898. The feeling in Congress was intense and all the more so because it had been so long suppressed, awaiting the President's action. A large majority of Congress was in favor of war to expel the Spaniards from Cuba, and most of the Democrats, assisted by some Republicans, desired, as a stage in the proceedings, to recognize the republic of the Cuban insurgents. Two days after the President's Message was sent to Congress, the members of the House met in "a state of frenzied excitement" with "partisan passion running high." During a passionate colloquy, a Republican member said to a Democrat, "You are a liar," when the Democrat seized a bound copy of the Congressional Record and hurled it at his opponent. The missile fell short; the two members rushed for one another, and the House, so a reporter wrote, "was in an uproar. Shouts of anger and indignation were heard on every hand. Members in the crush espoused the cause of the two original combatants, and there were several exciting collisions but no blows struck." At last, owing to the work of the Speaker and the Sergeant-at-Arms, the efforts of a dozen muscular members and an impassioned appeal by Dingley, the fighters were restrained, the angry members took their seats "and a resemblance of order was restored." [1]

> "Beware of entrance to a quarrel, but being in,
> Bear't that the opposed may beware of thee."

In such wise did the McKinley administration conduct the Spanish War.

Congress formally declared that war with Spain had existed since April 21. Excitement had given way to alarm in the public mind lest the Navy might not prove equal to the job when the country learned that the first successful blow had been struck in the Orient on May 1 by the Asiatic squadron, under the command of George Dewey. [2]

During the autumn of 1897, Dewey thought that we were drifting into a war with Spain and, of all things, he desired the command of the Asiatic squadron. Theodore Roosevelt, in his position of Assistant Secretary of the Navy, had made up his mind that Dewey was the man for the place, but political influence was pushing another officer who was his senior. [3] "I want you to go," Roosevelt said to him. "You are the man who will be equal to the emergency if one arises. Do you know any senators?"

"Senator Proctor," [4] was the reply, "is from my State. He is an old friend of the family and my father was of service to him when he was a young man."

---

[1] N. Y. Tribune, Apr. 14; Recollections of Henry S. Pritchett.

[2] "The newspapers of May 2 had a brief announcement of the victory." Dewey, Autobiography, 228. These first (May 2) announcements were from Spanish sources and gave no adequate idea of the completeness of the victory; the reading between the lines made it possible to arrive at a conclusion that made the headlines of victory justifiable.

[3] Theodore Roosevelt, Autobiography, 231.

[4] Redfield Proctor, "who was very ardent for the war." Ibid.

"You could not have a better sponsor," Roosevelt rejoined. "Lose no time in having him speak a word for you." Dewey at once enlisted the favor of Senator Proctor, whose influence with the President secured him the appointment.[1]

In a Japanese harbor on January 3, 1898, Dewey took over the command of the Asiatic squadron and hoisted his broad pennant on the *Olympia*. In his accurate and modest account of his work, written soon after his return to Washington in 1899,[2] he told of the careful preparation that he made for an attack on the Spanish fleet in the Philippines. Before he heard of the disaster to the *Maine*, the news of which reached him on February 17, he had decided to take the squadron to Hong Kong. An evidence of the common working of two minds bent on war is Roosevelt's despatch to Dewey of February 25, 1898. "Order the squadron to Hong Kong. Keep full of coal. In the event of declaration of war Spain, your duty will be to see that the Spanish squadron does not leave the Asiatic coast, and then offensive operations in Philippine Islands."[3]

In Dewey's account of the interchange of hospitalities among the ships assembled at Hong Kong during the month of March, he related a conversation that he had with Prince Henry of Prussia, brother of the Kaiser, who remarked "that he did not believe that the powers would ever allow the United States to annex Cuba."

"We do not wish to annex Cuba," Dewey answered, "but we cannot suffer the horrible condition of affairs,

---

[1] Dewey, Autobiography, 168.
[2] Dewey, Autobiography, vi. This account was not published until 1913.
[3] Dewey, Autobiography, 179.

which exists at present in that island at our very doors, to continue, and we are bound to put a stop to it."

"And what are you after? What does your country want?" the Prince asked jokingly on another occasion; [1] and, although a word in jest, it represented the European attitude which could see in our action only a desire to acquire a rich territory.

Having served under Farragut, Dewey looked upon him as a master. "Valuable as the training of Annapolis was," he wrote, "it was poor schooling beside that of serving under Farragut in time of war." [2]

On April 25 came this word from Secretary Long: "War has commenced between the United States and Spain. Proceed at once to the Philippine Islands. Commence operations at once, particularly against Spanish fleet. You must capture vessels or destroy. Use utmost endeavors." [3] Two days later Dewey set sail, on his 600-mile voyage to Manila Bay. The Hong Kong newspapers stated that Manila was impregnable, and in the Hong Kong club which was British, whose members were in thorough sympathy with the United States, it was not thought that Dewey would be successful in his attack. Arriving off Manila, he signalled for all the commanding officers to come on board his flag-ship and said to them, "We shall enter Manila Bay to-night, and you will follow the motions and movements of the flag-ship which will lead." [4]

That night (as he told the story) he asked himself,

---

[1] Dewey, Autobiography, 185.
[2] Dewey, Autobiography, 50.
[3] The New American Navy, Long, i. 182.
[4] Dewey, Autobiography, 206.

"What would Farragut do?" and he thought he would have done exactly as proposed.[1] On April 30 at 11.30 P.M., with all lights masked, the gun crews at their guns, Dewey entered the South Channel, and with eminent success ran by the batteries. After half of the squadron had passed, a battery opened fire but none of the shots took effect.[2] Now he was in Manila Bay in which was the Spanish fleet that he must "capture or destroy."

"In action," Dewey wrote, "we had six ships to the Spaniards' seven, but we were superior in class of vessel and in armaments."[3] Proceeding across the bay at slow speed at 5.15 in the morning of May 1, his squadron was fired upon by three batteries at Manila, two at Cavité[4] and by the anchored Spanish fleet. Still Dewey went forward to the attack, leading the column with his flag-ship *Olympia;* the rest of his command followed with a distance of 400 yards between ships. Two submarine mines exploded, but they were two miles ahead, "too far to be effective."[5] At 5.40 A.M., when two and one half miles away from their objective, the Spanish fleet, Dewey said to his captain, "You may fire when you are ready, Gridley."[6] At once the squadron opened fire. Firing without cessation as they moved, three runs were made from the eastward and two from the westward; the length of each run was about two miles. Approaching on the fifth run, when nearest, within 2000 yards, this rapid

---

[1] Autobiography, 60.

[2] Dewey's report, May 4. Appendix to the report of the Chief of the Bureau of Navigation, 70. This will be referred to as Crowninshield.

[3] Autobiography, 203; see also 212, 213.

[4] Cavité was ten miles from Manila, had 5000 people, a navy yard, arsenal and fortifications. Lodge, The War with Spain, 53.

[5] Report, Crowninshield, 70.

[6] Autobiography, 214.

and concentrated fire — "smothering," he called it — demolished the Spanish fleet.   At 7.35 A.M., an erroneous report was made to the Commodore that his ship was short of ammunition; this caused him to withdraw the squadron from action, and gave his men time for breakfast, as they had made the fight on coffee served in the early morning.   All but one of the Spanish fleet, however, had been destroyed, and as Dewey naïvely remarked, "Victory was already ours, though we did not know it." [1]   At 11.16 A.M., he returned with the squadron to the attack. "By this time," he said in his report, "the flag-ship and almost the entire Spanish fleet were in flames, and at 12.30 P.M. the squadron ceased firing, the batteries being silenced and the ships sunk, burnt, and deserted." [2]   The Spaniards lost at least thirteen vessels: three were sunk, eight burned [only seven of these were in line of battle]; two tugs and a number of small launches were captured. Their casualties were 381 men.[3]   In Dewey's squadron none was killed and only seven slightly wounded.   "The squadron," he reported, "is in as good condition now as before the battle." [4]

"The completeness of the result," wrote Senator Lodge, "which is the final test, gives Manila a great place in the history of naval battles and writes the name of George Dewey high up among the greatest of victorious admirals." [5]   The rapid and concentrated fire of the Americans destroyed the Spanish fleet.   This disconcerted the Spaniards whose valor was remarkable but whose fire was hasty and inaccurate.   Dewey told the secret of his suc-

---

[1] Autobiography, 218.   [2] Crowninshield, 70.
[3] Ibid., 71, 92.
[4] Ibid., 71.   [5] The War with Spain, 67.

cess. "It was," he wrote, "the ceaseless routine of hard work and preparation in time of peace that won Manila." [1]　It looked " 'so easy' after it was all done." [2] But let one imagine Dewey with his Americans on the defence in the position of the Spaniards with their many resources and incentive to preparation, and let one conceive the Spanish admiral and his fleet the attacking party, and the result would have been just the contrary. But in truth the Spanish admiral would not have attacked, nor would any American of "the respectable commonplace type." [3]　To attack a foe seven thousand miles from a base was a risk too great to take for any commander who did not pattern after Nelson and Farragut, as defeat or even "failure to gain a decisive victory" would have been a disaster. [4]　Dewey was long-headed as well as daring and took into account all the conditions of the game. "In the event of defeat," he wrote, "no ship of our Asiatic squadron would have been afloat to tell the story." [5]

Honors and congratulations came. The President made him a rear-admiral. Congress thanked him, his officers and men. In writing to him, his "old friend" John Hay spoke of his "mingled wisdom and daring." Roosevelt, who appreciated Dewey before and admired him greatly after the battle, cabled, "Every American is your debtor." [6]

It was the "man behind the gun" that did the business. The Spanish Captain-General in his war proclamation

---

[1] Autobiography, 231.　　　[2] The War with Spain, 62.
[3] Roosevelt Autobiography, 231.
[4] Admiral Luce, cited by Dewey, Autobiography, 189 *n.*
[5] Autobiography, 252.
[6] Dewey, Autobiography, 229.

had declared that the North American people "were constituted of all the social excrescences;" their squadron was "manned by foreigners possessing neither instruction nor discipline." As a matter of fact, the percentage of American-born seamen in Dewey's squadron was about eighty all told. The Archbishop of Manila who, it was said, had written the Captain-General's proclamation, visited the *Olympia* some months afterwards and Dewey had the ship's company paraded in his honor. "As he saw the fine young fellows march past," wrote the Admiral, "his surprise at their appearance was manifest." "Admiral," he said, "you must be very proud to command such a body of men." "Yes, I am," was the reply, "and I have just the same kind of men on board all the other ships in the harbor." "Admiral," the Archbishop rejoined, "I have been here for thirty years. I have seen the men-of-war of all the nations but never have I seen anything like this," as he pointed to the *Olympia's* crew.

Dewey paid tribute to his officers as well as to his men. "I doubt," he said in his report, "if any commander-in-chief under similar circumstances, was ever served by more loyal, efficient and gallant captains than those of the squadron now under my command." [1]

The moral effect of Dewey's victory was great. It gave the country confidence in her navy. It was generally thought that on paper the Spanish Navy was supe-

[1] My authorities for the battle of Manila Bay are Dewey's account printed in his Autobiography; reports of Dewey, Gridley, Coghlan, Walker, Dyer, Wood, Wildes, Montojo, the Spanish Admiral, printed by Crowninshield. I have also used The War with Spain, Lodge; The New American Navy, Long; and I have consulted the Autobiography of Roosevelt; Twenty Years of the Republic, Peck; America as a World Power, J. H. Latané (Hart's American Nation Series); *The Nation*, May 5, 12, 1898.

rior, and it might prove so in action. As a formidable fleet would certainly be sent across the ocean, imagination ran riot as to the destruction it might cause to the seaboard cities and to the summer resorts on the coast. Many Boston men took their securities inland to Worcester and Springfield. Roosevelt spoke of it as a "fairly comic panic" and wrote truly, "The state of nervousness along much of the seacoast was funny in view of the lack of foundation for it." [1] For the authorities in Washington, naval and otherwise, had perfect trust in the American Navy and felt that with a fair show it would destroy any Spanish squadron sent across the water to take a necessary part in the war. Now Dewey's victory showed the stuff in the officers and men of the American Navy and imparted a confidence to the general public that was sorely needed at the commencement of hostilities.

Sympathy in the large powers of Europe on the continent was with Spain, and especial manifestations were in Paris and Berlin. If there was any design to interfere in the conflict, it was checked by the attitude of England, who favored decidedly the United States. Dewey's victory strengthened the position of England by rendering any intervention on the part of the continental powers impossible. Sentiment on the continent was that, in the first encounters, Spain would be victorious, such was the confidence felt in her navy and distrust in the American sea power. Andrew D. White, our Ambassador to Germany, gave a vivid account of the sentiment, as shown in the German newspapers and in an interview granted by Mommsen, on the conduct of the United States toward

---

[1] Autobiography, 235.

Spain. This, White wrote, "was even more acrid than his previous utterances and exhibited sharply and at great length our alleged sins and shortcomings." [1] Following the Spanish newspapers, which liked to call their opponents "Yankee pigs," the "continental press teemed with the grossest caricatures, in which the Americans were drawn as swine." [2]

Anatole France in his novel "L'Anneau d'Améthyste" (226), published in 1899, gave this lively account of a conversation in a Paris salon : A general expressed the opinion that "in declaring war on Spain the Americans were imprudent and it may cost them dear. Having neither an Army nor a Navy it will be difficult for them to maintain a conflict with a trained army and experienced sailors. . . . The Americans are not prepared for war, and war requires long preparation."

"Now then, general," cried a lady, "do tell us that those American bandits will be beaten."

"Their success is doubtful," replied the general. "I should say that it would even be absurd, and would amount to an insolent contradiction of the whole system in vogue among military nations. In short the victory of the United States would constitute a practical criticism of principles adopted in the whole of Europe by the most competent military authorities. Such a result is neither to be expected nor desired."

"What luck!" exclaimed the lady, "Our friends the Spaniards will be victorious. Vive le roi!"

"Certain facts seem to indicate that the Americans are

---

[1] Autobiography, 11, 160, 178. White saw the proof sheets of the interview but it was never published.
[2] Peck, 544, 553.

beginning to repent of their rashness," said a gentleman of the party. "It is said that they are terrified. They expect any day to see Spanish warships appear on their Atlantic coast. Inhabitants of Boston, New York and Philadelphia are fleeing in great numbers toward the interior of the country. It is a general panic."

A servant brought in the mail. "Perhaps there will be news of the war," said the gentleman opening a newspaper. Amid an intense silence, he read aloud: "Commodore Dewey has destroyed the Spanish fleet in the port of Manila. The Americans did not lose a single man."

"On the 30th of April, 1898," wrote Dewey, "I had been practically unknown to the American public. In a day my name was on everyone's lips. The dash of our squadron into an Oriental bay seven thousand miles from home had the glamour of romance to the national imagination." [1]

After the battle of Manila Bay, Senator Redfield Proctor wrote to President McKinley: "Dewey will be as wise and safe, if there are political duties devolving on him, as he is forcible in action. There is no better man in discretion and safe judgment." [2] The sequel showed how profoundly the Senator comprehended the Admiral. After the battle, Dewey established a blockade of Manila which he aimed to maintain thoroughly and impartially. A good student of international law, he was guided in his conduct by the best of authorities, and his attitude to the men-of-war sent by several nations to Manila Bay for purposes of observation, was correct. The English, who

---

[1] Autobiography, 289.   [2] Ibid., 228.

thoroughly sympathized with the United States, the Japanese, who partially did so, and the French, whose feeling was favorable to the Spaniards, respected Dewey's authority and permitted him to prescribe rules for their guidance. Not so the Germans, who were a law unto themselves and chafed against the exercise of any authority not their own.

After Dewey's return to Washington, at a dinner at the White House given him by the President, the President desired to know the truth of the statements frequently made in the newspapers regarding the friction between him and the German Vice-Admiral. "There is no record of it at all on the files," McKinley said. "No, Mr. President," Dewey answered, "as I was on the spot and familiar with the situation from day to day, it seemed best that I look after it myself, at a time when you had worries enough of your own." [1] Dewey came into collision with the Germans a number of times before the arrival of the Vice-Admiral von Diedrichs. On June 12, he came in on his flag-ship, the *Kaiserin Augusta* making the third German cruiser in the harbor; another was expected and a transport had already arrived. In accordance with naval etiquette, Dewey made the first call upon Diedrichs and referred to the large German force and the limited German interest in the Philippines. The British, with a much larger commercial interest, with a greater number of resident subjects, with the largest naval force of any power in far Eastern waters, never had at any one time during the blockade more than three warships in Manila harbor. To Dewey's gentle

---

[1] Dewey, Autobiography, 252.

remonstrance Diedrichs answered, "I am here by order of the Kaiser, sir." [1]

Dewey properly entitled his chapter "A Period of Anxiety." He had news of a more powerful squadron than his own on the way from Spain to the Philippines; he awaited with great anxiety intelligence from Sampson's fleet in the Atlantic; at the same time it was evident from the action of the Germans that they did not accept his interpretation of the laws of the blockade. They were on the most cordial social terms with the Spaniards in Manila, and the talk of the town was that the Germans would intervene in favor of Spain. Dewey addressed a formal letter to Vice-Admiral von Diedrichs in which he said : "As a state of war exists between the United States and Spain, and as the entry into this blockaded port of the vessels of war of a neutral is permitted by the blockading squadron as a matter of international courtesy, such neutrals should necessarily satisfy the blockading vessels as to their identity. . . . I claim the right to communicate with all vessels entering this port, now blockaded with the forces under my command." [2] To this Diedrichs demurred and notified Dewey that "he would submit the point to a conference of all the senior officers of the men-of-war in the harbor." Only Captain Chichester of the British ship *Immortalité* answered the call, and his expressed opinion was decidedly on Dewey's side. Nevertheless it took further and peremptory action on the part of Dewey to convince the German that his orders in Manila Bay must be obeyed. [3]

---

[1] Dewey, Autobiography, 257.   [2] Dewey, Autobiography, 265.
[3] My authority is ch. xvii. of Dewey's Autobiography. But see A. D. White, Autobiography, ii. 160 *et seq.;* Chadwick, the Spanish-American War, ii. 364; Long, ii. iii.; Lodge, 195; Peck, 578.

The glamour of our entrance into the Orient through Dewey's victory could not take the public mind, nor that of the historian, off the real centre of the war, which was in Cuba, and from the direction of affairs, which lay in Washington. On April 22, President McKinley proclaimed a limited blockade of Cuban ports, and four days later he declared "that the policy of this government will be not to resort to privateering but to adhere to the rules of the Declaration of Paris." On April 23, he called for 125,000 volunteers and a little over a month later for 75,000 more.[1] The Secretary of War, Alger, wrote that, as events turned out, the additional call was unnecessary, as 136,000 volunteers did not leave the United States.[2] But it is a tradition in American administration that Lincoln in his first call for 75,000 demanded too small a number, so that McKinley, if he erred at all, was bound to err on the safe side; but a prolongation of the war would have justified the larger number.

Before the United States declared war the President had appointed Captain William T. Sampson commander of the North Atlantic squadron. Advanced over seventeen other officers, he was made rear-admiral at the outbreak of the war and placed in supreme command of all operations on the Atlantic coast. Appointed rear-admiral sixteen days before Dewey, the appointment came to him as a surprise, causing him to feel deep responsibility rather than any elation.[3]

---

[1] Richardson x. 202 et seq.   [2] The Spanish-American War, 19.

[3] The Relations of the United States and Spain: The Spanish War, Chadwick, i. 18 et seq. Chadwick was Captain of the flag-ship *New York* and also Sampson's chief of staff. This valuable and useful work is in two volumes published in 1911 and will be referred to as Chadwick, The Spanish American War i. and do. ii.; see also The New American Navy, Long, i. 211.

The "sinews of war" were carefully looked after. Two hundred million of an authorized loan of double that amount was offered to popular subscription and eagerly grasped at. Although paying but three per cent, it was oversubscribed seven and one half times, was entirely taken at home and went to a premium of six per cent within three months.[1] A revenue bill was carefully framed by Dingley and his Republican associates on the Ways and Means Committee and adroitly piloted through the House and eventually the Senate; it became a law on June 13.[2]

It was known that a Spanish fleet under command of Admiral Cervera had left Cape Verde Islands on April 29, and was steaming westward. The public was uncertain as to its destination, but the Navy Department felt sure that it was either Puerto Rico or Cuba. As it proceeded much more slowly than was estimated, it was a source of mysti-fication and alarm; it arrived at Martinique, a French island, on May 12, and one week later in Santiago harbor, Cuba. Cervera's choice of Santiago and decision to remain there made the battle, which finally took place, the decisive one of the war. In due time, his fleet was blockaded so that he could not make a sortie without a fight.

The President appreciated that to gain a decided re-sult the Army must coöperate with the Navy, and Cer-vera's entrance into Santiago fixed that place as the Army's objective point. Consequently an expedition was prepared to proceed thither. Theodore Roosevelt, a participator in the war and the historian of a phase of it,

---

[1] Noyes, American Finance, 279.
[2] Life of Nelson Dingley, Jr., 462 *et seq.*

called the chapter on it in his Autobiography "The War of America the Unready," and this title is true so far as it applied to the Army. With the charitable and intelligent view of men and affairs, which was a real distinction in a man of active life, he wrote, "Secretary Alger happened to be Secretary when war broke out, and all the responsibility for the shortcomings of the Department were visited upon his devoted head. He was made the scapegoat for our National shortcomings. The fault was not his; the fault and responsibility lay with us, the people, who for thirty-three years had permitted our representatives in Congress and in National executive office to bear themselves so that it was absolutely impossible to avoid the great bulk of all the trouble that occurred, and of all the shortcomings of which our people complained during the Spanish War." [1] But it was different in the Navy, as no one knew better than Roosevelt, who was Assistant Secretary when the war broke out. "The Navy," he wrote, "really was largely on a war footing, as any Navy which is even respectably cared for in time of peace must be. The admirals, captains and lieutenants were continually practicing their profession in almost precisely the way that it has to be practiced in time of war. Except actually shooting at a foe, most of the men on board ship went through in time of peace practically all that they would have to go through in time of war." [2]

If one desires to read a graphic account of the bad management and confusion attendant upon our getting 18,000 troops [3] from Tampa, Florida, to Santiago, let him read

---

[1] The Autobiography (1913), 244.   [2] Ibid., 242.
[3] Chadwick, The Spanish-American War, ii. 77.

Roosevelt's books.[1] "We were kept several days on the transport," he wrote, "which was jammed with men, so that it was hard to move about on deck. Then the fleet got under way, and we steamed slowly down to Santiago. Here we disembarked, higgledy-piggledy, just as we had embarked. Different parts of different outfits were jumbled together, and it was no light labor afterwards to assemble the various batteries. For instance, one transport had guns, and another the locks for the guns; the two not getting together for several days after one of them had been landed. Soldiers went here, provisions there; and who got ashore first largely depended upon individual activity." [2] In some way or other the Army

---

[1] The Rough Riders; Autobiography.

Roosevelt went to Cuba as Lieut. Colonel of the Rough Riders of which **Dr. Leonard Wood** was the Colonel. In a private letter to Dr. W. Sturgis Bigelow of March 29, 1898, Roosevelt wrote: "I do not know that I shall be able to go to Cuba if there is a war. . . . But if I am able to go I certainly shall. . . . I like life very much. I have always led a joyous life. I like thought and I like action, and it will be very bitter to me to leave my wife and children; and while I think I could face death with dignity, I have no desire before my time has come to go out into the everlasting darkness. So I shall not go into a war with any undue exhilaration of spirits or in a frame of mind in any way approaching recklessness or levity."— J. B. Bishop. *Scribner's Magazine*, Nov. 1919, 531.

[2] Autobiography, 255. Roosevelt wrote in his diary which was given in 1921 by Mrs. Theodore Roosevelt to the Roosevelt Memorial Association: "June 3 — Reached Tampa in morning. Railroad system in wildest confusion; it took us twelve hours to get into camp with our baggage.

"June 5 —No words can paint the confusion. No head; a breakdown of both the railroad and military systems of the country.

"June 6 —No plans; no staff officers; no instructions to us. Each officer finds out for himself and takes his chances.

"June 8—Told to go aboard transport. Worst confusion yet. No allotment of transports; no plans; utter confusion." — Boston *Herald*, Sept. 29, 1921.

Roosevelt wrote to his sister, Mrs. Robinson, on June 12 : "It seems to me that the people at Washington are inexcusable for putting us aboard ship and keeping us crowded to suffocation on these transports for six days in Tampa harbor in a semi-tropical sun." Previously one whole night had been spent "standing up opposite a railway track waiting for a train to come, and finally taking coal cars in the morning."— Mrs. Robinson's Roosevelt, 169.

was entirely ashore by June 27.[1] The General in command was Shafter, a regular army officer of talent.[2] but entirely unfitted for a tropical expedition. Sixty-three years of age, weighing over 300, with a tendency to the gout, mounting a horse with difficulty,[3] his physical disabilities weighed upon him to an extent to unfit him entirely for his dangerous and responsible job.

"I expect to attack Santiago to-morrow morning," Shafter wrote to Sampson on June 30.[4] He was as good as his word, and the battles of El Caney and San Juan Hill resulted. The fort at El Caney was captured, but the fight at San Juan Hill was the more important. Captain John Bigelow, who was a captain in the regular cavalry with the expedition, wrote: "The enemy's position was about as nearly ideal as a real position can be. I have seen the famous stone wall at Fredericksburg backed by Marye's Heights. It is hardly a circumstance to this position. San Juan was more suggestive of Gettysburg than of Fredericksburg. Our attack seemed hardly less desperate than that of Pickett's division. At Gettysburg a cannonade of several hours' duration designed to shake the *morale* of the defence, preceded the advance of the attacking infantry which, during this period of preparation, was kept out of fire. At San Juan there was

---

[1] "The Army was in a region with a character wholly unlike that of any in its experience. Nearly the whole of the regular force of which it was composed had been accustomed to harrying Indians over treeless plains or arid mountains. In this case however it found itself in a country covered with brush so heavy that, almost impassable to the individual man, it was altogether so to troops in formation." Chadwick, The Spanish-American War, ii. 62.

[2] Chadwick, Spanish-American War, ii. 6; Alger.

[3] Chadwick, ii. 110; R. H. Davis, The Cuban and Porto Rican Campaigns, 185.

[4] Chadwick, Spanish-American War, ii. 75.

hardly any preparation by artillery, and the infantry and dismounted cavalry, who made the attack, were exposed to the enemy's fire for about an hour immediately preceding their advance, most of them not being able or permitted to fire back." [1] The work was done by the regular troops, "the flower of the American standing army," Senator Lodge so termed them.[2] They were assisted by three volunteer regiments, only one of which, the Rough Riders, under the command of Theodore Roosevelt,[3] did effective service. The Cuban insurgents helped the Americans by doing their part in cutting off the supplies from Santiago, but were not as valuable support as had been expected. San Juan Heights was taken on this July first. "The attack," wrote Chadwick, "was indeed one of high heroism . . . as gallant a deed as was ever done." [4]

No word of praise can be too high for the work of the soldiers that day, but their creature comforts were not looked after. They fought on empty stomachs, as the commissariat was badly managed; they were also short of tobacco so highly prized by soldiers in the field. "Their woolen clothing," said Roosevelt, "was exactly what I

---

[1] Reminiscences of the Santiago Campaign, 127.
[2] P. 130. Chadwick wrote : "Our first army was one of extraordinary quality; such probably as will never again take the field, as the conditions of its training can never be repeated. It was the product of long years of war against the wiliest and most capable of savage races. Schooled in every trick of savage warfare, inured to every privation of heat and cold, individualized as no other soldier ever has been, these men of the plains were accustomed to fighting their own battles, and took with them to San Juan Hill the qualities and character which made this a force, which it is not too much to say, has never been equalled in general efficiency." ii. 12.
[3] Wood had been advanced to a brigade command which made Roosevelt colonel of the Rough Riders.   [4] ii. 96.

would have used in Montana in the fall." [1] The Spaniards were better armed and equipped and had a larger supply of smokeless powder. Nevertheless, the events justified the charge on the fortified position, as Spanish firing was less deadly than the climate. But the loss at El Caney and San Juan Hill was over ten per cent of the men engaged; the casualties among the officers were unusually heavy.[2]

Next day, July 2, while the Spaniards made no attempt to retake San Juan Heights they kept up an incessant firing. This and the heavy losses of July 1 completely demoralized Shafter who, suffering from malarial fever, almost always accompanied by mental depression, was thoroughly despondent when, on July 3, he telegraphed to Washington, "I am seriously considering withdrawing about five miles and taking up a new position." [3] Other officers of the army shared his anxiety but nevertheless two captains of the regular troops came to Roosevelt desiring him to protest against any retirement. Roosevelt, who always disliked the word retreat, cordially agreed with them "that it would be far worse than a blunder to abandon our position." [4] But Shafter had not forgotten the American game of bluff and at 8.30 that morning demanded the surrender of Santiago, which was peremptorily declined by the Spanish commander.

Senator Lodge gave a graphic account of the feeling in Washington on July 3. "It was the one really dark day of the war," he wrote, "and the long hot hours of that memorable Sunday were heavy with doubt, apprehen-

---

[1] Chadwick, ii. 66.
[2] Chadwick, The Spanish-American War, ii. 100.
[3] Chadwick, The Spanish-American War, ii. 109.
[4] The Rough Riders, 148; Chadwick, ii. 108.

sion and anxiety." [1] But if the administration in Washington and Shafter could have known the sentiment of the Spanish camp, their despondency would have given way to elation. For Santiago was reaching the point of capitulation; while the fleet had food for about a month longer, the army and the city had been reduced to rice.[2] The fleet, however, was the important thing. "The eyes of every nation," wrote Captain-General Blanco to Cervera from Havana, "are at present fixed on your squadron on which the honor of our country depends." [3] Before this Blanco had suggested to Madrid that all the land and naval forces in the Western waters be placed under his supreme command and his suggestion had been complied with.[4] Admiral Cervera, the commander of the Spanish squadron, was discouraged at the outlook. He wrote on June 25, eight days before the dark day in Washington, to the Spanish general in command at Santiago; "I have considered the squadron lost ever since it left Cape Verde. . . . To-day I consider the squadron lost as much as ever, and the dilemma is whether to lose it by destroying it, if Santiago is not able to resist, after having contributed to its defence, or whether to lose it by sacrificing to vanity the majority of its crews and depriving Santiago of their coöperation, thereby precipitating its fall. . . . It is therefore for the Captain-General to decide whether I am to go out to suicide, dragging along with me those 2000 sons of Spain." On the same day he telegraphed to the Captain-General, "In my opinion the sortie will entail the certain loss of

---

[1] P. 133.
[2] Chadwick, ii. 114.   [3] June 26, ibid., 119.
[4] June 20-25, ibid., 115.

the squadron and majority of its crews." [1]   Blanco desired the escape made "from that prison in which the squadron is unfortunately shut in" on a dark night and in bad weather, but to this Cervera replied, "With the harbor entrance blockaded as it now is, the sortie at night is more perilous than in daytime, on account of ships being closer inshore." [2]

Thus stood affairs until the army made the attack of July 1, after which the Spanish general in command reported the "exhausted and serious condition of Santiago." The result of that battle brought the Spanish authorities to a decision. Cervera had lent his "landing forces" to the army for the defence of Santiago, and to make a proper sortie he must have them reëmbarked. He received an order from Blanco on July 1 to reëmbark "the crews" and to hasten the sortie from the harbor. This was followed up by a despatch next day to go out immediately. A telegram to the general in command showed plainly the thought that dwelt in Blanco's mind: "Main thing is that squadron go out at once, for if Americans take possession of it, Spain will be morally defeated and must ask for peace at mercy of enemy. A city lost can be recovered; the loss of the squadron under these circumstances is final and cannot be recovered." [3]   It was impossible to make the sortie in the afternoon of July 2, so the morning of July 3 was decided upon.

The historian is able to look into both camps — a look of course impossible to either Sampson or Cervera. There was friction between Sampson and Shafter as well

---

[1] Chadwick, ii. 116, 118.   [2] Ibid., ii. 118, 119.
[3] Ibid., ii. 122, 124.

as between the Army and Navy departments in Washington. When the Naval Board announced — an announcement which was endorsed by the Secretary — that it was better to sacrifice a number of soldiers rather than to lose one battleship, such an opinion was regarded as inhuman although probably based on good naval strategy. Shafter, appalled at the losses of July 1, did not want to sacrifice further his men, and desired Sampson to force an entrance into the harbor on the Farragut plan, which, on his part, Sampson did not want to do on account of the risk of losing a battleship. Shafter was ill and telegraphed to Washington on July 3 : "I have been unable to be out during the heat of the day for four days,[1] but am retaining the command. . . . I am urging Admiral Sampson to attempt to force the entrance of the harbor and will have consultation with him this morning." [2] This conference was to be had at Shafter's headquarters, for which place Sampson on his armored cruiser, the *New York*, started on the morning of July 3. The port at which he proposed to land was eight miles from his position in the blockading squadron. No fortune could have been worse for Sampson. Since June 1 he had maintained a perfect blockade of Santiago Harbor. "The faithful search-light" [3] made him feel secure at night. "When I wake up," he said, "and can see from where I lie the operation of the search-light, I can fall asleep quite contented, knowing that everything is all right." Among the eventualities which he considered, was the escape of

---

[1] On July 4, after the naval battle of Santiago, Shafter wrote to the Adjutant-General in Washington, "I am still very much exhausted, eating a little this P.M. for the first time in four days." Chadwick, ii. 192.
[2] Ibid., 109.   [3] Long, ii. 7.

ships from the harbor, and he had issued the order, "If the enemy tries to escape, the ships must close and engage as soon as possible, and endeavor to sink his vessels or force them to run ashore"; [1] but he could have had no idea that the plan of battle which he had considered and carefully thought out would be put into force on that day. Not only was the commander-in-chief and his cruiser *New York* absent, but the *Massachusetts* had gone away forty miles in order to coal.

The Spanish squadron consisted of the armored cruisers *Infanta Maria Teresa, Oquendo, Vizcaya, Cristóbal Colón* and two torpedo-boat destroyers; the American, of the armored cruiser *Brooklyn*, the battleships *Texas, Iowa, Oregon, Indiana* and the auxiliaries *Gloucester* and *Vixen*. The Spanish vessels came out of the harbor of Santiago on this Sunday morning, July 3, "a superb day," [2] between 9.35 and 10; the flag-ship *Maria Teresa* was in advance and, following at a distance of about 800 yards, were the *Vizcaya, Cristóbal Colón* and the *Oquendo* and at a greater distance the torpedo-boat destroyers. The men on the American ships were at Sunday "quarters for inspection," which was to be followed by divine service. But their officers were on the alert and, at the first sight of the Spaniards, the American ships, carrying out Sampson's standing orders, closed in and began the work of destruction which their careful labor of preparation and accurate firing enabled them to do. The Spaniards advanced with coolness and courage. The *Maria Teresa* "presented a magnificent appearance," wrote Robley Evans, Captain of the *Iowa*, and the fleet "came at us like mad

---

[1] Long, ii. 7.   [2] Wilson, The Downfall of Spain, 295.

bulls." [1]   At first the fire of the *Maria Teresa* was rapid
and accurate, but as the American fire "smothered" her,
it grew "ragged and inaccurate." [2]   "I felt sure," wrote
Cervera, "that the disaster was inevitable . . . although I did not think our destruction would be so sudden." [3]

Between ten and half past the *Maria Teresa* and *Oquendo*,
"with large volumes of smoke rising from their lower
decks aft, gave up both fight and flight and ran in on the
beach" when about seven miles from Santiago.   At quarter past eleven the *Vizcaya*, when fifteen miles from Santiago, "turned in shore and was beached"; she "was
burning fiercely and her reserves of ammunition were
already beginning to explode." [4]   Meanwhile the Spanish
torpedo-boat destroyers had been smashed by the fire
of the battleships and especially by that of the auxiliary,
Gloucester, a converted yacht. Remained "the sleek
foxy *Colón*," [5] the "best and fastest vessel" [6] of the Spanish fleet, which was overhauled by the *Brooklyn* and
Oregon; at twenty minutes past one, forty-eight miles
from Santiago, she hauled down her colors and surrendered.

"I regard," wrote Sampson in his Official Report, "this
complete and important victory over the Spanish forces
as the successful finish of several weeks of arduous and
close blockade, so stringent and effective during the night
that the enemy was deterred from making the attempt

---

[1] A Sailor's Log, 445.   [2] Ibid., 446.   [3] Chadwick, ii. 138, 185.
[4] Admiral Sampson's Official Report, July 15.   Crowninshield, 507 *et seq.*
[5] Spears, Our Navy in the War with Spain, 319.
[6] Sampson.

to escape at night and deliberately elected to make the attempt in daylight." [1]

President Roosevelt, with a comprehension of naval affairs such as few or no civilians had, after a careful review of all the facts, wrote, "It was a captains' fight." [2]

The casualties of the Spanish squadron, which numbered 2227, did not exceed 474 and were probably fewer; the American loss was one killed, one seriously wounded. [3] "It is safe to say," wrote H. W. Wilson, an English authority, "that most Englishmen, with their knowledge of 1812 and the feats of the Civil War, confidently expected the Americans to win. It is equally safe to say that no one anticipated that two important victories would be secured at the cost of but one American life. . . . After less than five hours' fighting a modern squadron was completely annihilated with infinitesimal loss and infinitesimal damage to the victors. It is the low cost at which victory was purchased that renders this great battle so honorable to the American Navy." [4]

The naval battle of Santiago was a great victory and decisive of the war. "Do not Europeans regard us as barbarians?" was asked of a man, who, though not a

---

[1] Crowninshield, 509. Secretary Long wrote: "The battle of July 3 was actually fought and the great victory won in accordance with the plan of the commander-in-chief," ii. 8. President Roosevelt wrote, Feb. 18, 1902: "Sampson's real claim for credit rests upon his work as commander-in-chief; upon the excellence of the blockade; upon the preparedness of the squadron; upon the arrangement of the ships head-on in a semicircle around the harbor; and the standing order with which they instantly moved to the attack of the Spaniards when the latter appeared." Long, ii. 208.

[2] Long, ii. 208.

[3] Chadwick, ii. 176. According to Spanish authority the Spaniards had 323 killed and 151 wounded.

[4] The Downfall of Spain, 69, 334.

native American, had passed enough time in the United
States to speak and write English well and, although
devoted artistically to Europe, had gained a thorough
comprehension of Americans. "They did," was the reply,
"until you smashed two Spanish fleets, but they think so
no longer." Such is the judgment of the civilized world.
Our work toward the elevation of humanity, toward the
greater diffusion of education, are counted as naught in
contrast with these naval victories.

Noteworthy as was the victory of Santiago it was supplemented by humane action. "As the *Maria Teresa*
struck the rock, the tars of the *Texas* . . . began to
cheer." But their Captain Philip exclaimed, "Don't
cheer, boys; the poor devils are dying." [1] When Captain Robley Evans instantly handed back the surrendered
sword to the Captain of the *Vizcaya*, his "blue shirts"
cheered lustily.[2] "So long," he wrote in his report of
July 4, "as the enemy showed his flag they fought like
American seamen; but when the flag came down they
were as gentle and tender as American women." [3] "This
rescue of prisoners," wrote Admiral Sampson in his report, "including the wounded from the burning Spanish
vessels was the occasion of some of the most daring and
gallant conduct of the day. The ships were burning fore
and aft, their guns and reserve ammunition were exploding, and it was not known at what moment the fire would
reach the main magazines. In addition to this a heavy
surf was running just inside of the Spanish ships. But no
risk deterred our officers and men until their work of humanity was complete." [4] Cervera in his report eulogized

[1] Long, ii. 39.   [2] A Sailor's Log, 451.   [3] Crowninshield, 539.
[4] Crowninshield, 509.

"the chivalry and courtesy of the enemy. They clothed the naked," he wrote, "giving them everything they needed; they suppressed the shouts of joy in order not to increase the suffering of the defeated, and all vied in making their captivity as easy as possible."[1] He wrote to the Captain of the *St. Louis* when "at sea" on his way home, "I thank you for the delicate and manifold acts of kindness through which you have endeavored to alleviate the sore burden of our great misfortune."[2] In other words, the American seamen fought like gentlemen and not like brutes. Exactly the same may be said of the American soldiers who contended before Santiago.[3]

As has been previously stated, the naval battle of Santiago was the decisive one of the war. Blanco thought that the squadron must make a fight to save Spanish honor but he recognized that its destruction meant that the game was up. The annihilation of the fleet, wrote Captain Concas, the acting chief-of-staff of Cervera, deprived "Spain of the only power still of value to her, without which a million soldiers could do nothing to serve her; of the only power which could have weight in a treaty of peace; a power which, once destroyed, would leave Spain, the old Spain of Europe, not Cuba as so many ignorant persons believed, completely at the mercy of the enemy."[4]

The fall of Santiago quickly followed. Puerto Rico was also captured. "In comparison to the Santiago

---

[1] Crowninshield, 562. See also Cervera to Blanco and Sampson. Chadwick, ii. 189, 190.
[2] Foreign Relations, 1898, 798.
[3] Chadwick, ii. 262; Peck, 598.   [4] Chadwick, ii. 128.

nightmare," wrote Richard Harding Davis, "the Porto Rican expedition was a 'fête des fleurs.'" [1]

Meanwhile it was learned that the reserve fleet of Spain was despatched to the Philippines, and soon thereafter an American squadron was collected, the destination of which should be the Spanish coast. This was publicly announced. The reserve Spanish fleet went through the Suez Canal, but the public announcement of the destination of the American fleet, together with the news of the destruction of Cervera's squadron, compelled its return to Spain.

A glance must now be had at the Orient. Troops were sent at different times until on August 6 there were about 8500 men ashore in the Philippines. General Merritt commanded the land forces and, in conjunction with Dewey, demanded the surrender of Manila and the Spanish forces in occupation. On August 13, an attack was begun which soon terminated, as arranged through "the good offices of the Belgian consul," by the surrender. [2]

The 10,000 Filipino insurgents under Aguinaldo had rendered valuable assistance in the investment of Manila and now made "a passing demand for joint occupation of the city" and, as the situation was difficult, Merritt and Dewey asked for instructions from Washington. President McKinley in reply directed that there "must be no joint occupation with the insurgents." [3]

"Had not the cable been cut," wrote Dewey, "there would have been no attack on August 13, for while our ships — counting the twelve hours' difference in time

---

[1] The Cuban and Porto Rican Campaigns, 296.
[2] Chadwick, ii. 408.
[3] Chadwick, ii. 423; Richardson, x. 217.

between the two hemispheres — were moving into position and our troops were holding themselves in readiness for a dash upon the Spanish works, the Protocol was being signed at Washington. The absence of immediate cable connection had allowed no interruption to the fateful progress of events which was to establish our authority in the Philippines." [1]

The smashing of the two fleets decided the war, and this was acknowledged by the Spaniards themselves. They had made resistance to save their honor but recognized that, when the fortunes of war decided against them, it was useless to prolong the conflict. Through a letter from the Spanish Minister of State to President McKinley [2] they started negotiations through Jules Cambon, the French Ambassador, who showed wonderful qualities. Frankly on the Spanish side, he saw clearly the American position, appreciated the magnitude of the naval victories and the helplessness of Spain. He found McKinley inflexible and disposed to drive a hard bargain. Believing that the "Conqueror resolved to procure all the profit possible from the advantages it has obtained," [3] he advised Spain to give him authority to sign the Protocol. This was done and the Protocol was signed by him and Secretary of State Day. [4]

The Protocol provided that Spain should relinquish all claim of sovereignty over Cuba, that she should cede to the United States Puerto Rico and an island in the Ladrones. This cession was in lieu of a pecuniary in-

---

[1] Autobiography, 282.   [2] Olcott, ii. 59.   [3] Chadwick, ii, 440.
[4] Elihu Root said when Secretary of War (Nov. 15, 1902) that Cambon was an " ideal ambassador," the " sympathetic representative and defender " of Spain. Miscellaneous Addresses, 145, 147.

demnity for the cost of the war. Furthermore, "The United States will occupy and hold the city, bay and harbor of Manila, pending the conclusion of a treaty of peace which shall determine the control, disposition and government of the Philippines."

Five Commissioners on the part of the United States and five on the part of Spain should meet in Paris not later than October 1 to negotiate and conclude a treaty of peace, subject to ratification by the constitutional authorities of both countries. This Protocol was signed on August 12 and involved a total suspension of hostilities.[1]

The war was over, having lasted 113 days [April 21 to August 12], less than four months.[2]

---

[1] Foreign Relations, 1898, 828.

[2] Authorities on the Spanish-American War: First, and foremost, the two volumes of Admiral French E. Chadwick. Chadwick has used the Spanish as well as the American documents with the result that he has enabled us to see both camps at the same time. He has written an impartial account. His action on the New York before and during the naval battle of Santiago made him an excellent interpreter of the documents, showing no animosity whatever to Spain. At the end of Vol. ii. he has given an excellent bibliography.

Reports of Battle of Santiago by Sampson; Schley and Cook of the Brooklyn; Chadwick of the New York; Clark of the Oregon; Philip of the Texas; Taylor of the Indiana; Evans of the Iowa; Wainwright of the Gloucester; Report of Cervera; Crowninshield, 506 et seq.; Autobiography of George Dewey; Foreign Relations, 1898; The New American Navy, Long; Lodge, The War with Spain; Theodore Roosevelt, Autobiography, Rough Riders; R. A. Alger, The Spanish-American War; Evans, A Sailor's Log; John Bigelow, Jr., Reminiscences of the Santiago Campaign; H. W. Wilson, The Downfall of Spain; R. H. Davis, The Cuban and Porto Rican Campaigns; F. D. Millet, The Expedition to the Philippines; Spear's Our Navy in the War with Spain; Mahan, Lessons of the War with Spain; Peck; Latané, America as a World Power, Hart's American Nation series.

Secretary Long wrote that the trip of the Oregon "has no parallel in history," ii. 54. Admiral Sampson spoke of her "brilliant record" under Captain Clark, Crowninshield, 510. "Her performance," wrote Chadwick, "was one unprecedented in battleship history and was one which will probably long preserve its unique distinction," i. 16. On "the Oregon's famous run," see Spear's chap. xii. For Hobson's exploit, see Chadwick, i. 338; Long, ii. 71.

CHAPTER V

In the first article of the Protocol, Spain relinquished Cuba. This rich island might fall to the United States. It was a ripe plum [1] that needed only the plucking. But there stood in the way the sentiment of a majority of the American people embodied in the so-called Teller Amendment to the resolutions adopted by Congress when the United States went to war with Spain. Although long a favorite policy that Cuba ought to belong to the United States, she now disclaimed any intention of taking the island, but proposed to leave it to the Cubans themselves. Any other large country would not probably in the first place have adopted the Teller Amendment but, even had it done so, its occupancy would have been made the prelude on one pretext or another to an eventual absorption. Undoubtedly a powerful minority would have supported McKinley in such a policy, but he deserves credit that, believing in the terms of the Teller Amendment when adopted, he held to them firmly, after the quick result of the war, and wrote a glorious page in his country's history as the pledge was faithfully carried out. In lieu of a pecuniary indemnity for the cost of the war and because it was desirable that Spain should quit the Western Hemisphere, Puerto Rico and other islands under the Spanish dominion in the West Indies were taken. Also on the ground of pecuniary indemnity an island in the Ladrones was required; this article resulted in the

---

[1] Substantially the same remark was made in chap. iii.

99

selection of Guam. Remained the Philippines, which caused much discussion in the Cabinet, country and with the Spanish Peace Commissioners, who by the terms of the Protocol, met in Paris those sent from the United States to negotiate a treaty of peace.

When the letter of the Spanish Minister of State was received [July 26] [1] the President on a hot afternoon took the members of the Cabinet on a lighthouse tender for a trip down the Potomac, when were thoroughly discussed the terms of peace. This resulted later in the submission by Secretary Day of an article which proposed to "relinquish all of the Philippine Islands to Spain except sufficient ground for a naval station." [2] On this proposition the Cabinet was about equally divided. It is easy to see that had the President then decided not to take the Philippines he would have had a powerful backing. During the war he had displayed a shrewd trading instinct thus expressed, "While we are conducting war and until its conclusion we must keep all we get; when the war is over we must keep what we want." [3] Now he did not desire to come to a positive decision, and preferred to leave the matter open for the development of circumstances and until we had more information and especially some enlightening word from Dewey. The President said to Jules Cambon: "The negotiators of the two countries will be the ones to decide what will be the permanent advantages that we shall demand in the archipelago and finally the control, disposition and government of the Philippines. The Madrid government may be assured that up to this time there is nothing determined *à priori*

---

[1] This is printed by Olcott, ii. 59.
[2] Life of McKinley, Olcott, ii. 61.   [3] Ibid., 165.

in my mind against Spain; likewise I consider there is
nothing decided against the United States." [1] Therefore,
Article III in the Protocol, agreed to with Jules Cambon,
left the disposition of the Philippines until a formal treaty
of peace should be concluded.

The Protocol provided for the appointment of five
Commissioners to meet in Paris an equal number from
Spain. The President named William R. Day, Cushman
K. Davis, chairman of the Senate Foreign Relations Committee, William P. Frye, Senator from Maine, Whitelaw
Reid, editor and proprietor of the New York *Tribune*
and ex-minister to France, and George Gray, Senator
from Delaware, the only Democrat on the Commission.
The discussion between the Peace Commissioners and
the different despatches of the Americans to Washington make interesting reading, but it is apparent that the
decision of the main points rested with the President,
who used the communications from the Commissioners
as materials on which to base his own judgment. He
decided at once that neither the United States nor any
government which she might set up in Cuba would assume any portion of the so-called Cuban debt which had
been largely incurred in fighting two insurrections.

The greatest contention, however, was in regard to the
Philippines. These consisted of a number of islands with
a combined area of 115,000 square miles, nearly as large
as England, Scotland, Ireland and Wales. The largest is
Luzon with nearly 41,000 square miles, substantially the
size of Ohio. The total population was more than seven
and one half millions; the population of Luzon was

---

[1] Despatch of Cambon to Spain, Aug. 4, Chadwick, ii. 436.

3,798,507 and that of Manila, the chief city, 219,928.[1]
"The Philippines were a rich prize for any ambitious
power," was Dewey's opinion after his victory.[2]

After the Protocol was signed, the President inclined
toward taking the Philippines. Of his five Peace Commissioners, three, Davis, Frye and Reid, were avowed imperialists. In his instruction to the Commission of September 16,[3] he wrote that we must have the island of
Luzon and on October 26 he had his Secretary of State,
John Hay,[4] telegraph as follows to Commissioner Day:
"The information which has come to the President since
your departure convinces him that the acceptance of the
cession of Luzon alone, leaving the rest of the islands
subject to the Spanish rule, or to be the subject of future
contention, cannot be justified on political, commercial or
humanitarian grounds. The cession must be of the whole
archipelago or none. The latter is wholly inadmissible
and the former must therefore be required. The President reaches this conclusion after most thorough consideration of the whole subject, and is deeply sensible of the
grave responsibilities it will impose, believing that this
course will entail less trouble than any other, and besides
will best subserve the interests of the people involved,
for whose welfare we cannot escape responsibility." [5]

---

[1] Life of McKinley, ii. 145; Foreign Relations, 1898, 925. "The entire population, according to the census of 1903, was 7,635,426. Of these
6,987,686 were classed as civilized and 647,740 as wild. The civilized native inhabitants are practically all adherents of the Roman Catholic
Church. Of the wild tribes at least two-fifths are Mohammedan Moros.
With the exception of the aboriginal Negritos, who are widely dispersed
through the mountain regions, all the natives are believed to be Malays."
Latané, 79.

[2] Autobiography, 251.   [3] Foreign Relations, 904.
[4] John Hay had become Secretary of State succeeding William R. Day.
[5] Hay to Day, Foreign Relations, 1898, 935.

Between October 10 and 22 McKinley visited the
Omaha Trans-Mississippi Exposition ; in going thither and
returning he made a number of speeches at convenient
rail stops.[1] Senator Hoar called it "his famous Western
journey." [2] Unquestionably Hoar is correct in attribut-
ing to McKinley too great a reliance on the sentiment
exhibited by the enthusiastic crowds that he addressed,
but in truth his deductions from the meetings only confirmed what he had already determined.

By direction of the President, General Merritt went
from Manila to Paris and gave a full report to the Peace
Commission. While he was careful not to express himself
positively in response to certain questions, a fair inference
from his testimony is that it was desirable to take the
whole group.[3]

The President had before him Dewey's report, from
which it may be gathered that the Admiral favored the
retention of Luzon alone, but General Greene, who
brought to the White House this report, with whom
McKinley had a "long talk" and whom he found
"thoroughly well informed," approved decidedly our
taking all of the Philippines.[4] The President had also

---

[1] For these speeches, see New York *Tribune*, Oct. 11–23, 1898.
[2] Autobiography, ii. 311.   [3] Foreign Relations, 1898, 918.
[4] "Luzon is in almost all respects the most desirable of these islands
and therefore the one to retain." — Dewey, Aug. 29. General Greene
said in his Memorandum of August 27 which represented his opinion when
he had the "long talk" with McKinley on September 28 : "If the United
States evacuate these islands, anarchy and civil war will immediately
ensue and lead to foreign intervention. The insurgents were furnished
arms and the moral support of the Navy prior to our arrival, and we cannot ignore obligations, either to the insurgents or to foreign nations, which
our own acts have imposed upon us. The Spanish Government is completely demoralized and Spanish power is dead beyond possibility of res-
urrection. Spain would be unable to govern these islands if we surrendered them. . . . On the other hand, the Filipinos cannot govern the

before him the opinion of the several members of the Peace Commission before it was necessary to arrive at a final decision. The opinions of the three imperialists, Davis, Frye and Reid, tallied with his own; that of Day was a compromise,[1] but Senator Gray's opinion deserves consideration. "I cannot agree," he said, "that it is wise to take Philippines in whole or in part. To do so would be to reverse accepted continental policy of country, declared and acted upon throughout our history. Propinquity governs case of Cuba and Puerto Rico. Policy proposed introduces us into European politics and the entangling alliances, against which Washington and all American statesmen have protested. . . . Attacked Manila as part of legitimate war against Spain. If we had captured Cadiz and Carlists had helped us, would not owe duty to stay by them at conclusion of war. On contrary interest and duty would require us to abandon both Manila and Cadiz. . . .

"So much from standpoint of interest. But even conceding all benefits claimed for annexation we thereby abandon the infinitely greater benefit to accrue from acting the part of a great, powerful and Christian nation; we exchange the moral grandeur and strength to be gained by keeping our word to nations of the world and by exhibiting a magnanimity and moderation in hour of victory that becomes the advanced civilization we claim, for doubtful material advantages and shameful stepping down from high moral position boastfully assumed. We

---

country without the support of some strong nation."—Senate docs. 8, no. 62; Treaty of Peace between United States and Spain, 374, 383; Foreign Relations, 1898, 915, 917.

[1] Foreign Relations, 1898, 932 et seq.

should set example in these respects, not follow the selfish and vulgar greed for territory which Europe has inherited from mediæval times. Our declaration of war upon Spain was accompanied by a solemn and deliberate definition of our purpose. Now that we have achieved all and more than our object, let us simply keep our word." [1]

Admiral Chadwick, after citing Gray's dissent, wrote: "There is no questioning the cogency of Judge Gray's argument, nor the nobility of its sentiment. To demand the Philippines was undoubtedly to alter the moral position of the United States and change its attitude from one of altruism to one of self-interest. This much is self-evident and scarcely requires statement." [2] But McKinley stuck to his determination and had Hay telegraph it to Commissioner Day on October 28: "The sentiment in the United States," he said, "is almost universal that the people of the Philippines, whatever else is done, must be liberated from Spanish domination. In this sentiment the President fully concurs. Nor can we permit Spain to transfer any of the islands to another power. Nor can we invite another power or powers to join the United States in sovereignty over them. We must either hold them or turn them back to Spain.

"Consequently, grave as are the responsibilities and unforeseen as are the difficulties which are before us, the President can see but one plain path of duty — the acceptance of the archipelago. Greater difficulties and more serious complications, administrative and international, would follow any other course. The President has given to the

---

[1] Oct. 25, Foreign Relations, 1898, 934.   [2] ii. 461.

views of the Commissioners the fullest consideration, and
in reaching the conclusion above announced, in the light
of information communicated to the Commission and to
the President since your departure, he has been influenced
by the single consideration of duty and humanity." [1]

On November 13, the President's idea was further
elaborated by Hay's despatch again to Commissioner
Day. "Do we not owe an obligation to the people of
the Philippines which will not permit us to return them
to the sovereignty of Spain?" he asked. "You are
therefore instructed to insist upon the cession of the whole
of the Philippines and, if necessary, pay to Spain
$10,000,000 to $20,000,000. . . . The trade and commercial side as well as the indemnity for the cost of the war
are questions we might yield. They might be waived or
compromised but the questions of duty and humanity
appeal to the President so strongly that he can find no
appropriate answer but the one he has here marked out." [2]

The biographer of McKinley shows us the working of
his mind in some words he addressed to his Methodist
brethren: "The truth is," he said, "I didn't want the
Philippines and when they came to us as a gift from the
gods, I did not know what to do with them. . . .
I sought counsel from all sides — Democrats as well as
Republicans — but got little help. I thought first we
would take only Manila; then Luzon; then other islands,
perhaps, also. I walked the floor of the White House
night after night until midnight; and I am not ashamed
to tell you, gentlemen, that I went down on my knees

---

[1] Foreign Relations, 1898, 937.
[2] Ibid., 949. For an interesting account of the work of the Peace Commission, see Life of Whitelaw Reid, Cortissoz, ii. chap. xiii.

and prayed Almighty God for light and guidance more
than one night. And one night late it came to me this
way — I don't know how it was, but it came: (1) that
we could not give them back to Spain — that would be
cowardly and dishonorable; (2) that we could not turn
them over to France or Germany — our commercial
rivals in the Orient — that would be bad business and discreditable; (3) that we could not leave them to themselves — they were unfit for self-government — and they
would soon have anarchy and misrule over there worse
than Spain's was; and (4) that there was nothing left
for us to do but to take them all, and to educate the
Filipinos, and uplift and civilize and Christianize them,
and by God's grace do the very best we could by them as
our fellow-men for whom Christ also died. And then I
went to bed, and went to sleep and slept soundly." [1]

It is true that McKinley was inconsistent in his public
words. In his message of December, 1897, he had said,
"Forcible annexation . . . cannot be thought of; that,
by our code of morality, would be criminal aggression." [2]
One cannot read the proceedings of the Peace Commission in Paris and see in any other light than that our taking of the Philippines was "forcible annexation." In his
instructions to the Commissioners of September 16, 1898,
he had said that the United States must be "scrupulous
and magnanimous in the concluding settlement." It
should not be tempted into "excessive demands or into
an adventurous departure on untried paths." [3] But our
attitude to Spain denied the injunction to show magnanimity, and our demand for and the taking of the

---

[1] Interview, Nov. 21, 1899.   Life of McKinley, ii. 109.
[2] Richardson, x. 131.   [3] Foreign Relations, 1898, 907.

Philippines was an excessive demand and a venture on untried paths.

Yet McKinley was entirely sincere. He was truly religious, and when he told his Methodist brethren of the working of his mind, he told exactly the truth as he saw it. When he wrote, "The war has brought us new duties and responsibilities which we must meet and discharge as becomes a great nation on whose growth and career from the beginning the Ruler of Nations has plainly written the high command and pledge of civilization,"[1] he meant what he said; and many good moral and religious men were entirely of his mind. Indeed it was a troublesome question to decide. The opinion of a majority of the American people was opposed to allowing the islands to go back to Spain; and yet as we see it now, that was the only alternative. They and the President did not believe that things should be permitted in the Eastern Hemisphere that they had gone to war to stop in Cuba. While the humanitarian impulse did the President honor, he had no right to commit his country to a dangerous course, to run the risk of "an adventurous departure on untried paths," on account of a religious sentiment. Despite the obvious opinion of the majority, which with "his ear close to the ground"[2] he well knew, his hold on the country was so great, increased as it was by a victorious war, that he could have led it to accept any conditions that he deemed necessary for the conclusion of a peace. The only possible alternative, leaving the islands to Spain, might have been done under conditions suggested by Commissioner Day.[3] Such con-

---

[1] Foreign Relations, 1898, 907.
[2] Peck, 659.   [3] Foreign Relations, 1898, 926, 934.

ditions would have filled the measure of humanity; but there would naturally have been the query whether Spain would or could carry them out.[1]

An American condition, however, should have influenced the President without fail. The Monroe Doctrine had come to be regarded as sacred and the spirit of it, if not the letter, was violated when we annexed the Philippines. We held that no European Power should take territory or increase what she possessed in the Western Hemisphere. In other words we said, "You keep away from us and we will keep away from you."[2] By the same token we were bound not to encroach on the Eastern Hemisphere. A cartoon in *Punch* entitled "Doctrine and Practice" represented Dame Europa in a garden, her attitude haughty, saying coldly to an intruder, "To whom do I owe the pleasure of this intrusion?" The intruder, in face, figure and get-up of the well-known type, replied "Ma'am — my name is Uncle Sam!" When came the rejoinder, "Any relation of the late Colonel Monroe?"[3] True it was urged that we had grown too large to be confined by the Monroe Doctrine, that the teachings of Washington, Monroe and John Quincy Adams applied to the country as it was then and had no longer application.[4] Others reasoned that the Monroe

---

[1] General MacArthur said in his Testimony before the Senate Committee on the Philippines on April 11, 1902: "When we landed [MacArthur sailed for Manila from San Francisco on June 27, 1898] we found the entire population [of the Philippines] in open, violent, vindictive resentment against Spain, as an expression of their desire to be emancipated from that monarchy. . . . I think if they had been granted the reforms which were extended to the people of the peninsula [of Spain] that the Filipinos would have been loyal Spaniards to-day." — Part ii. 1384.

[2] *The Nation*, Nov. 10, 1898, 345.

[3] *Punch*, Aug. 6, 1898; Winslow Warren in Boston *Herald*, Apr. 18, 1919.

[4] See *The Nation*, May 19, 1898, 376.

Doctrine only obliged us to keep out of Europe and had no reference to Asia.[1]   But it was entirely easy for President McKinley to set aside such reasonings did he so desire.

The Secretary of State, John Hay, was influenced by the opinion of England as she had been the sole large European power on our side during the Spanish War. "The dull hostility between us and England which existed a year ago," he wrote while Ambassador, has been changed into a firm friendship.   "If we give up the Philippines it will be a considerable disappointment to our English friends. . . .   I have no doubt that Germany has been intriguing both with Aguinaldo and with Spain. They are most anxious to get a foothold there; but if they do there will be danger of grave complication with other European powers."[2]

With the determination of the President, events moved forward to the Treaty of Peace which was signed on December 10, 1898.   It followed the Protocol as regards Cuba, Puerto Rico and the island in the Ladrones [Guam], but it further provided for the cession of the Philippine Islands and the payment by the United States to Spain of twenty million dollars.   Neither the Cuban nor the Philippine debt was assumed.   McKinley had a difficult time in getting his Treaty confirmed by the Senate which considered it from January 4 to February 6, 1899, and finally ratified it by 57 : 27, only one vote more than the necessary two thirds.   Senator Gray signed the Treaty, advocated it in the Senate and afterwards accepted the position of judge from President McKinley.   Naturally

---

[1] Latané, 259.
[2] Letters of Aug. 2, Sept. 9. Life of McKinley, ii. 135.

his after-conduct does not agree with the heretofore cited opinion anent taking the Philippines ; but in a newspaper interview and in his speech in the Senate for the Treaty he explained his change of mind.[1] Both Senators Hoar and Hale, Republicans, opposed it, but Bryan came to Washington during its pendency and urged enough of Democrats to vote for it to secure its ratification.[2]

Two days before the ratification of the Treaty, the Filipinos, whose leader Aguinaldo was exasperated at the non-establishment of a Philippine Republic with himself at the head of it, attacked the American soldiers at Manila[3] and war began, which, with an ensuing guerilla warfare, continued for more than three years. In truth the United States had paid twenty millions for "a white elephant." It was "scarcely comprehended," wrote Dewey, "that a rebellion was included with the purchase."[4] It cost the United States to subdue the Philip-

---

[1] Jan. 20, 1899; Jan. 31, Feb. 1, 1899, New York *Tribune*.

[2] Life of McKinley, ii. 139; George F. Hoar, Autobiography, ii. 322; Latané, 77.

[3] The following I believe to be the truth about the much disputed question, who began the actual hostilities : "About 8.30 on the night of February 4, four Filipinos approached within five yards of an American outpost near the San Juan bridge and, ignoring the command to halt, were fired upon by the sentry. A Filipino detachment near by returned the fire and the firing soon became general along the entire line. . . . The Filipinos at that particular hour were unprepared for attack or defence. The expected battle came when they were off their guard, most of the higher officers being absent at Malolos." — The Philippines, Charles B. Elliott (1916), i. 452. J. A. Le Roy wrote: "The strained condition of affairs between the American and Filipino forces, having reached a climax, virtually brought on trouble of itself; a subordinate Filipino officer, unchecked by the discipline of his superiors, was the chief *deus ex machina* of the affray of February 4; the American authorities in Manila, having taken a more positive stand at the close of that week regarding encroachments upon their line, let loose the dogs of war they had been holding ready, and promptly followed up the provocation given." The Americans in the Philippines (1914), J. A. Le Roy, ii. 16.

[4] Autobiography, 284.

pine insurgents nearly one hundred and seventy millions,[1] while the cost of the Spanish War was three hundred million.[2] The one was attended with glory, the other with apology, despite the splendid results accruing from our rule.

Nearly all writers agree that the annexation of Hawaii [3] was brought on by the Spanish-American War, and by the taking of the Philippines. Hawaii, wrote John W. Foster, was a link in the chain of our possessions in the Pacific.[4] Like Cuba it had long been coveted by some American officials and a crisis occurring in January, 1893, furnished the fit occasion. "The Hawaiian pear is now fully ripe, and this is the golden hour for the United States to pluck it," wrote our minister.[5] A revolution, assisted by the United States forces, took place; the corrupt and despotic government of the Queen was overthrown and a provisional government established in its place. This government at once despatched a Commission to Washington with a treaty of annexation which had the thorough sympathy of President Harrison, who on February 14, 1893, signed it and submitted it to the Senate. The Treaty was favorably reported but, before action could

---

[1] Peck, 615; Senate docs., 57th Cong. 1st Sess. no. 416. June 20, 1902.
[2] Life of McKinley, ii. 112.
[3] "The Hawaiian Islands constitute a group of several islands in the mid Pacific having a total area of 6449 square miles. According to the United States census of 1900 their total population was 154,001 (or, deducting 274 persons in the military and naval service of the United States, 153,727). The latter number was made up of 61,122 Chinese, 25,742 Japanese, 29,834 Hawaiians, 7835 part Hawaiians, 28,533 Americans, 407 South Sea Islanders, and 254 Negroes." — Willoughby, Territories and Dependencies of the United States, 61.
[4] American Diplomacy in the Orient, 384.
[5] February 1, 1893. Pres. Cleveland's message of Dec. 18, 1893. Richardson, ix. 464.

be taken on it, Cleveland became President and during
March, 1893, withdrew it; in his special message of December 18, 1893, he gave the reason for this withdrawal
and for his subsequent action.   Believing that a grievous
wrong had been done to the government of the Queen
by the United States forces, he endeavored to restore her
to her preëxisting power, but his movement was defeated
by the recalcitrant action of the Queen herself.   With
his sturdy sense of justice Cleveland could do no other
than permanently to withdraw the treaty of annexation,
but his attempt to restore the Queen was at the time unpopular and does not now merit approval.   As the United
States would not have Hawaii and the Queen's government was impossible, the revolutionary parties established a republican form of government which was recognized by the Powers, including the United States.   This
new government administered affairs "through a period of
four years," so John W. Foster [1] wrote, "in which the
country enjoyed unexampled peace and prosperity.
Never before in its history had there been such honesty
in administration, such economy in expenditures, such
uniform justice in the enforcement of the laws and respect for the officials, such advance in education and such
encouragement of commerce and protection to life and
property." [2]

When McKinley became President Hawaii was annexed
by joint resolution of Congress.[3]   This form was used as

---

[1] Foster was Secretary of State under Harrison at the time the treaty
of annexation was presented.

[2] American Diplomacy in the Orient, 381.

[3] A treaty of annexation was signed June 16, 1897, and submitted the
same day to the Senate, which body removed the injunction of secrecy on
it the next day. — Senate Jour., 55th Cong. 1st Sess., 181, 183.

doubt existed whether a two-thirds vote for the ratification of a treaty could be secured in the Senate. "What is to be thought of a body," wrote John Hay in a private letter from London, "which will not take Hawaii as a gift and is clamoring to hold the Philippines?"[1] But on July 7, 1898, Hawaii became part of the United States by a two-thirds vote in both Houses,[2] a little over two months after Dewey's victory at Manila.

Had it not been for the foreshadowed policy in regard to the Philippines, it was a case of let well enough alone. A good government under a republican form was functioning in Hawaii and it was taking too great a risk to annex territory 2089 miles away.[3]

"The story of alternating 'booms' and panics," wrote Noyes, "is largely the story of modern industrial progress."[4] Those who believe in the periodicity of panics and recovery therefrom may note with elation that it was twenty years from the panic of 1873 to that of 1893, and twenty years from the "boom" of 1879 to that of 1899. As in the earlier case, recovery began sooner than was generally appreciated and is placed by Noyes in the middle of 1897.[5] Certain it is that the revival would have been in full swing had it not been for the Spanish War. War is a disturbing factor in finance and business and, when it was declared, no one would have dared to prophesy its brief duration. The "boom" year of 1899 resembles that of 1879. Both were the result of recupera-

---

[1] May 27, 1898, Life of Hay, Thayer, ii. 170.
[2] Foster, 383.
[3] Authorities: Foster; Willoughby, Territories and Dependencies of the United States; Cleveland's special message of Dec. 18, 1893; Peck.
[4] American Finance, 258.   [5] P. 262.

tive years after panics and both were attended with large crops in the United States, a failure in Europe, or, as Noyes expressed it, "A European famine and a bumper crop at home," immense exportations of breadstuffs, an import of gold and a buying-back of securities which Europe had taken in former years. Hay and Adams in their walks, discoursed of "the insolent prosperity of the United States." [1] While the dominant characteristics of 1879 were an advance in the price of pig iron and railroad shares, 1899 was noted for its "boom" in industrials and putting railroads on their feet.

John Pierpont Morgan is the hero of 1899 and of the succeeding years, and he came into public notice from his reorganization of railroads which had been badly hurt by the panic of 1893 and by conditions prevailing before and after. While circumstances favored his operations, they were really marvellous and may be fully appreciated by putting the question whether any other man in the country could have accomplished what he did. Not by affability and not by any strong hold on public sentiment did he work his results; for he was reticent, taciturn, decisive and blunt; his manner was stern and brusque; endowed with great energy, he was ruthless. He lacked a wide range of knowledge, but somehow he arrived quickly at decisions involving millions to the amazement of the beholder. He rarely read books and, on a constitutional question, he once displayed an ignorance that would have disgraced a College freshman. But the apologists for a mathematical training may point to Morgan as a shining example. From the English High

----

[1] Hay, Letters, iii. 140.

School of Boston he went to the University of Göttingen where he so distinguished himself in mathematics that the professor, under whom he sat, wanted him to remain. "You would have been my assistant as long as I lived," he said, "and unquestionably at my death you would have been appointed professor of mathematics in my place."[1] This incident Morgan used to tell in the day of his success with justifiable pride. His action showed "precision" and "wariness of mind" which John Stuart Mill mentioned as some of the "excellencies of mathematical discipline."[2]

The railroads had tried competition with the result that large numbers of them were in the hands of receivers and the sounder ones had difficulty in making both ends meet. Morgan substituted combination for competition. In the parlance of the street his first name was Jupiter and this was properly bestowed, for his word was "I command." Those who wished a reorganization of their railroads must accept his terms; and the result proved their justification. A contrast of the condition of the railroads in 1899 and before that year is one between excellent business management and the proper payment of interest and dividends, and a cut-throat competition that did no one, except perhaps speculators, any good. Naturally Morgan added to his great reputation of a banker that of a reorganizer of railroads. He always bore in mind what his father told him. Junius S. Morgan was one of America's first men of business who developed an influential London banking house. This was the advice he gave to his son:

---

[1] Life of Morgan, Hovey, 316.   [2] See my vol. ii. 333.

"Remember one thing always. Any man who is a bear on the future of the United States will go broke. There will be many times when things look dark and cloudy in America, when everyone will think there has been over development. But remember yourself that the growth of that vast country will take care of it all. Always be a 'bull' on America." [1]

Along with the reënhancement of the railroads was the revival of industrial conditions. Captains of industry showed their ability and power and forged to the front with their manufactures, so that Europe began to hear of what they called the "American invasion." "European nations," said the Austrian Minister of Foreign Affairs, "must close their ranks and fight shoulder to shoulder, in order successfully to defend their existence." [2]

A conspicuous development was in the steel industry which is fully represented in a report of Charles M. Schwab, dated May 15, 1899. "I know positively," he wrote, "that England cannot produce pig iron at actual cost for less than $11.50 per ton, even allowing no profit on raw materials, and cannot put pig iron into a rail with their most efficient works for less than $7.50 per ton. This would make rails at net cost to them of $19.00. We can sell at this price and ship abroad so as to net us $16.00 at works for foreign business, nearly as good as home business has been. . . . As a result of this we are going to control the steel business of the world. You know we can make rails for less than $12.00 per ton, leaving a nice margin on foreign business." [3] Schwab

---

[1] *McClure's Magazine*, Nov., 1910, 16.   [2] Noyes, 273.
[3] The Inside History of the Carnegie Steel Co., Bridge, 314.

was President of the Carnegie Steel Co. and his report was to Henry Clay Frick, chairman, his superior officer, but both were under Andrew Carnegie, who, despite his obvious faults, was the greatest iron master of the world, was now at the head of the best equipped steel works and could make steel cheaper than anyone else.

"Between 1893 and 1899 our export of manufactures actually doubled." [1]

In the old school-books it was set down that the development of a State lay in commerce, manufactures, and agriculture. Agriculture was the largest single interest in the United States and commerce and manufactures owed more to it than it owed to the others. In 1899 the farmer was prosperous. "Every barn in Kansas and Nebraska has had a new coat of paint." "For anyone," wrote Ray Stannard Baker, "who knew the West of 1895 and 1896, with its bare weather-stained homes, its dilapidated barns, its farm machinery standing out in the rain, its ruinous 'boom' towns, its discontented inhabitants crying out for legislation to relieve their distress, this bit of observation raises a picture of improvement and smiling comfort such as no array of figures, however convincing, could produce. The West painted again: how much that means! The farmer has provided himself with food in plenty and the means for seeding his fields for another year; he has clothed himself and his family anew; he has bought an improved harvester, a buggy and a sewing machine; and now with the deliberation which is born of a surplus and a sturdy confidence in himself and in the future, he is painting his

---

[1] Noyes, 275.

barn. Paint signifies all of these preliminary comforts. And after paint comes a new front porch, a piano and the boys off to college." [1] Baker might have added that cancelled farm mortgages were reckoned by the carload.[2]

Since the campaign of 1896, there had been an enormous increase in the production of gold so that circumstances were ripe for the Republicans to fulfil the promises they had made in their platform of 1896 and during that lively canvass. Unquestionably the gold Democrats, who had supported McKinley, were disappointed that financial legislation was not enacted as the result of his victory, but those who believed in a protective tariff dominated the councils of the party and before they tackled the subject of finance they felt that the tariff demanded their attention: hence the Dingley Tariff Bill. McKinley and his immediate advisers had come to believe in a gold standard and were right in their conviction that a better law could be later secured than in 1897. But this conviction was based on the education of their party, as they could not have foreseen how Nature was going to work on their side.

On March 14, 1900, a law was enacted declaring the gold dollar to be the standard unit of value. It provided that "United States notes [greenbacks] and Treasury notes" issued under the Act of 1890 "shall be redeemed in gold coin; and, in order to secure the prompt and certain redemption of such notes, it shall be the duty of the Secretary of the Treasury to set apart a reserve fund of

[1] Ray Stannard Baker, The New Prosperity, *McClure's Magazine*, May, 1900, 86.
[2] In addition to authorities already cited, I have used *The Nation* for 1899, and conversations with Mark Hanna and J. P. Morgan.

one hundred and fifty millions in gold, which fund shall be used for such redemption purposes only." If that fund should fall below one hundred millions it should be the duty of the Secretary of the Treasury to replenish it to the maximum sum of one hundred and fifty millions. by the sale of three per cent bonds, of which the interest and principal should be payable in gold. The proceeds of these bonds should not "be used to meet deficiencies in the current revenues." United States notes, when redeemed and reissued, should be held "in the reserve fund until exchanged for gold." The legal tender quality of the silver dollar was unaffected.[1]

During the summer of 1900 affairs in China claimed the attention of the State Department, and Hay as its head directed the admirable course of the United States, showing great ability in state-craft.

John Hay, as he gave an account of himself, "was born in Indiana, grew up in Illinois, was educated in Rhode Island. I learned my law," he continued, "in Springfield and my politics in Washington, my diplomacy in Europe, Asia and Africa."[2] He had an innate sense of refinement but his cultivated manner never obscured his Western raciness. He loved society and talk. Residing ten years in Cleveland, he organized a dinner club, called the Vampire, of which he was the life. Hay used to come to the dinners primed with circumstances and anecdotes and, eating and drinking little, he gave himself up to talk and was listened to with interest and delight. Not infrequently one of the wits of the club

---

[1] U. S. Statutes, xxxi. 45.
[2] Life of Hay, Thayer, i. 2.

would prod Hay and, with his rare sense of humor a
witticism of the sort served for an additional display.
Occasionally he would fall into a serious strain and talk
of political events or his acquaintances in New York or
England, but always replete with intelligence. Sometimes, although with seeming reluctance, he would speak
of his work on Lincoln, on which he was then engaged,
and the business men, who gathered at that round table,
were eager to hear of the processes of a live author. But
it was a common remark that he never repeated himself.

> " What things have we seen
> Done at the Mermaid [Union Club of Cleveland] heard words that
>   have been
> So nimble and so full of subtile flame."

"There is no longer the play of wit and raillery,"
wrote Professor Matthews, "the brilliancy, the concentration, the rapid glancing at a hundred subjects in succession, which there used to be in the attic nights of Johnson, Burke, Garrick and Sheridan."[1] But had the
Professor dined with the Vampire, when Hay was at his
best, he might have thought it an attic night.

Hay was the soul of the club and when in 1879 he felt
compelled to accept the position of Assistant Secretary
of State, offered him by William M. Evarts, he left a
void, which, although the dinners went on, was not filled
until his return to Cleveland, when he was welcomed
with glee.

Hay was not a trained historian in the way of knowing
thoroughly the masters of the art. He did not read with
rapt attention Gibbon, Macaulay, Parkman or any other

---

[1] The Great Conversers (1874), 42.

historian except Henry Adams. He was apt to have at
hand some high class French novel or Memoirs. He was
especially fond of Tourguéneff. Is there in literature,
he asked, such another story of a suicide so dramatically
told, as that of Nejdanof in Terres Viorges? During a
long acquaintance I never heard him talk of historians
except of his friend Henry Adams, but he had at his
tongue's end what we used to call belles-lettres and his
conversation thereon was a profit and delight. In his
familiar letters written to his coadjutor Nicolay in regard to the History, when he spoke of condensation or
the troubles of narration, there is never a question how
Macaulay or Parkman would have treated the one or
solved the other. We "must seize every chance to con-
dense," he wrote. "We could cut down a good deal and
present what would be a continuous narrative in about
half the space we have taken for our book." [1] Unquestionably had he followed out this idea, the History would
have been more popular and less criticized.

Although Hay did not possess the power of generalization of Gibbon he had two qualities invaluable for a historian — that of narration and a skepticism that influenced in a marked degree his judgment of men and of
events. And no writers in America ever had more priceless material. As private secretaries of Lincoln, feeling
that he was the central figure of the time, thinking that
some day they might write a history of these eventful
years, they made memoranda and garnered up their impressions. Robert T. Lincoln, the President's son, had
a large body of material which he placed at their dis-

---

[1] Thayer, ii. 28, 35.

posal. The two merits which Gibbon ascribed as those of a historian, diligence and accuracy, they possessed. The ten volumes of the History testify to their diligence; that they rarely, if ever, failed in the correctness of a quotation or a reference is a warrant of their accuracy.

Hay was a partisan and he carried partisanship into his historical work, but he aimed at impartiality. "We ought to write," he said, "the history of those times like two everlasting angels who know everything, judge everything, tell the truth about everything, and don't care a twang of their harps about one side or the other." Yet in the same letter he wrote, "I am of that age and imbued with all its prejudices," and "We are Lincoln men all through."[1] Therein lay an unconscious partisanship. Nicolay and Hay made Lincoln out a saint and, when he came into contact with other men, the saint was always right.

"No man," Hay wrote in a private letter, "can be a great historian who is not a good fellow." A "good fellow," a genuine man was Hay in every respect.

An earnest Republican, he took great interest in politics and coöperated with the managers of the Republican cause in Ohio and in the country at large. Those who knew him best thought that, until McKinley appointed him in 1897, his ability was not appreciated by those high in power, as the offers to him of office were below his merits. He helped Hanna in the nomination of McKinley and when McKinley was elected, among the large number of well-backed aspirants for the English mission, Hanna's voice was for Hay; as Hay jocosely wrote,

---

[1] Thayer, ii. 33.

"Hanna is a good judge of men and he recognizes infallibility when he sees it." McKinley named him Ambassador to Great Britain, a position which pleased him immensely and which he was abundantly qualified to fill.

McKinley and Hay took to one another, drawn together by an innate sense of refinement, for McKinley appreciated culture. Hay was decidedly a cultivated man. His natural propensity for culture was fostered by the reading of books and by mingling in the best society. Having a notable aptitude for acquiring knowledge at second hand he used this knowledge in his talk with wonderful skill. Always meeting interesting people he absorbed incidents that in turn set off his own conversation. He loved wit and humor and any manifestation of them was to his latest day a passport to his favor. He was a remarkable dinner-table talker and, in a discussion of the subject, a man of wide experience could think only of two shining lights of Boston and Cambridge who were his equal or superior.

In August, 1898, McKinley offered Hay the position of Secretary of State for which he had no wish, as he would have preferred to remain Ambassador to Great Britain.[1] Thus he wrote during September to his brother-in-law: "I did not want the place and was greatly grieved and shocked when it came — but of course I could not refuse to do the best I could. It was impossible, after the President had been so generous, to pick and choose, and say, 'I will have this and not that.' But I look forward to the next year with gloomy forebodings."[2]

---

[1] The Education of Henry Adams, 364; Life of Hay, Thayer, ii. 173 et seq.

[2] Thayer, ii. 183.

The correspondence between McKinley and Hay, when Hay's first canal treaty was rejected by the Senate, is honorable to them both. Hay showed consideration for the President in offering his resignation and McKinley in declining it, affirmed his loyalty to his Secretary of State. "Your administration of the State Department," he wrote, "has had my warm approval. As in all matters you have taken my counsel, I will cheerfully bear whatever criticism or condemnation may come."[1] In his sympathetic eulogy delivered before the Congress, Hay rose to a sublime height, as he depicted the ability, moral greatness and success of his master. His countenance was the picture of his mind and heart. "His face," he said, "was cast in a classic mold; you see faces like it in antique marble, in the galleries of the Vatican; . . . his voice was the voice of the perfect orator."[2]

China, devoted to Oriental civilization, did not wish for Western modern improvements, had no desire for railroads and telegraphs, the importation of English and American cotton fabrics and of American petroleum. She could see no use in them; they disturbed her calculations and her mode of life; she was satisfied to be let alone. To the European nations she seemed inert — a fat goose for the plucking — and therefore, on one account and another, these foreign nations claimed and obtained "spheres of influence or interest." Especially was this the case with Great Britain, Germany and Russia, and, from their point of view, such spheres in China were economically and politically like their own territory. The China trade was important to the United

---

[1] Thayer, ii. 228.
[2] Memorial Address, Feb. 27, 1902.

States and the American manufacturers desired part of the consumption of the three hundred and fifty million Chinese. Did these nations adopt preferential tariffs in their spheres of interest, the American manufacturers would suffer, and for aid they looked to the State Department which was alive to the situation.

On September 6, 1899, Hay addressed a note to Great Britain in which his English predilection tallied with her traditional and declared policy for freedom of trade, and he asked her to maintain the "open door" policy which meant that the commerce and navigation of the world should receive equality of treatment within the "spheres of influence or interest." On the same day, he addressed notes to Germany and Russia pleading to these protective tariff countries for the "open door" policy within their spheres of interest, although to them he did not use the term "open door." On November 30 England replied that she would declare for the "open door" provided that the other powers concerned would do likewise. During December Germany and Russia answered, affirming the principle under like conditions. Meanwhile Hay addressed similar notes to Japan, France and Italy, from all of whom he received satisfactory answers. This led to his note of March 20, 1900, to the several six nations, giving the course of his negotiations and saying that as each nation had "accepted the declaration suggested by the United States concerning foreign trade in China" he considered the assent of each one addressed "as final and definitive." [1] Hay's sanguine anticipations were substantially realized.

---

[1] Corr. concerning Amer. Commercial Rights in China, Foreign Relations, 1899.

But the game of grab had received a check. The worm trodden on will turn. Before 1900, there were mutterings of the coming storm which is known as the Boxer uprising. The Boxers were a secret Chinese society and their name may be freely translated as "The Fist of Righteous Harmony." Sir Robert Hart "looked upon the Boxer movement as a national and patriotic one for freeing China of the foreigners to whom, rightly or wrongly, is attributed all the country's misfortunes during the last half century." [1] Hart was properly called by the Encyclopædia Britannica, an Anglo-Chinese statesman and his remark was made after the suppression of the uprising which had individually cost him much; it stated a condition that the Boxers, dominated by the fanatics, sought to remedy, but the remedy was worse than the disease. The Empress Dowager who sympathized with the fanatical Boxers said in a secret edict, "The various powers cast upon us looks of tigerlike voracity, hustling each other in their endeavors to be the first to seize upon our innermost territories." [2] A Chinese politician declared that the Boxer movement "was due to the deepseated hatred of the Chinese people towards foreigners. China had been oppressed, trampled upon, coerced, cajoled, her territory taken, her usages flouted." [3] While this feeling against foreigners as such was undoubtedly the main cause of the Boxer uprising, it was mixed with antagonism toward Christian missionaries who were trying to convert the Chinese to an alien religion. Material conditions likewise fostered the movement. In De-

---

[1] Foreign Relations, 1900, 207.
[2] Nov. 21, 1899.   Foreign Relations, 1900, 85.
[3] J. W. Foster, Amer. Diplomacy in the Orient, 416.

cember, 1899, our minister E. H. Conger wrote to John Hay, "Crops have failed on account of the drought; great poverty and want prevail." [1] Little wonder was it that a placard was issued saying, "The Roman Catholic and Protestant religions have ruined and destroyed Buddhism. Their adherents . . . have irritated heaven and in consequence no rain has fallen. . . . If foreigners are not swept away no rain will fall." [2] Swayed by these different impulses the Peking Boxers attacked the foreign legations. On June 11, 1900, Conger wrote to Hay: "We are besieged in Peking, entirely cut off from outside communication. . . . In a civilized country of course there would be no question as to our safety, but here, with practically no government, and the army only a mutinous horde of savage ruffians, there can be no predicting what they may attempt." [3] Ordinarily, government soldiers would protect foreign legations but in this case the armed Boxers, who were looked upon as patriots, were assisted by the Imperial troops. The entire city of Peking, wrote Conger on June 15, is "in the possession of a rioting, murdering mob, with no visible effort being made by the government in any way to restrain it." [4] Five days later the German Minister, who had ventured out on an official errand, was murdered. Nearly all the foreigners repaired to the British legation, which was made a veritable fortress; their lines of defence were quickly shortened and straightened; trenches and barricades were built. "The Chinese army," related Conger on August 17 after relief came, "had turned out against us; the whole quarter of

---

[1] Dec. 7, 1899. Foreign Relations, 1900, 77.
[2] Apr. 30, 1900. Foreign Relations, 123.   [3] Ibid., 145.
[4] Foreign Relations, 154.

the city in which the legations are situated was surrounded by its soldiers, firing began on all sides and the
battle against the representatives of all foreign governments in China was begun. . . . Until July 17 there
was scarcely an hour during which there was not firing
upon some part of our lines . . . varying from a single
shot to a general and continuous attack along the whole
line. Artillery was planted on all sides of us." [1]

Culminating by July 17, a thrill of horror ran through
Europe and the United States at the idea that the legations to an ostensibly friendly country were besieged and
in danger of massacre. London, Paris and Berlin believing that the worst had happened, mourned for those
who had suffered this conjectured untimely fate. On
July 16 it was stated in the House of Commons that the
government entertained "no further hope for the safety
of the foreign community in Peking." The London
Times, the most conspicuous journal in Europe, which contained this news, printed in the same issue conventional
eulogies of the British Minister, of the *Times* correspondent and of Sir Robert Hart, and gave a list of British
officials and others who were in the Chinese capital.
While those connected with the American press were inclined to the belief of their confrères over the sea, the Chinese Minister in Washington, Wu, Secretary John Hay and
President McKinley doubted the story of a general massacre. Amid a period of excitement Hay and McKinley did not lose their heads and coöperated in efforts to
relieve the suffering garrison. Hay was determined to
get correct news and through Minister Wu sent a des-

---

[1] Foreign Relations, 162.

patch to Conger on July 11, "Communicate tidings bearer." Conger replied under date of July 16, received in Washington four days later: "For one month we have been besieged in British legation under continued shot and shell from Chinese troops. Quick relief only can prevent general massacre." [1] Five days later (not received in Washington until August 5) Conger telegraphed through the Consul-General at Shanghai: "All well. No fighting since 16th by agreement. Enough provisions; little ammunition. Hope for speedy relief." [2] In his despatch of July 21, Conger was somewhat too optimistic as the situation was one of ebb and flow. Nevertheless relief was at hand and he had the satisfaction of announcing on August 14, "We are safe." [3]

The occupying forces [4] restored order and organized a provincial administration, which gave way eventually to a reëstablished Chinese government. Protracted negotiations followed, with the result that suitable punishment was meted out to the guilty and an indemnity in a lump sum agreed upon. The success of President McKinley and Secretary Hay lay in their confidence in the Southern viceroys. As Hay said in his eulogy on McKin-

---

[1] Foreign Relations, 155, 156. "Your telegram was the first communication received by anyone from outside since the siege began and mine the first sent out." Conger to Hay, ibid., 161.

[2] Ibid., 156.

[3] Ibid., 160. The paraphrase of Conger's message of Aug. 17 ran: "Excepting the Imperial palace the entire city is occupied by 2000 Americans, 2000 British, 3000 Russians, 8000 Japanese and 200 French and is being apportioned for police supervision. The Chinese army has fled. The Imperial family and court have gone westward. . . . There are no representatives of the Chinese government in sight. The palace will be taken at once. . . . Conditions chaotic." It must be noted that our rapid action of relief was due to our having troops in the Philippines.

[4] For what the occupying forces were which relieved the foreign community in Peking, see note 3.

ley, "While the legations were fighting for their lives against bands of infuriated fanatics, the President decided that we were at peace with China; and while that conclusion did not hinder him from taking the most energetic measures to rescue our imperilled citizens, it enabled him to maintain close and friendly relations with the wise and heroic viceroys of the south, whose resolute stand saved that ancient Empire from anarchy and spoliation." [1] They also believed Minister Wu; and their voices, as friends of China, were for the preservation of her integrity and for moderation in every respect. "Hay's achievement," wrote Thayer, "in this Chinese contest gave him an immense prestige. Throughout the world he was now looked upon as a statesman, honest, disinterested, resourceful and brilliant." [2] Reference is had to the "open door" correspondence as well as to his conduct during the Boxer uprising; lapse of time confirms fully this effective statement. The brother Vampires who listened to Hay's brilliant talk when he was forty were not surprised at the development of his parts until he became Secretary of State. They were prepared for the History, knew that he would be an excellent Ambassador to Great Britain, but were amazed at the able statecraft he displayed in handling Chinese affairs.[3]

---

[1] Addresses, 162.
[2] Life of Hay, ii. 249.
[3] Authorities: Foreign Relations, 1900; Life of Hay, Thayer; Life of McKinley, Olcott; President's Messages of Dec. 1900 and Dec. 1901; Peck.

CHAPTER VI

PRESIDENT making was a concern of the year 1900, which in this case meant practically the action of the Republican Convention that assembled in Philadelphia during June. There was no difference as to the presidential candidate, none as to the platform. According to the prevailing sentiment McKinley had deserved well of the party and the country, and was entitled to another term. The platform was on the point-with-pride order and gloried in the achievements of the Republican party. Merited indeed was all that it said about the Republican opposition to the free coinage of silver and the preservation of the gold standard; for the action of the Republican party had been in line with what believers in sound money advocated. While the platform commended the foreign policy of the President it could not ignore entirely the bloody suppression of the Philippine rebellion which was still on foot, so that the statement regarding the Philippines limped and took no account of patent facts as I have stated them. The platform was adopted with unanimity; there is not "a particle of objection to it," a delegate from New Jersey declared,[1] and he spoke the unanimous voice of the Convention.

The nomination of McKinley and the platform had practically been decided by public opinion freely expressed in various ways in a pre-convention canvass, and traversed Ostrogorski's statement that a National Convention is "a colossal travesty of popular institutions."[2]

---

[1] Official Proceedings of the Repub. Nat. Com. of 1900, 108.   [2] ii. 278.

The Convention and the Republican party were well represented in the words of Theodore Roosevelt, a delegate at large from New York State, who seconded McKinley's nomination. "We nominate President McKinley," he said, "because he stands indeed for honesty at home and for honor abroad; because he stands for the continuance of the material prosperity which has brought comfort to every home in the Union; and because he stands for that kind of policy which consists in making performance square with promise." [1]

The whole ticket of 1896 could not be renominated as Hobart, the Vice-President, had during the year previous passed away. A new candidate must therefore be chosen and the convention is remarkable for its choice. The services of Theodore Roosevelt during the Spanish-American War made him Governor of New York State, where he came into collision with Senator Platt and the Republican organization who were influenced by "the big corporation men." [2] Roosevelt desired a renomination for governor by the New York State Convention, which would be held subsequent to the National Convention in Philadelphia, as the governorship interested him and he had policies which he desired to perfect and carry out; and he did not want to be sidetracked as Vice-President. He positively declined a number of times to be a candidate for that office. Hanna regarded Roosevelt as erratic and "unsafe" and was emphatically opposed to his nomination as Vice-President. The natural antagonism between the two became publicly known at this Convention. Hanna was for the old order with an

[1] Official Proceedings, 119.   [2] Roosevelt, Autobiography, 110.

important modification, Roosevelt for the new. And President McKinley in an unobtrusive way let it be known that he did not want Roosevelt as a running mate. Roosevelt arrived in Philadelphia on Saturday, June 16, and next day had an interview with Hanna, in which he said frankly to the Senator, "I am not a candidate for Vice-President and I don't want the nomination. What I want is to be Governor of New York." [1] Roosevelt's own account of the matter may be set down as true history: "Senator Hanna appeared on the surface to have control of the Convention. He was anxious that I should not be nominated as Vice-President. Senator Platt was anxious that I should be nominated as Vice-President in order to get me out of the New York Governorship. . . . My supporters in New York State did not wish me nominated for Vice-President because they wished me to continue as Governor; but in every other State all the people who admired me were bound that I should be nominated as Vice-President." [2] A supplement to this is a telephone despatch to President McKinley which reached him late on Sunday evening, June 17: "The Roosevelt boom is let loose and it has swept everything. It starts with the support of Pennsylvania and New York practically solid and with California and Colorado back of it also. The feeling is that the thing is going pell-mell like a tidal wave." [3]

On this Sunday Hanna and Roosevelt failed to reckon the strength of popular sentiment. Roosevelt, on ac-

---

[1] Olcott, ii. 275.   [2] Autobiography, 332.
[3] Olcott, ii. 271. In the midst of the excitement Mrs. Robinson, who had hastened to Philadelphia at Roosevelt's request, found him in his hotel room reading the "History of Josephus." My Brother, T. Roosevelt, Mrs. Robinson, 196.

count of his course during the Spanish-American War and the governorship of New York was one of the most popular men in the country especially in the West, of the inhabitants of which he was fond. He could not ignore the manifestation in his favor and was forced to bow to the will of the people thus expressed. McKinley also arrived at the same opinion by the Tuesday and thus telephoned: "The President's close friends must not undertake to commit the Administration to any candidate. It has no candidate. The convention must make the nomination; the Administration would not if it could. The President's close friends should be satisfied with his unanimous nomination and not interfere with the vice-presidential nomination. The Administration wants the choice of the convention and the President's friends must not dictate to the convention." [1] As soon as Hanna knew of the President's wishes, he abandoned his opposition and favored unanimity. This was effected on Thursday, June 21; Roosevelt received on the ballot taken the vote of every delegate except his own. [2]

The Democratic Convention was held in Kansas City on July 4. Bryan had made so gallant a fight four years previously that no one else was talked of for presidential candidate. He had the nomination for the asking and he purposed dictating the policy of his party. His article in the *North American Review* for June showed what was passing in his mind. "The issue presented in the campaign of 1900," he wrote, "is the issue between plutoc-

---

[1] Olcott, ii. 279.

[2] Besides the Life of McKinley and Roosevelt's Autobiography I have used freely the Life of Hanna by Croly, and the Official Proceedings. I have also consulted *The Nation, passim;* the Life of Foraker, ii.; Platt's Autobiography, chap. xix.

racy and democracy.   All the questions under discussion will, in their last analysis, disclose the conflict between the dollar and the man."   Later on he came to details. "To-day," he wrote, "three questions contest for primacy — the money question, the trust question and imperialism." [1]   In placing the money question to the fore, Bryan displayed greater consistency than wisdom, but as he had made the contest of 1896 on the remonetization of silver on the basis of 16 : 1, he was determined that the question should not now be ignored.   He dominated the committee on resolutions and the Convention in Kansas City.   They therefore demanded the "free and unlimited coinage of silver . . . at the present legal ratio of 16 : 1 without waiting for the aid or consent of any other nation"; but in an earlier resolution they declared that "the burning issue of imperialism" was the paramount one of the campaign.

On the first ballot Bryan was unanimously nominated for President and at Indianapolis on August 8 accepted the nomination in what he regarded "as one of the most if not the most important of his political speeches."   The speech in the authorized volume "revised and arranged by himself" is entitled "Imperialism" and is mainly devoted to the Republican management of the Philippines.

The Philippine Islands were acquired as the result of the Treaty with Spain and it was a well-known fact that the Treaty could not have been ratified without Democratic votes.   This is tersely stated by Senator Hoar in his Autobiography.   "Seventeen of the followers of Mr.

---

[1] Pp. 753, 758.

Bryan voted for the Treaty.[1] The Treaty would have
been defeated, not only lacking the needful two-thirds
but by a majority of the Senate but for the votes of Democrats and Populists. Mr. Bryan in the height of the
contest came to Washington for the express purpose of
urging upon his followers that it was best to support the
Treaty, end the war, and let the question of what should
be done with our conquest be settled in the coming campaign." [2] In his speech on "Imperialism," Bryan acknowledged the truth of this statement, defended his
position in a careful argument, and then addressed himself to the question, What should we do with the Philippines? He and the Democratic party say, treat the Filipinos as we have promised to treat the Cubans. Why
ought not the Filipinos "of right to be free and independent" as well as the Cubans? Admiral Dewey reported
that the Filipinos were more capable of self-government
than the Cubans, and Bryan stated plainly his purpose.
"If elected," he said, "I will convene Congress in extraordinary session as soon as inaugurated and recommend
an immediate declaration of the nation's purpose, first,
to establish a stable form of government in the Philippine
Islands, just as we are now establishing a stable form of
government in Cuba; second, to give independence to
the Filipinos as we have promised to give independence
to the Cubans; third, to protect the Filipinos from outside interference while they work out their destiny just
as we have protected the republics of Central and South
America, and are, by the Monroe Doctrine pledged to

---

[1] Ten of these were Democrats.
[2] ii. 322. This has been briefly stated in chap. v.

protect Cuba." [1]   Bryan enforced his argument by a poetical citation:

> "Would we tread in the paths of tyranny,
>   Nor reckon the tyrant's cost?
>   Who taketh another's liberty
>   His freedom is also lost.
>   Would we win as the strong have ever won,
>   Make ready to pay the debt,
>   For the God who reigned over Babylon
>   Is the God who is reigning yet." [2]

The important printed contributions to the campaign are this speech of Bryan's and McKinley's letter of acceptance of September 8; of this two-thirds are devoted to the Philippines and a defence of his management. The letter is in effect a reply to the speech and on the whole may be deemed an effective answer. The majority of voters probably thought so, although the quotable portions of McKinley's speech of July 12 may have had the greater influence. We have fulfilled the pledges we made in 1896, he declared, "We have prosperity at home and prestige abroad," yet by the action of the Democratic party, "the menace of 16:1 still hangs over us. The Philippines are ours and American authority must be supreme throughout the archipelago. . . . There must be no scuttle policy." "No blow has been struck except for liberty and humanity and none will be." The Republican party "broke the shackles of 4,000,000 slaves" and now it has liberated 10,000,000 "from the yoke of imperialism." [3]   Kipling's words represent McKinley's action:

---

[1] Speeches, ii. 46.

[2] In a courteous letter to D. M. Matteson, William J. Bryan says the citation was from a poem written by James A. Edgerton.

[3] Official Proceedings, pp. 148, 149, 150.

"Take up the White Man's burden . . .

. . . .

By open speech and simple
An hundred times made plain,
To seek another's profit,
And work another's gain."

The decisive jury was the thirteen and a half million voters. The logical result of Democratic policy was to turn over the Philippines to Aguinaldo and his associates, and there were many who thought as did Senator Lodge, the permanent chairman of the Republican convention, that Aguinaldo was "a self-seeking adventurer and usurper." While the bloody suppression of the Philippine rebellion militated against Republican success, there seemed no other way out. Even if we had an undesirable acquisition, it was ours and our authority must be preserved.

McKinley and Hay, who took an eager though impersonal [1] view of the contest, were solicitous that Hanna should continue as chairman of the Republican National Committee and, when he decided to do so, the President wrote to him: "I am delighted that you have accepted the chairmanship of the National Committee. It is a great task and will be to you a great sacrifice." [2] As we see it now, the election of McKinley appeared a foregone conclusion, but during the canvass there was anxiety among the knowing ones. On September 25 Hay wrote to Henry Adams: "Hanna has been crying wolf all summer, and he has been much derided for his fears, but now everybody shares them. Bryan comes out a frank anarchist again in his letter of acceptance; and Mitchell

---

[1] See letter to Samuel Mather, Life by Thayer, ii. 254.   [2] Croly, 319.

with his coal strike has thrown at least a hundred thousand votes to him." [1]   The anthracite coal strike disturbed Hanna and he used his influence with the coal operators to get it settled before election.[2]

Hanna was unquestionably the chief man on the Republican side. All of his executive ability and his knack at raising money were exercised in behalf of his candidate and party. So far, it was 1896 over again, but he had learned to make effective speeches on the stump and, as he was much in demand from the several committees, he appeared before many audiences throughout the country. The burden of his talk was that Republican success and administration had given prosperity to the manufacturer, merchant and financier, and the full dinner pail to the laborer. His more effective work was through his personality. Westerners beyond Ohio had the idea that he was a "bloated millionaire," and when they came to see a man of easy bearing, of democratic ways, placing himself on a par with the common man and hear his rough speech adapted to their easy comprehension, they were converted to the Hanna cult. "This trip," wrote Croly with singular penetration, "helped to make Mr. Hanna personally popular throughout the West, just as his first stumping tour in Ohio had made him personally popular in his own State. As soon as he became known, the virulence and malignity with which he had been abused reacted in his favor. When he appeared on the platform, the crowd, instead of seeing a monster, found him to be just the kind of man whom Americans best understand

---

[1] Letters Privately Printed, iii. 196.
[2] Croly, 328; *The Nation*, Nov. 1, 1900, 342.

and most heartily like.　He was not separated from them
by differences of standards and tastes or by any intellectual or professional sophistication.　The roughness of
much of his public speaking and its lack of form which
makes it comparatively poor reading, were an essential
part of its actual success.　He stamped himself on his
speeches just as he had stamped himself upon his business.　His audiences had to pass judgment on the man
more than on the message and the man could not but
look good to them." [1]

"I have never wondered," said Senator Dolliver of Iowa,
"as so many have, that Hanna suddenly developed into a
great orator. . . .　I was present in 1900 at the stock yards
in Chicago when I had a glimpse of the colossal personality of this man which made a very profound impression
on my mind.　We took him down there to speak to the
working people of Chicago, and curiously enough — a
very strange anomaly under institutions like ours — a
large part of the audience had assembled there, not to
listen to him but to prevent him from speaking; and
with noise, riot, tumult, disturbance, and breach of peace
. . . that surging multitude for one hour and thirty
minutes fought an unequal battle with the genius of a
single man; and at 10 o'clock, the audience calmed, controlled, fascinated, he began one of the most remarkable
political speeches it was ever my good fortune to hear." [2]

Next in importance was Roosevelt's stumping.　If we
may judge his speeches by his letter of acceptance, he
defended Republican policy and administration.　He insisted that the remonetization of silver meant disaster,

[1] P. 340.　　　　[2] Address, April 7, 1904.

and that our acquisition of new provinces was in the line of national development; it meant expansion and not "imperialism or militarism." [1]   He added strength to the ticket and his appearance and manner increased his strong personal popularity. "His attitude as speaker," wrote Thayer, "his gestures, the way in which his pent-up thoughts seemed almost to strangle him before he could utter them, his smile showing the white rows of teeth, his fist clenched as if to strike an invisible adversary, the sudden dropping of his voice, and levelling of his forefinger as he became almost conversational in tone, and seemed to address special individuals in the crowd before him, the strokes of sarcasm, stern and cutting, and the swift flashes of humor which set the great multitude in a roar, became in that summer and autumn familiar to millions of his countrymen; and the cartoonists made his features and gestures familiar to many other millions." [2]

As was the case four years previously, Bryan was indefatigable on the stump. By his and the Democratic criticism of the Republican management of the Philippines, he gained the support of the anti-Imperialists, at the head of whom was Carl Schurz, but as *The Nation* remarked on another occasion, "Those who sup with the devil, even with a long spoon, are sure to have to swallow a nauseous portion at the end." [3]   Bryan had the cordial support of Tammany Hall and showed his appreciation of it when he came to New York, declaring "Great is Tammany! And Croker is its prophet." This disgusted Carl Schurz, who wrote, "Bah! Wasn't it awful!" [4]

---

[1] Official Proceedings, 180.
[2] Roosevelt, 151.   [3] June 28, 1900.
[4] Reminiscences, iii. 447.

Despite the strength of the cause and the candidates, there will be hours of depression among those destined to victory. While 1900 must be put down as a year of prosperity, there were weeks when business halted owing partly to a reaction from the flush times of 1899, partly to the depression usual in a presidential year and partly to a real alarm by financiers at the prospect of Bryan's success. His policy was distrusted and his administrative power feared. This feeling is well reflected in John Hay's private letter of October 31 : "This last week of the campaign is getting on everybody's nerves. There is a vague uneasiness among Republicans, which there is nothing in the elaborate canvasses of the Committee to account for. I do not believe defeat to be possible, though it is evident that this last month of Bryan, roaring out his desperate appeals to hate and envy, is having its effect on the dangerous classes."[1] Also Hay wrote to Henry Adams on the same day, "Our folks are curiously nervous about next Tuesday. The canvass is all right — the betting also. But nobody knows what Jack Cade may do."[2]

Forty-five States voted on November 6, giving McKinley 292 electoral votes to Bryan's 155, and a plurality in the popular vote of 849,000, — the greatest Republican victory since 1872.[3] Bryan carried only four Northern States, Colorado, Idaho, Montana and Nevada; as compared with 1896 he lost his own State of Nebraska, Kansas, Utah, Washington, South Dakota and Wyoming.

---

[1] To Samuel Mather, Life of Hay, Thayer, ii. 256.
[2] Letters Privately Printed, iii. 201.
[3] Grant in 1872 had a greater percentage of the popular vote. In 1896 Kentucky gave McKinley 12 of her 13 votes. All went to Bryan in 1900.

Hanna and Roosevelt undoubtedly contributed to the result west of the Missouri River.

By McKinley's reëlection in 1900, wrote Croly, "The Republicans had received a clear mandate to govern the country in the interest of business expansion." [1]   J. Pierpont Morgan, with his great reputation of railroad reorganizer as well as banker, now turned his attention to the iron and steel business, where it was thought his faculties would have full play.   Under the régime of competition, men bid against one another for trade.   Pig iron manufacturers were eager for the custom of the steel mills, who in turn sought to sell to the railroads.   Confining our attention to the period from the close of the Civil War to 1900, fluctuations had been great.   A glut of pig iron naturally induced low prices, a large capacity for the manufacture of steel resulted in the enterprising managers bidding against one another for whatever trade was in sight.   Fostered by the "hard times" following the panic of 1873, long-headed men developed the manufacture of "specialties" in steel, but every pound so made took the place of the same quantity of iron with the result that mills devoted exclusively to iron could not in dull periods make the two ends meet.   Failures came and the list of bankruptcies in the iron trade was appalling.   It was always a "feast or a famine" was a common expression and the hard years were followed by the "Benner boom" of 1879 when prices went beyond all reason.   This, with less violent fluctuations after 1881, was the history of the iron trade to the panic of 1893.   Requiring large capital and managing ability, the number of steel

---

[1] Life of Hanna, 341.

mills was not large, but the feeling among them was not
harmonious unless the common dislike of all the others
for Andrew Carnegie and his methods might draw them
together in sympathy. Between 1893 and 1900 a process of consolidation had been going on so that a large
part of the steel business of the country had become cen-
tred in seven concerns outside of the Carnegie Steel
Company. The consolidation was effected by promoters
and "water" was a component part of all of the common
and preferred stocks which made up the capitalization.
The rebound from the panic of 1893 made easy the
flotation of these securities and in some of the concerns
Morgan had an interest. The question arose after the
election outcome of 1900, Could not these seven be united
into one concern? and with one accord it seemed to be
agreed that Morgan was the man to finance the enterprise. Attracted to it, he went to work and soon had
under way the combination of the seven, which would
have been a huge concern with the Carnegie Steel Company its chief opponent.[1]

Andrew Carnegie came from Scotland to America as
a poor boy and got a job in a cotton mill in Allegheny
City at the wage of $1.20 per week. He told of his ex-
perience: "For a lad of twelve to rise and breakfast every
morning, except the blessed Sunday morning, and go into
the streets and find his way to the factory and begin to
work while it was still dark outside and not be released until after darkness came again in the evening, forty minutes

---

[1] A convenient list of these seven plus the Carnegie Steel Co., the American Bridge Co., and the Lake Superior Consolidated Iron Mines is given
by Cotter, 22. See likewise Berglund, 102. "The American Bridge Co.,
and the Lake Superior Consolidated Iron Mines entered the Steel Corporation soon after its organization."

only being allowed at noon, was a terrible task."[1] At
fourteen he became a messenger boy in a telegraph office,
attracted the attention of Thomas A. Scott who asked
him to be his "clerk and operator." Scott took a fancy
to Carnegie and suggested investments, so that he developed into what his boy friends termed a "capitalist."
When Scott became Vice-President of the Pennsylvania
Railroad, Carnegie became superintendent of the Pittsburg division and remained for a number of years in the
service of this great company. Prospering in his investments he organized the Keystone Bridge Works, which
was among the first, if not the first, to construct successful iron bridges.[2] Thus, becoming a business man, working on his own account, he resigned his position on the
Pennsylvania Railroad, and devoted his attention first
to the making of pig iron and then by a natural development to the manufacture of steel. Financial vicissitudes,
differences with partners, manufacturing difficulties had
to be overcome, but in 1900 he was the greatest steel-
maker in the world and could produce steel rails cheaper
than anywhere else on earth. His history has been told
in an unsympathetic yet truthful way by J. H. Bridge,
who had been private secretary of Herbert Spencer and
literary assistant to Carnegie himself ; yet from a careful
reading of this book one cannot be otherwise than convinced that, in this day of material progress, Carnegie
was a great man.

Carnegie's faults were those of many self-made men
and lay on the surface. He was egotistical and con-

---

[1] The Gospel of Wealth, x. "The hours hung heavily upon me and in
the work itself I took no pleasure." — Carnegie's Autobiography, 34.

[2] See Carnegie's Autobiography, 115, 122.

ceited and had an opinion dogmatically expressed on many subjects on which confessed ignorance would have been better. Apparently without reverence for those who had made study the pursuit of a lifetime, he took issue with Greek scholars on the desirability of a study of Greek; and there was scarcely a subject in English or American politics as to which he had not a positive opinion. Dispensing a generous hospitality from his Scotch retreat of Skibo Castle he was much run after for contributions to all sort of enterprises. This phase of his life is well represented in a contemporary cartoon.[1] Was it not humiliating, said an observer, "to see people in a London drawing-room cringing before him in order to get a cheque?" But it was no better in the United States, where he was besieged by all sorts of men for money contributions to their favorite enterprises. "With sincerity," said Confucius, "unite a desire for self-culture." Carnegie was sincere. "The man who dies rich, dies disgraced," he wrote in 1899.[2] He was not then rolling in superabundant wealth, but when he possessed it after the event I am about to relate he carried out his dictum of years before. That he had a desire for self-culture is evident from his reading of books which he displayed in his writings and from his benefactions. When he was a working-boy in Pittsburg he had constant recourse to a free library, and he told of his "intense longing" for a new book. "I resolved," he wrote, "that if ever wealth came to me, it should be used to establish free libraries."[3] The Anglo-Saxon world knows how well this resolution was carried out.

---

[1] Cleveland *Plain Dealer; Cosmopolitan Mag.*, Sept. 1901.
[2] The Gospel of Wealth, 19.   [3] Ibid., 28.

Such was Andrew Carnegie, the poor boy, the great manufacturer of steel and after 1901 the possessor of two hundred and fifty millions. Of course he was helped by the high tariff and he took advantage of all the conditions in the country that he had made his own.

Men may poke fun at him because he wrote, "I sympathize with the rich man's boy and congratulate the poor man's boy," for most of the "immortals" have been born to "the precious heritage of poverty,"[1] but it was the sincere observation of a poor boy, who during his life had amassed millions.

We now return to the organization of the United States Steel Corporation in which were displayed some of Morgan's best and doubtful qualities. He was keen enough to see that the Carnegie Steel Company must be in the combination and while Carnegie was desirous of selling, the Scotchman was determined to get a good price. His policy of threat was effectually used. According to Bridge, he wrought through a "press agent" and by newspaper interviews. It was given out that owing to a disagreement with the Pennsylvania Railroad he would give all possible business to the railroad running from Pittsburg to Conneaut, the Lake Erie terminus, and would also take advantage of the cheap water transportation. Striking thus directly at the Pennsylvania Railroad, he also threatened to build at Conneaut the largest

---

[1] The Gospel of Wealth, xii. In his Autobiography, 31, Carnegie gave a charming picture of the life of his family after they had left Scotland and settled in Allegheny City and then wrote: "The children of honest poverty have the most precious of all advantages over those of wealth. The mother, nurse, cook, governess, teacher, saint, all in one; the father, exemplar, guide, counsellor and friend! Thus were my brother and I brought up. What has the child of millionaire or nobleman that counts compared to such a heritage?"

and best equipped tube works in the country, giving a direct blow to Morgan who was largely interested in the National Tube Company, one of the combining concerns. It was likewise well known that the Carnegie Steel Company could make steel cheaper than any other company in the world. Carnegie had his price which Morgan, with apparently little hesitation, paid. It was said at the time that the canny Scotchman had outwitted the New England Yankee. Thus the so-called "billion dollar trust" was launched. It consisted of 550 million common stock, 550 million preferred, and 304 million [1] 5 per cent bonds; all of the bonds went to the Carnegie Steel Company of which Andrew Carnegie got the lion's share. The Carnegie Steel Company also received $98,277,120 in preferred stock and $90,279,040 in common stock at par. Reckoning the bonds of $303,450,000 worth one hundred cents on the dollar, the preferred stock at 82 and the common stock at 38, the Carnegie Steel Company received $418,343,273 for their property. It was no wonder then that Andrew Carnegie was counted worth $250,-000,000.

The other combining companies [2] took stock. Of the 1,100,000,000 stock all of the common and some of the preferred was "water"; but as there was an abundance of "water" in the combining companies, the increase of stock and the increase of "water" do not seem to have been objected to. For their services the Morgan syndicate received 649,897 shares of the common stock of the

---

[1] Probably $303,450,000. There were also about 56 million of bonds owned by the combining companies which the U. S. Steel Corporation assumed. Berglund, 71.

[2] See again Cotter, 22; Berglund, 102.

United States Steel Corporation and an equal number of the preferred. At $38 a share for the common and $82 a share for the preferred, this amounted to $77,987,640. This was all effected on a cash capital of 25 millions, which the syndicate received back, plus 200 per cent in dividends.[1] Although J. P. Morgan himself never speculated in the way of buying or selling stocks on a margin, he comprehended the stock market well and engaged a celebrated manipulator to market the shares, which were put upon the market as paying dividends of four per cent on the common and seven per cent on the preferred. Starting on the curb at 38 for "steel common" and 82¾ for "steel preferred," these stocks were soon admitted on the Stock Exchange and within a month advanced to 55 and 101⅞ respectively, although perhaps considerable of this advance was due merely to "matching of orders." [2]

It was popularly supposed that the United States Steel Corporation possessed about two-thirds of the Lake Superior iron ore and Connellsville coal of the country, although the actual figures of production do not substantiate the popular belief. In the four years, 1902–1905 inclusive, the United States Steel Corporation shipped 56 per cent of the Lake Superior ore, produced 36 per cent of the Connellsville coke, 70 per cent of Bessemer steel ingots, 60 per cent of Bessemer steel rails and 51 per cent of open hearth steel ingots and castings. There was naturally some efficiency in operation by bringing so many plants under one head and management, and there was

---

[1] American Finance, Noyes, 300; Life of Morgan, Hovey, 216.
[2] Noyes, 300.

a praiseworthy effort to get workingmen, superintend-
ents and other employés interested in the Company by
selling them shares at lucrative rates. The United States
Steel Corporation constantly stabilized prices. After its
formation there was no violent enhancement of values
during a time of "boom," no "runaway market" in steel.
On the other hand, during times of depression, prices
never went below what would give a fair profit.

The distribution of interests by Jupiter does not work
in our common world and did not under Morgan. In
short, the United States Steel Corporation was too big
for effective work. As Morgan discovered, it is exceedingly difficult to find a man of sufficient ability and character to head so large a concern. His first efforts were
failures and while the present [1] "chief executive officer,"
Judge Elbert H. Gary, is a decided success, it is doubtful
whether his successor will possess his eminent qualities.
But at no time has the United States Steel Corporation
made steel absolutely or comparatively as cheap as did
the Carnegie Steel Company just before the combination
was made. Carnegie said that "his partners knew nothing about making stocks and bonds but only the making of steel." [2] The difference lies in the combination of
companies and the adjustment of interests with a sharp-
ened pencil on a writing pad in a Wall Street office and
presence at the works among the men where steel is
turned out. Charles M. Schwab, the first President
of the United States Steel Corporation, in New York

---

[1] 1920.

[2] Trusts of To-Day, Montague, 37. "America is soon to change
from being the dearest steel manufacturing country to the cheapest."—
Written before the sale to J. P. Morgan. Autobiography of Andrew
Carnegie, 227.

City and Europe, was a different Schwab from him who, in the grime and dirt of Pittsburg, administered the affairs of the Carnegie Steel Company. "Schwab had graduated at Braddock under Captain Jones and, displaying exceptional ability as a manager of men, had quickly won his way from one of the lowest positions in the yards to the highest in the office. His cheery friendliness made him especially popular among the workmen." [1] Anyone who knew personally William R. Jones, or as he was familiarly called, Captain Bill Jones, and what he stood for, may well join in this tribute which Bridge paid him: "Greater than all of Jones's inventions was his progressive policy. . . . The young men whom he trained ably seconded him. . . . The famous scrap heap for outgrown, not outworn, machinery was instituted by Jones, who never hesitated to throw away a tool that had cost half a million if a better one became available. And as his own inventions saved the company a fortune every year, he was given a free hand. Under this greatest of all the captains of the American steel industry [Jones] a group of younger men grew up, trained in his broad views and habituated to his progressive methods; so that when in 1889 he was killed in a horribly tragic way by the explosion of one of his furnaces, there were men ready trained to take up his work and continue it." [2] Carnegie said that he owed his success to Jones and to Schwab; [3] and

---

[1] Bridge, 245. Schwab wrote, July 24, 1919, on his photograph which is reproduced in Carnegie's Autobiography opposite 256: "To my dearest friend and ' Master ' with the sincere love of ' His Boy.' "

[2] Bridge, 105.

[3] Cotter, 89. " Jones," so wrote Andrew Carnegie in his Autobiography, "bore traces of his Welsh descent. . . . He came to us a two-dollar-

he once suggested for his epitaph, "Here lies the man who knew how to get around him men who were cleverer than himself." [1] He said, "The nation that makes the cheapest steel has the other nations at its feet." [2] Hendrick also affirmed that Carnegie did not like "this Wall Street coterie." [3] What a pity that, with his desire to get out of business, such inducements were offered that he must perforce go in with them! For the United States Steel Corporation has never been the asset for the country that the Carnegie Steel Company was or might have been. Carnegie in the United States was greater than Krupp in Germany. The one made the implements of peace; the other was skilful in the production of necessaries of war. Carnegie had a fit successor in Henry Clay Frick to carry on his work while he might have devoted himself to his noble benefactions. Unfortunately however, the two had quarrelled.

While the Carnegie foibles are apparent, he was ahead of his age in his devotion to "gentle Peace." How much he thought of it, why the world ought to have it, why

---

a-day mechanic from the neighboring works at Johnstown. . . . He had volunteered as a private during The Civil War and carried himself so finely that he became captain of a company which was never known to flinch. Much of the success of the Edgar Thomson Works belongs to this man." In later years, Carnegie offered him an interest which would have made him a millionaire without entailing any financial responsibility. This Jones declined saying, "No, I don't want to have my thoughts running on business. I have enough trouble looking after these works. Just give me a big salary if you think I am worth it." "All right, Captain, the salary of the President of the United States is yours." "That's the talk," rejoined Jones. P. 203.

"Captain Jones described me as having been born with two rows of teeth and holes punched for more, so insatiable was my appetite for new works and increased production." — Ibid., 112.

[1] The Age of Big Business, B. J. Hendrick, 68.
[2] The Age of Big Business, Hendrick, 60.   [3] P. 81.

war was the worst of evils, are amply testified to in his writings, private letters, expressed desires and by his benefactions. No wonder then that the great war of 1914 broke his heart.[1]

Different from Carnegie, J. P. Morgan had inherited wealth and a good education; he possessed the confidence of the investing public. It was thought in 1901 and 1902 that he could accomplish anything. Ex-Mayor Grace's experience was that of many. One morning he received a brief letter by post saying that he had been awarded a hundred thousand dollar share in the Underwriting syndicate of the United States Steel Corporation. Having had no conversation with Morgan on the subject, knowing only by hearsay of the organization of the "billion dollar" trust, he sent his cheque for what was asked for, being $8000, from his entire confidence in the banker. Although liable up to the amount of $100,000 he never got a further call for more but in due time received back the money he had sent and his share of the enormous profits of the Underwriting. "I never made money as easy as that," he said.[2]

The organization of the "billion dollar steel trust," as the Steel Corporation was called, the impetus of McKinley's second election, the rebound from the panic of 1893, the war of 1898 and the stock depression of 1899 turned men's heads in 1901. Stocks went up, money was easily made, thoughts ran in hundred millions, men and women were extravagant, champagne corks popped, the assertion was made that the day of panics had passed

---

[1] Preface to Carnegie's Autobiography by Mrs. Carnegie, v.
[2] Life of Morgan, Hovey, 216.

and all went as merry as a marriage bell. "The out-
burst of speculation during April 1901," wrote Noyes,
"was something rarely paralleled in the history of speculative manias." Men who were made millionaires by
their sales of United States Steel Corporation shares became speculators in Wall Street. "The 'outside public'
meantime seemed to lose all restraint. A stream of excited customers of every description brought their money
to New York and spent their days in offices near the Stock
Exchange. . . . The newspapers were full of stories of
hotel waiters, clerks in business offices, even doorkeepers
and dressmakers, who had won considerable fortunes in
their speculations." [1] Happily this booming condition
was for a time brought to an end by a quarrel between
Edward H. Harriman on one side and Morgan and James
J. Hill on the other. Both parties desired control of the
Northern Pacific Railroad and began bidding against
one another for its possession. The stock ran up from
160 to 1000 but "all other stocks broke violently" and
a good part of Wall Street was for two hours on that day
of May 9, 1901, "technically insolvent." [2] Those who
term this a real panic and are fond of historical parallels
may refer to 1881 and point to the facts that the Indian
corn crop in 1901 was with two exceptions [3] the smallest
in twenty years and that a President was also assassi-
nated. The strife for the Northern Pacific was a battle
of financial giants but all this turmoil would have been
avoided had they composed their differences before instead of after this Wall Street shock.

[1] Noyes, 301.

[2] Noyes, 306. [3] 1881, 1894. In

1900 the crop was	2,105,000,000
1901 the crop was	1,522,000,000
1902 the crop was	2,523,000,000

Elated with his success in the Steel combination Morgan attempted a similar enterprise in connection with transport across the Atlantic Ocean. He got hold of the Dominion Line, the American and Red Star, the Atlantic Transport Company, the White Star Line and the Leyland, paying for the ships more than they were worth. The chairman of the Leyland Company told the shareholders that Morgan's offer was so high "that no management had a right to refuse it." [1] Morgan attempted to get hold of the German lines and the Cunard Company but these for similar reasons would not sell their ships.

As I have previously written, the whole amount of cash in the flotation of the United States Steel Corporation was twenty-five millions; the rest was faith in Morgan. It may be readily conceded that he alone in the country could effect such an organization but, was it worth while to abuse that faith and put upon the market at a supposedly valuable price more than 550 millions of "water"? True, Morgan's friends argued that the capitalization was based upon earnings and not upon the value of the property; but what consolation was that to "widows and orphans" who had invested in Steel Common at from 38 to 55 because it paid four per cent, when the Corporation suspended dividends on the Common and the stock went below 10 as it did in 1903? The decline in the market was from 101 for the Preferred down to 49, and from 55 for the Common to 10. No wonder that Morgan was depressed coming as it did with the utter failure of his ship combine. Morgan has "fallen down" in his steamship combination, was a usual remark.

This depression in 1903 was called "the rich men's

---

[1] Noyes, 303.

panic." After what is known as the Northern Pacific Railroad corner, speculation again grew rampant as the "bumper wheat crop" in 1901 made up for the shortage of corn, but early in 1903 it became apparent that the old rules of business and finance remained in force and the "little panic" between two economic crises occurred. As Morgan said in a newspaper interview it was a case of "undigested securities." [1]

The Boston *Herald* of January 10, 1920, commented on "The Greatest Epic in the History of Big Business" by which it meant the Standard Oil Company, that is typified by John D. Rockefeller. In the constituent companies which made up the United States Steel Corporation one finds the "Lake Superior Consolidated Iron Mines," which is put down as the "Rockefeller interests" and which was necessary to the Corporation as owning a large quantity of Lake Superior iron ore. Lake Superior ore had become the basis of the steel industry from its quantity and, while the Bessemer process ruled, from so much of it being low in phosphorus. Ores high in phosphorus were inadmissible as that element was at enmity with steel. The "Rockefeller interests" were not absorbed until after the Carnegie Steel Company. The transaction is simply related by Rockefeller. "After some negotiation," he wrote, "Morgan made an offer which we accepted whereby the whole plant — mines, ships, railways, etc. — should become a part of the United

---

[1] Noyes, 308. Besides works already referred to, I have used in this account, Trusts of To-Day, G. H. Montague; Commercial and Financial Chronicle, 1900, 1901; *The Nation*, 1900, 1901; Articles of Gleed, Macchen, Ely, *Cosmopolitan Mag.*, 1901; article of R. S. Baker, *McClure's Mag.*, Nov. 1901; Peck; Life of Hill, Pyle, ii.

States Steel Corporation. The price paid was, we felt, very moderate considering the present and prospective value of the property." [1]

John D. Rockefeller was one of the directors of the huge corporation and he is comprehensible to us from a study of Napoleon I and from a remark made by Herbert Spencer in 1882 when he was considered a great philosopher, "Practically business has been substituted for war as the purpose of existence." [2] From a bookkeeper Rockefeller had become a partner in a small commission house on the Cuyahoga River in Cleveland, when the discovery of petroleum in Western Pennsylvania started many men in Cleveland, bent on making their fortunes, in that direction. Nothing like the excitement had been known since the discovery of gold in California.[3] Samuel Andrews had invented an easy and cheap process of cleansing the crude oil with sulphuric acid and oil refineries went up in Cleveland as if by magic. Rockefeller, like Cassius, was not fat and thought much and he made up his mind that for him success lay in oil; he embarked on its manufacture, made a copartnership with Andrews and H. M. Flagler and the three went into the business as did many others. For a while the demand for "the light of the world" could not be supplied but eventually the supply became greater than the demand and Cleveland manufacturers were confronted with the fact that the refining of oil in Cleveland for the whole trade of the

---

[1] Random Reminiscences, 131.

[2] After-dinner speech in New York, Nov. 9, 1882. Essays, iii. 484.

[3] An animated account of the discovery of oil and the excitement ensuing is given by Oberholtzer in his History of the United States, i. 250 *et seq.*

world was a geographical absurdity, as the bulk of the trade lay east of the oil regions. The Cleveland refiners were engaged in a cutthroat policy; they bid against one another in the purchase of the crude oil from Pennsylvania, and in the other direction were intense competitors for the sale of the refined.   In 1870 the Standard Oil Company was formed with Rockefeller as the directing agent, who conceived the idea of uniting all under one head by the purchase of all of the Cleveland refineries.   This he did, paying a fair price and giving the owners the choice of Standard stock or cash for their works.   Those who took cash thought that they were getting a bargain; those who took stock became rich.

Rockefeller had difficulty in raising money to meet his desires as the financial "bigwigs" of Cleveland, with two exceptions, were opposed to his scheme and thought that he was taking too many and too great chances.   At this time he would have preferred to pay for the refineries that he was buying in stock rather than in money, as the one commodity was more plenty than the other.   "We invariably," he wrote, "offered those who wanted to sell the option of taking cash or stock in the company.   We very much preferred to have them take the stock because a dollar in those days looked as large as a cart-wheel, but as a matter of business policy we found it desirable to offer them the option and, in most cases, they were even precipitate in their choice of the cash.   They knew what a dollar would buy but they were very skeptical in regard to the possibilities of resurrecting the oil business and giving any permanent value to these shares." [1]   The tale

---

[1] Random Reminiscences, 95.

of Rockefeller's financial anxieties seems strange to the younger generation which associates him with unlimited amounts of money, but those whose memory goes back to the time know how true is his account and that he does not exaggerate in any way his difficulties. "We had our troubles and setbacks," he wrote, "we suffered from severe fires; and the supply of crude oil was most uncertain. . . . At best it was a speculative trade and I wonder that we managed to pull through so often." [1]

The Standard Oil Company was thus launched.[2] If Rockefeller did not say it, he thought that, "The coal oil business belongs to us."[3]   Keeping in mind the similarity and the difference between war and trade how like Napoleon's expression in 1811, "Three years more and I am lord of the universe!"[4]   With great method and untiring zeal Rockefeller wrought for the control of the manufacture and business of refined oil. He acted in accordance with the conditions of his time. After the panic of 1873 railroad business became poor and the railroads were "cutting one another's throats" for whatever business was in sight. Rockefeller took in the situation and, by his control of a large amount of desirable freight, compelled rebates not only on his own shipments but on those of his competitors.

William H. Vanderbilt, who succeeded his father in the control of the New York Central and Lake Shore Railways, important lines of communication for the oil

[1] Random Reminiscences, 83.
[2] I do not digress into a history of the South Improvement Company, believing that it died in embryo. See Wealth against Commonwealth, Henry D. Lloyd, 59.
[3] History of the Standard Oil Company, Tarbell, ii. 34.
[4] Sloane's Napoleon, ii. 235.

business, was then supposed to be the richest man in the country, worth $200,000,000. Only one man in the world, the Duke of Westminster, had an equal amount, but his return from this capital was not as great as Vanderbilt's. His appreciation of the ability shown in the management of this enterprise is therefore important. Vanderbilt testified in 1879: "These men [the Standard Oil Company managers] are smarter than I am a great deal. They are very enterprising and smart men. I never came in contact with any class of men so smart and able as they are in their business." [1]

Rockefeller's handling of the railroads placed him in a commanding position. Herbert Spencer said in the speech already quoted, "I hear that a great trader among you deliberately endeavored to crush out everyone whose business competed with his own." [2] This was unquestionably Rockefeller's method but he was absolutely fair to all of his stockholders and gentle to competing refineries who would work with him on his own terms, which in every case turned out advantageously for those manufacturers. The crude oil producers looked upon him "with superstitious awe," so Miss Tarbell wrote. "Their notion of him was very like that which the English common people had for Napoleon in the first part of the nineteenth century . . . a dread power, cruel, omniscient, always ready to spring." [3] He undoubtedly squeezed the crude oil producers as he did recalcitrant partners of friends whom he started in outside operations. It was owing to these tactics that the man who from nothing

---

[1] Tarbell, The History of the Standard Oil Company, ii. 252.
[2] Essays, iii. 484.
[3] Tarbell, The History of the Standard Oil Company, ii. 63.

had made a billion, had to be guarded by detectives.   He could have no such funeral as Peter Cooper had, of which a journalist at the time said Jay Gould, a rich man of the day, with all of his money, could not buy such a funeral.

Rockefeller accepted the conditions of the game and played it accordingly.   The management of the Standard was one of efficiency in every direction.   "It seemed absolutely necessary," Rockefeller wrote, "to extend the market for oil by exporting to foreign countries which required a long and most difficult development." [1]   This was in exact keeping with the ideas of the day and expressed a thought in many minds.   Rockefeller put the idea in active operation, and, while making money for the Standard made it an important factor in the country's foreign trade.[2]   When the "spellbinders" declaimed that the tariff was the mother of all trusts, the Standard Oil Company must be excepted, as its operations were not dependent on the tariff legislation of Congress.

In line with efficiency, every bit of waste was carefully looked after.   His scientific men were encouraged in the development of by-products which were sold cheaply, brought comfort to many households and swelled the foreign exports.   Rockefeller himself was a remarkable judge of men and gathered around him a number of able lieutenants who wrought loyally under his direction. While he himself was a puritan in life he never made his personal system of morality a guide in the choice of those

---

[1] Random Reminiscences, 82.
[2] Exports fiscal years 1870–71 to 1899–1900 in value, Corn $1,073,333,-598, Wheat $2,495,182,543, Wheat Flour $1,382,075,300, Cotton $6,409,-112,711, Refined Mineral Oil $1,294,953,816.

under him. Was the man equal to his job? seemed to
be the sole test. For efficient coöperation the United
States never saw the equal of the Standard.

Rockefeller was the first to develop on a large scale
the sale of a natural product direct from the producer
to the consumer. He suppressed the middleman and
of course made enemies. A man who had a small broker-
age business dependent upon the Standard, on which
he supported in economic ease a small family, could
not refrain from exclaiming, when deprived of his means
of living, as he thought of the work of this powerful rich
man, "He has taken from me my one ewe lamb." To
such considerations Rockefeller was callous. Mercy in
business never entered into his calculations. Not unlikely
he ascribed talk, critical of his work, to envy, which he
illustrated in his Reminiscences with the action of an
Irish neighbor who built an extremely ugly house, the
bright colors of which were offensive, as he looked out
from his windows; therefore he moved some large trees
to shut out the house from his view. Why are those
large trees moved? the Irishman was asked, to which
came the quick reply, "It's invy, they can't stand looking
at the evidence of me prosperity." [1]

Rockefeller quoted the expression of an old and experienced Boston merchant, "I am opposed on principle
to the whole system of rebates and drawbacks — unless
I am in it." [2] This was undoubtedly the opinion
of business men until this practice was forbidden by the
Interstate Commerce Law of 1887. But before 1887 the
Standard had developed its system and, as it increased

---

[1] Random Reminiscences, 72.   [2] Ibid., 112.

in power and wealth, dictated to those high in command of the railroads, getting low rates which enabled it to crush competitors, or when that was unnecessary, to amass hitherto unheard of wealth.

As Rockefeller's operations were successful he had no difficulty in obtaining all of the money that he desired, so that we see in the Standard a corporation efficiently directed with a real genius at its head and an ever ready supply of cash. To develop the foreign trade and to supply the East it was soon seen that the crude oil must be refined at the seaboard, hence refineries were established at Brooklyn, Bayonne in New Jersey, Philadelphia and Baltimore. Having made dictatorial arrangements with the railroads, organized trade with Europe, Asia, Africa, the East and West of his own country, a common man would have rested on his oars satisfied with his great accomplishments. Not so Rockefeller who was ever on the watch. Pipe-lines had early been in operation to gather the oil from the wells to the railroads, of which the Standard had its share, but in 1879 it was demonstrated by an opposition company that crude oil could be pumped over the mountains and so reach the seaboard. Pipe-line transportation was much cheaper than railroad even if the railroads cut down their carrying charges to cost. Under this new competition all of Rockefeller's carefully made contracts with the railroads, so far as the carrying of crude oil was concerned, were for naught, but he was equal to the emergency. Within five years he owned all of the pipe-lines to the seaboard or had them under his control. With great effect he wrote in his book: "The entire oil business is dependent upon the pipe-line. Without it every well would be less valuable and every market at home and abroad would be more difficult to serve or retain." [1]

Constantly in litigation the Standard employed the best lawyers to fight its cases. Its policy ever to get hold of the ablest was in this particular exemplified with good results.

Did the Standard make the light of the world cheaper? An affirmative answer is at once given by its apologists, a negative by its critics. For ourselves we shall do well to accept the judgment of the intelligent historian of the Standard Oil Company, Gilbert H. Montague, who with the energy of youth investigated fully the matter. "The vexed question," he wrote, "of the effect of the Standard Oil combination on the price of refined oil will probably never be settled." [2] It certainly stabilized prices. Under Cleveland competition, as it existed before 1871, there would have been an era of low prices succeeded by one of high, in entire accordance with the law of supply and demand. Under Standard management the price could not have been excessive or it would have lacked candid defenders. On the other hand there were the large dividends and the fact that everyone connected with the Standard grew rich.

Henry D. Lloyd in "Wealth against Commonwealth" makes a sharp criticism of the Standard Oil Company, and his remedy for the evils it and other trusts caused is State Socialism. This discussion will go on as long as socialists and individualists exist. But the student of men and affairs cannot overlook that "government is

---

[1] Random Reminiscences, 84.
[2] The Rise and Progress of the Standard Oil Company, 136.

some of us, and those not the best of us, put over the rest of us." [1] After a careful reading of this book of Lloyd's one inclined to individualism cannot fail to approve the statement of the reviewer of *The Nation*, "Were we not satisfied from evidence *aliunde*," it said, "that the managers of the Standard Oil Company had violated both law and justice in their attempts to suppress competition, we should be inclined to acquit them after reading this screed. It is quite beyond belief that these men should be capable of the height and depth of wickedness attributed to them, even if they possessed the superhuman powers with which they are credited. It is plain upon Mr. Lloyd's showing that their competitors would be no better than they if they had similar opportunities and it is impossible to arouse sympathy for men whose complaint is that they were not allowed to make enormous profits, for it appears to have been the policy of the Standard Company to buy out its rivals at reasonable rates." [2]

Miss Tarbell, from a number of articles in *McClure's Magazine*, devoted to muckraking, has written two volumes entitled "The History of the Standard Oil Company" in which her industrious research can do no other than compel admiration from anyone who seeks historic truth. Her examination of documents that bear upon the subject seems thorough and no one can attempt a consideration of the Standard without recourse to the many facts that she has uncovered. All the same, the feeling grows that she had determined on her thesis and in her book had sought facts which should support her preconceived impressions. Again must one have recourse to *The*

---

[1] Cited from memory but the remark was, I think, made by Professor W. G. Sumner. [2] *The Nation*, Nov. 8, 1894, 348.

Nation. "The writer" [*i.e.* Miss Tarbell], it said, "has
either a vague conception of the nature of proof or she
is willing to blacken the character of John D. Rockefeller
by insinuation and detraction." But he "has been
caught in no worse crimes than underselling his competitors and getting rebates from railroads. . . . It is matter of public notoriety that Mr. Rockefeller is offensively
reticent. . . . In impassioned . . . language a desperate
struggle is described between the powers of evil incarnate
in the Standard Oil Company and the powers of goodness
appearing in a metaphysical entity called the 'Oil Region.'
This being, it appears, loved virtue for its own sake; it
believed in independence and fair play; it hated the rebates and secret rates; it hated, but it also feared, its
adversary. . . . The 'Oil Region' means a number of
men engaged in the wildest kind of speculation, many
of whom proved themselves willing to engage in every
kind of wickedness of which the Standard Oil Company
was accused." It "might say like the French deputy to
his constituents, 'So intense was the corruption that even
I did not altogether escape.'" [1]

A careful consideration of the subject, with a thorough
reading of Lloyd's and Miss Tarbell's books cannot fail
to impress an inquirer with the great ability shown by
Rockefeller, who was to business what Napoleon was to
war and to civic society. In Rockefeller may be seen a
ripe development of the application of energy to resources.
This quiet, reticent man, thinking and listening,
as he stropped his penknife over the heel of his boot,
like the traditional Yankee whittling a stick, made combinations which startled the world. Always given to

[1] *The Nation*, Jan. 5, 1905, 15.

reflection when not taking needed physical exercise, reading no book but "Ben Hur," [1] he moved men upon his chess-board like pawns in the game.   Sincerely religious, it must have been a surprise to him that his methods were questioned when he simply played the game as he found its conditions, and supposed that he never violated the tenets of the Christian religion as commonly understood.   Outside of religion and physical exercise he pursued one single idea and was eminently successful from the grasp of his mind.

The question must arise, Is it well for the State to have such huge fortunes as those of Rockefeller and Carnegie accumulated in a lifetime?   It must be said in their defence that they accomplished the difficult art of giving, that their benefactions were noble and that they set a pattern for other rich men, whose gifts and bequests have been on the side of civilization.   In the amassing of such wealth it is well that they or their descendants did not spend it in luxurious or riotous living; that they themselves obeyed the call of duty and were as systematic and wise in their dispensations as in their acquirements. That their gifts made for the good of civilization, however, will fail to convince the mass of voters, who cannot see that fine pictures, well-collected libraries, endowed universities, cure of disease and prophylactic treatment compensate them for a deprivation of their share of the cake in favor of Rockefeller, Carnegie and others. [2]

---

[1] Up to 1918.   The Bible of course excepted.

[2] For authorities not specifically referred to I have consulted Industrial Commission Reports, vol. i. 19.   House docs., 1899–1900, vol. 93; 1901–1902, vol. 82;   Trusts of To-Day, Montague; Noyes, Forty Years of American Finance;   Burton J. Hendrick, Age of Big Business;   Peck; *The Nation*, 1900, 1901.

McKinley's second inaugural address (March 4, 1901)
was a pæan to the successful accomplishment of the past
four years. Then there was a deficit, now a surplus;
then depression, now activity. "The national verdict
of 1896," he declared, "has for the most part been exe-
cuted." His personal bearing, action and amiability had
contributed much to the achievement of what he stated
in fitting words : " Sectionalism has disappeared. Division
on public questions can no longer be traced by the war
maps of 1861." [1] "I can no longer be called the President of a party," he said to his Secretary; "I am now the
President of the whole people." [2]

Between the second inauguration and his death
McKinley enjoyed his office and the hold which he had
on the people;   his content was marred by the alarming
illness of his wife during a trip to the Pacific coast. On
his return to Washington, he was obliged, because of her
condition, to decline an invitation to the Commencement of Harvard University and receive the honorary
degree of Doctor of Laws. In answer to repeated public
requests that he should again be a candidate for the presidency, he made an open statement that under no circumstances would he accept a nomination for a third
term.

He had promised to visit the Buffalo fair, believing,
as he there said, "Expositions are the timekeepers of
progress. They record the world's advancement." " The
crowning and original feature of this Exposition,"
wrote Robert Grant, was the illumination by the electric

[1] Messages and Papers, Supplement, 163.
[2] Life of McKinley, Olcott, ii. 296.

lights; the power for the electricity was furnished by
Niagara Falls. "The time fixed for the ceremony of
illumination," continued Grant, "is half-past eight, just
as the summer twilight is deepening into darkness. . . .
There is a deep silence and all eyes are riveted on the
electric tower. Suddenly . . . we have a veritable fairy-
land; the triumph not of Aladdin's lamp but of the masters of modern science over the nature-god, Electricity." [1]
Dooley likewise visited the fair. "They tell me," he
wrote, "that at th' Pan-American show in th' city iv
Buffalo th' ilicthric light is made be Niag'ra Falls. . . .
Hogan seen it, an' he says it makes th' moon look like
a dark lanthern. They speak iv th' sun in Buffalo th'
way a motorman on a trolley line wud shpeak iv a horse
car. 'Th' sun is settin' earlier,' says he to Conners, th'
thruckman that wus towin' him. 'Since th' fair begun,'
says Conners, 'it hasn't showed after eight o'clock. We
'seldom hear iv it nowadays. We set our clocks be th'
risin' an' settin' iv th' lights.'" [2]

The President's visit to the Buffalo fair was delayed
until September when, during a crowded reception, he
was shot by an anarchist (September 6) who, in the line
of approaching people, pretending to have an injured
hand, concealed, in the handkerchief wrapped around it,
a revolver from which two shots dealt the death-blow
to the President. The fatal shot was fired on a Friday
afternoon. McKinley lingered for over a week and at
times strong hopes were entertained for his recovery, but
these were vain, and early on Saturday morning, September 14, he passed away.

---

[1] *Cosmopolitan Magazine*, Sept. 1901, 453.
[2] *Cosmopolitan Magazine*, Sept. 1901, 478.

The crowd, amazed at the attempt on the life of their beloved President, threatened to lynch the assassin but McKinley, stricken to death, showed his respect for the law in his words, "Don't let them hurt him."[1] Then his thoughts dwelt upon his wife, who, accompanying him to Buffalo, was at a neighboring house. "My wife — be careful, Cortelyou, how you tell her — oh, be careful!" A week later when he and all of his friends knew that the end was near, he said, "It is God's way. His will, not ours, be done"; then he repeated some lines of his favorite hymn, "Nearer, my God, to Thee."[2] Involuntarily came to many lips, "See how a Christian can die." The journalist who had sneered at "the pious McKinley" could not, from his skeptical view, appreciate the depth and sincerity of McKinley's religious nature.

Roosevelt, on hearing of the assassination, hurried to Buffalo but, on the assurance that the President would recover, left for the Adirondacks whence he was hastily summoned again. Before his arrival McKinley had passed away and, when reaching Buffalo, Roosevelt was met by a request from Secretary Elihu Root, the ranking member of the Cabinet who was there, that he "take the constitutional oath of President of the United States." To this he replied: "I shall take the oath at once in accordance with your request, and in this hour of deep and terrible national bereavement I wish to state that it shall be my aim to continue absolutely unbroken the policy of President McKinley for the peace and prosperity and honor of our beloved country."[3]

[1] For the trial and execution of McKinley's assassin, see my vol. viii. 151.

[2] Life of McKinley, Olcott, ch. xxxiv.

[3] Messages and Papers, Supplement, 298.

Elihu Root, McKinley's Secretary of War, said: "I have talked with him [McKinley] again and again before a Cabinet meeting and found that his ideas were fixed and his mind firmly made up. He would then present the subject to the Cabinet in such a way as not to express his own decision, but yet bring about an agreement exactly along the lines of his own original ideas, while the members often thought the ideas were theirs. . . . He cared nothing about the credit but McKinley *always had his way*. . . . He had vast influence with Congress. He led them by the power of affectionate esteem not by fear. He never bullied Congress." [1] Shelby M. Cullom, Senator from Illinois for thirty years, wrote: "We have never had a President who had more influence with Congress than McKinley. . . . I have never heard of even the slightest friction between him and the party leaders in Senate and House. . . . He looked and acted the ideal President. He was always thoroughly self-poised and deliberate; nothing ever seemed to excite him and he always maintained a proper dignity." [2] President Roosevelt said in his first Message to Congress: "At the time of President McKinley's death he was the most widely loved man in all the United States; while we have never had any public man of his position who has been so wholly free from the bitter animosities incident to public life. . . . To a standard of lofty integrity in public life he united the tender affections and home virtues which are all-important in the make-up of national character." [3]

From my point of view it will ever be a regret that the

---

[1] Olcott, ii. 346.   [2] Fifty Years, 275.
[3] Messages and Papers, Supplement, 315.

long-standing distrust of and enmity to Spain should have
come to a head during McKinley's administration. For
he was essentially a peace minister. Coming before the
public, the high-priest of protection, he had, through the
exercise of executive authority, modified his views. He
was diligent in the enforcement of the reciprocity provision of the Dingley Act and named John A. Kasson to
negotiate in accordance therewith reciprocity agreements.
It was not necessary that these agreements should be
ratified by the Senate but some Senators, who were more
strongly high tariff than McKinley himself, thought that
France had gotten the better of Kasson in the bargain.[1]
Nor was McKinley's recommendation of free trade with
Puerto Rico immediately adopted. In his message of
December, 1899, he said, "Our plain duty is to abolish
all customs tariffs between the United States and Puerto
Rico and give her products free access to our markets."
It took him a little over a year and a half to accomplish
this but he had the satisfaction before his death of seeing
complete free trade with the island.[2]   In the speech that
he made in Buffalo the day before his assassination, he
showed how far behind him he had left the doctrines of
ultra-protection.   "A system," he said, "which provides
a mutual exchange of commodities, is manifestly essential
to the continued and healthful growth of our export trade.

---

[1] Kasson made the agreement with France on May 28, 1898; it was
proclaimed on May 30. He made an agreement with Italy on Feb. 8,
1900; it was proclaimed on July 18, 1900; another with Portugal on
May 22, 1899; it was proclaimed on July 12, 1900.

There were later made the following agreements, but not by Kasson:
Germany, proclaimed July 13, 1900. Switzerland, proclaimed Jan. 1, 1906.
Spain, signed Aug. 1, 1906. Bulgaria, proclaimed Sept. 15, 1906. Great
Britain, proclaimed Dec. 5, 1907. Netherlands, proclaimed Aug. 12, 1908.

[2] Willoughby, Territories and Dependencies, 113.

We must not repose in fancied security that we can for-
ever sell everything and buy little or nothing. If such a
thing were possible, it would not be best for us or for those
with whom we deal. We should take from our customers
such of their products as we can use without harm to our
industries and labor. . . . The period of exclusiveness is
past. The expansion of our trade and commerce is the
pressing problem. Commercial wars are unprofitable.
A policy of good will and friendly trade relations will
prevent reprisals. Reciprocity treaties are in harmony
with the spirit of the times, measures of retaliation are
not." "We find our long-time principles echoed," declared *The Nation*, " to our unfeigned satisfaction." [1]

McKinley, however, did not live up to the expectations
of the Civil Service reformers, inferred from his expressions and attitude when a member of the House. The
testimony of William D. Foulke of Indiana is of high
value. Singularly in favor of Civil Service reform, on
excellent terms with Eaton, Curtis, Schurz, Dana and
others who labored in the vineyard, he supported by
speech and action McKinley in 1896 and 1900 and was a
level-headed man who could look on both sides of any
question. By his order of July 27, 1897, asserted Foulke,
McKinley "greatly strengthened the competitive service"; it provided that no removal should be made "except for just cause." In his Annual Message of December, 1897, he said that the merit system "has the approval
of the people and it will be my endeavor to uphold and
extend it," and in the ensuing session of Congress "he
opposed all efforts to repeal or change the law. But in

---

[1] Sept. 12, 1901, 197.

the administration of it," continued Foulke, "the executive department showed great weakness." An anticipated and forecasted order was promulgated on May 29, 1899, which marked "the first considerable reduction in the area of the merit system since the Civil Service law was enacted in 1883." As a quasi-atonement he extended the merit system to the Philippine Islands "by his instructions to the Philippine Commission in April, 1900." "As the campaign of 1900 drew near," Foulke went on to say, "the opinions of Civil Service reformers were divided." The anti-imperialists, among whom was Carl Schurz, "felt a deep resentment at the backslidings of McKinley and could see nothing of his extension of the competitive system to the Philippines which could atone for breaking his promises regarding that system in the United States." [1]

McKinley's action in regard to Civil Service reform was tortuous. He seemed swayed by opposing forces. Undoubtedly the one opposed to Civil Service reform was represented by Mark Hanna who sincerely believed that, for the good of the country and the party, he himself, the heads of the departments, the senators and representatives could make better appointments than could be secured by any system of competitive examination.[2]

---

[1] W. D. Foulke, Fighting the Spoilsman, 119, 122, 123, 125. See Richard H. Dana's review, *Amer. Polit. Science Rev.*, Feb. 1920.

[2] Authorities not specifically mentioned. Proceedings of National Civil Service Reform League, 1900, 1901; Carl Schurz, Speeches, Correspondence, etc., vi.; Foraker, Notes of a Busy Life, ii.; *The Nation*, *passim*.

CHAPTER VII

WITH our new colonies it has been impossible to preserve a chronological unity of narrative. It is now necessary to enter upon an account of Puerto Rico, Cuba and the Philippines, going back to a point beyond which the narrative has already taken us and terminating ahead of the time to which the history of our domestic transactions will be carried.

Puerto Rico may be easily disposed of. In the words of Archibald C. Coolidge, its annexation, "being a natural consequence of the Spanish War, met with little opposition from any quarter." Writing in 1908 he sums up with, "All told, the record of American rule has been satisfactory and creditable."[1] This is supported by the words of a competent and intelligent English authority, Eustace Percy, who wrote about 1919, "In Porto Rico the United States has pursued a most liberal and progressive policy."[2] To Joseph B. Foraker, chairman of the Senate Committee on Puerto Rico, fell the duty of drafting the organic act which determined our relations with Puerto Rico. This became a law in 1900, is known as the Foraker Act, was upheld somewhat over a year later as constitutional by the United States Supreme Court, and is thus referred to with commendable pride by the author, "The mere fact that this law has continued in force, practically without change, ever since it was

---

[1] The United States as a World Power, 143, 145.
[2] The Responsibilities of the League, 87.

176

enacted, now full fifteen years ago, is enough to indicate that it proved satisfactory when put into practical operation." [1] "This Act," wrote William F. Willoughby, "is in every respect an important document. It may be said to stand to our new insular possessions in much the same relation as the Northwest Ordinance did to our dependent territory on the mainland." Willoughby was Treasurer of Puerto Rico from 1901 to 1907 and, while in that office, wrote a book in which he gave an excellent account and analysis of the Foraker Act summing up with, "The problem that Congress had to meet when it framed the organic act — that of providing a system of government that should at once grant a maximum of local autonomy and at the same time make provision for sufficient central control — was an exceedingly difficult one. If it has erred, it has been in immediately granting too much rather than too little." [2]

"Whatever may be the fate of Cuba in the future," wrote Archibald C. Coolidge, "the treatment she has received at the hands of the United States in the decade since she was made free will remain something to be proud of." [3] The pledge contained in the Teller Amendment was faithfully kept. After the Treaty of Paris the government of Cuba was for a while under the direction of the American Army. Elihu Root had become Secretary of War and he was insistent that Cubans be prepared for a civil government to be administered by themselves.

---

[1] Notes of a Busy Life, Foraker, ii. 82. This was published in February, 1916. The statute is printed in U. S. Statutes at large, 56th Cong., vol. 31, p. 77.

[2] Territories and Dependencies of the United States, 83, 117.

[3] The United States as a World Power, 130.

But before the American Army left, a great work was accomplished in sanitation — "the marvel of the age," Latané terms it.[1] "Read the story of yellow fever in Havana and Brazil," wrote Dr. William Osler, "if you wish to get an idea of the powers of experimental medicine; there is nothing to match it in the history of human achievement." [2] The work in Cuba is well stated by Secretary Root in his report of November 27, 1901. "The eastern part of the island," he wrote, "is entirely free from yellow fever. The western part is practically free there being but a few cases in or about Habana. This dreaded disease has passed from one of the leading causes of death to one of the least frequent. The reduction of death rate in Habana alone, as compared with the former death rate, shows an average of approximately 3700 lives per year saved, and Habana has changed its position from one of the most unhealthy cities to one of the most healthy. The control of yellow fever, acting upon the results of investigation as to its causes, prosecuted under the direction of the military government, appears to be now practically absolute." [3]

The chief credit is of course due to General Wood without whose command nothing could be done, but associated with him in this "extraordinary service in ridding the island of yellow fever" were Major Walter Reed and Major William C. Gorgas. "The name of Dr. Jesse W. Lazear, contract surgeon," continued Secretary Root, "who voluntarily permitted himself to be inoculated with the yellow fever germ, in order to furnish a necessary

---

[1] The United States as a World Power, 182.
[2] "Man's Redemption of Man," in *American Mag.*, Dec., 1910, 251.
[3] Report, House Docs., 57th Cong. 1st Sess., 39.

experimental test in the course of the investigation, and
who died of the disease, should be written in the list of
the martyrs who have died in the cause of humanity." [1]

A census was taken showing a population of 1,572,797,
of whom 34 per cent were able to read and write, while
66 per cent were illiterate. The desire and need of popular education were great and both private and public
efforts were made in this direction. The wise President
of Harvard University, Charles W. Eliot, was to the fore,
raised a fund for the purpose and invited a number of
Cuban teachers to the summer school in Cambridge where
they could learn from masters of the art how to instruct
others eager for education but ignorant of the way to get
it. These teachers, 1281 in number, spent the summer
in attending the school and in a study of neighboring
institutions of art and practical manufacture, and, before
they went home, were given a free visit to New York
City and Washington. [2]

All the while, progress was making toward the training
of the people of Cuba for self-government. A basis of
suffrage was agreed upon [3] and on June 16, 1900, municipal officers throughout the entire island were elected. As
soon as the new municipal governments were fairly in-
stalled, a call for a constitutional convention was made,
and thirty-one delegates to it were orderly chosen. The
convention met in Havana on November 5, 1900, and was
opened by General Wood. But before Cuba could be
let go, the relations between the island and the United
States must be defined. This was done in the Platt

---

[1] Report of Dec. 1, 1902. House Docs. 57, Cong. 2d Sess., 10.
[2] Military and Colonial Policy, Root, 198.
[3] For restrictions on universal suffrage, ibid., 194.

Amendment to the Army Appropriation Bill which became a law on March 2, 1901. The author of this was Orville H. Platt of Connecticut who is fitly described by his biographer, Louis A. Coolidge, as "an old-fashioned senator," and the biography is said to be "the story of a life unselfishly devoted to the public service." He feared that he could not pass the measure independently through the Senate at the short session and so had recourse to a rider to an appropriation bill.

The Platt Amendment provided that:

I. The independence of Cuba should not in any way be impaired by any compact with a foreign power.

II. A proper limitation was made as to the amount of any public debt that Cuba should contract.

III. Cuba consented to the intervention of the United States "for the preservation of Cuban independence, the maintenance of a government adequate for the protection of life, property and individual liberty and for discharging the obligations imposed by the Treaty of Paris on the United States."

IV. The acts of the United States during the military occupancy should be validated.

V. Cuba would maintain "and as far as necessary" extend the work of sanitation.

VI. The Isle of Pines should be omitted "from the proposed constitutional boundaries of Cuba."

VII. Cuba was to furnish the United States "lands necessary for coaling or naval stations." [1]

Article III caused the greatest amount of opposition in the Cuban constitutional convention and this was

---

[1] See America as a World Power, Latané, Hart's American Nation Series, 189.

finally quieted by a statement of Senator Platt and an official communication to a committee of the convention by the Secretary of War.[1] Then the provisions of the Platt Amendment were appended to the Cuban Constitution.

Like many important documents the authorship of these wise provisions has been in dispute. The editors of the series of the Root publications have maintained that it was drafted by Secretary Root and this claim was made indeed during the lifetime of Senator Platt. The true genesis of the Platt Amendment, however, is truthfully and effectively told by Senator Platt in a private letter of January 1, 1904: "The original draft was my own. . . . It was changed from time to time, somewhat in language but not in spirit, in consultation both with Republicans of the Committee, President McKinley and Secretary Root. A final consultation between myself and Senator Spooner put the document in its complete form."[2] Root's titles to greatness were so many that he would be the last man to claim aught that was not fully his own, while Senator Platt's admiration at an early day for Root was unbounded. He, said the Senator, is discharging the duties of Secretary of War better than any other man could. But he could fill any position in the Cabinet and indeed he might serve as President with capacity and wisdom.

"At any rate," wrote the Senator in a private letter, "the United States will always, under the so-called Platt Amendment, be in a position to straighten out things if they get seriously bad."[3]

[1] Life of Platt, Coolidge, 344; Military and Colonial Policy, Root, 214.
[2] Life of Platt, Coolidge, 351, et ante; Military and Colonial Policy, Root, viii.   [3] Life of Platt, Coolidge, 349.

Elections were held in Cuba under the Constitution on the last day of December, 1901, when governors of provinces, members of the House of Representatives and presidential and senatorial electors were chosen; these electors met during the following February and elected a President, Vice-President and senators.   The civil government of Cuba was duly inaugurated and the American troops withdrawn on May 20, 1902.   With pardonable pride Elihu Root wrote as Secretary of War in his report of 1902: "I know of no chapter in American history more satisfactory than that which will record the conduct of the military government of Cuba.   The credit for it is due, first of all, to General Leonard Wood."   In his order of July 4, 1902, Root said that the officers and enlisted men "have with sincere kindness helped the Cuban people to take all the successive steps necessary to the establishment of their own constitutional government; . . . they have governed Cuba wisely, regarding justice and respecting individual liberty; have honestly collected and expended for the best interests of the Cuban people the revenues" of the island.[1]

The peace, the health, the independence of Cuba are necessary to the United States.   A commercial arrangement should be made with her under which she can live, said Root in his report of November 27, 1901.[2]   This meant that in a reciprocal arrangement the duties on her sugar and tobacco should be reduced.   This proved to be a long and tedious process owing to the opposition of some selfishly protected interests, but the arrangement was finally submitted to both Houses of Congress.

---

[1] Report of Dec. 1, 1902, 9, 14.   [2] P. 53.

Through the influence of President Roosevelt and the work of Senator Orville H. Platt (to mention some of the agencies working to this end) a treaty of reciprocity between Cuba and the United States was ratified late in 1903. During the contest Senator Platt wrote in a private letter: "The reduction on Cuban imports will not hurt the sugar or tobacco industry one particle. Neither the sugar trust nor the tobacco trust will derive the slightest benefit from it. The talk about it has been the greatest exhibition of expansive bosh that I have ever known." [1]

By the Platt Amendment it was provided that a treaty between the two countries should embody its provisions. This was made. Our course towards Cuba is well summed up by Theodore Roosevelt: "We made the promise to give Cuba independence; and we kept the promise. . . . We also by treaty gave the Cubans substantial advantages in our markets. Then we left the island, turning the government over to its own people." [2]

The Philippines is a knotty question. It has been a political issue and the course of the administration has aroused sentimental objection. The literature on the subject is enormous and observers, who have remained long and have written candid accounts, have arrived at opposite conclusions. [3] It is best, therefore, in the maze

---

[1] Life of Platt, Coolidge, 381.

[2] Autobiography, 545. In this study of Cuba I have been much helped by Latané's "America as a World Power." See the Chapter in Life of Platt on "Cuban Scandals and Allowances."

[3] Charles B. Elliott wrote: "Many writers, American and English, who have favored the public with their views on the Philippines . . . sug-

of contradictions to rely on the man, who, more than any other one, is responsible for our policy — Elihu Root. It will be told later how he came into administrative office. For the moment it suffices to say that he regarded the United States as the greatest of his clients, and that an ambassador of the Russian Czar said that having met most of the public men of Europe, he knew no one who was as able as Elihu Root.

Before he called Root to his aid President McKinley had inaugurated the government of the Philippines. His message to Otis, who was the military commander in the islands, stated the mission of the United States but in it he said that we had succeeded to the "sovereignty of Spain" and that our aim was "benevolent assimilation." Now McKinley was entirely sincere and the anti-Imperialists, who afterwards played upon those words, failed to comprehend the depth of his religious nature. The overpowering feeling which swayed him was religious and this cannot be better stated than in the private letter to him of Senator Orville H. Platt of August 15, 1898. "I feel that I ought to say," he wrote, "that during the past week I have been well over the State of Connecticut and I am satisfied that nine-tenths of the people of the State have an intense feeling that we should insist upon the cession of all the Philippine Islands. Those who be-

---

gest Kipling's famous 'Pagett M. P.' who visited India in winter and 'spoke of the heat of India as the Asia solar myth.' " As his entertainer returned homeward he wrote:

> "And I laughed as I drove from the station but
> the mirth died out on my lips
> As I thought of the fools like Pagett who write
> of their Eastern Trips."

The Philippines to the End of the Commission Government, 376.

lieve in Providence see, or think they see, that God has placed upon this government the solemn duty of providing for the people of these islands, a government based upon the principle of liberty, no matter how many difficulties the problem may present. They feel that it is our duty to attempt its solution. Among Christian thoughtful people the sentiment is akin to that which has maintained the missionary work of the last century in foreign lands. I assure you that it is difficult to overestimate the strength and intensity of this sentiment. If, in the negotiations for peace, Spain is permitted to retain any portion of the Philippines it will be regarded as a failure on the part of this nation to discharge the greatest moral obligation which could be conceived." [1]

Connecticut is a small State but it has great influence especially in the Western States through which President McKinley made his "famous Western journey" and had his own opinion confirmed. The attempt of many anti-Imperialists to hint that love of gain was the prime cause of our taking the Philippines is not borne out by the record.

The first interference by Congress with the Commission government was by the Spooner Amendment to the Army Appropriation Bill, which was approved on March 2, 1901; this was decidedly opposed to any attempt to exploit the islands. [2] The Philippine Commission, in their report to the Secretary of War of November 1, 1902, spoke of "the burdensome restrictions upon the investment of

---

[1] Life of Platt, Coolidge, 287.
[2] The Spooner Amendment is printed in Root, Milit. and Colonial Policy, 255. See speech of Senator Lodge on an earlier bill. Speeches and Addresses, 317.

capital in lands and mines in these islands. . . . The re-quirements," they continued, "that no corporation shall own more than 2500 acres, stops absolutely the invest-ment of new capital in the sugar industry and in the to-bacco industry. It takes away any hope of bringing prosperity to these islands by the extending of the acreage in the cultivation of these two important products of the archipelago. It very much interferes with the invest-ment of capital in railroad enterprises, because they are naturally connected with the possibilities of transporta-tion of sugar and tobacco from the interior to the sea-ports." [1] In their report of December 23, 1903, they re-turned to the subject and recommended that "the limi-tation ought either to be removed entirely or be increased so as to allow the acquisition of at least 25,000 acres of land." [2]

The charge that our acquisition was "a greedy land-grabbing game" may have come from the open plans of promoters of new enterprises. So far as I have been able to discover there were no extravagant profits except those made out of the 70,000 American soldiers by some half dozen "American trading companies," who acquired "quick and large profits" referred to by Civil Governor William H. Taft in his report of November 15, 1903.[3] It was the old story of Pistol,

"I shall sutler be
Unto the Camp and profits will accrue." [4]

While on this subject the idea may at once be dismissed that the United States made any money out of the Phil-ippines. Archibald C. Coolidge, whose authority can-

---

[1] Report, 7.   [2] Report, 9.
[3] P. 49.   [4] King Henry V., act ii., scene 1.

not be gainsaid, wrote in 1908: "American capital has not come in in the way that was expected, partly on account of the legislation passed to protect the natives against exploitation, but more particularly because people have found it safer and more profitable to invest their money nearer home."[1] It is true that the manipulation of the tariff, although a concession was made to the products of the Philippine Islands, was not enlightened policy. Governor Taft desired absolute free trade with the islands but it took a number of years, and then under his own presidency (1909), to effect this consummation.

President McKinley was a conscientious Methodist, and he fully believed that in the Philippines the white man's burden was laid upon the United States. As men act from mingled motives, the idea of personal fame doubtless was bound up in his action. He was a student of American history and knew it well for the years that came within his personal remembrance. Every American President since 1865 has emulated the fame of Lincoln, as did McKinley, when in his speech accepting the nomination in 1900, he declared: "The Republican Party . . . broke the shackles of 4,000,000 slaves and made them free, and to the party of Lincoln has come another supreme opportunity which it has bravely met in the liberation of 10,000,000 of the human family from the yoke of imperialism."[2] He likewise believed that the possession of the Philippines would be an assistance to our growing trade in the Orient.

No one can write on this subject without devoting a large amount of study to the arguments of the anti-

[1] The United States as a World Power, 170.
[2] Life of McKinley, Olcott. ii. 287. This was then stated

Imperialists with whose statements, so far as they can be tortured into reasoning that we had no business trying to govern people 7000 miles away, I am in entire sympathy. Moorfield Storey's acute logic and large present intelligence would make one almost feel that Charles Sumner was on earth again interpreting the Constitution and the acts of the President by the truths of the Declaration of Independence. His opposition to our work in the Philippines was sincere and was urged by a sacrifice of present ease and earthly honors. For he was of the stuff of which martyrs are made and, in earlier days, would have suffered for his opinions at the stake. Carl Schurz, according to a personal friend, was a revolutionist and thus he showed himself in his opposition to the Philippine policy. His speeches were those of an orator and his well-rounded periods put his position with great force. His argument, which was generally concurred in by the anti-Imperialists that we should treat the Philippines as we had treated Cuba, was well put, attested as it was by the despatch of Admiral Dewey that the Filipinos "are far superior in their intelligence and more capable of self-government than the natives of Cuba, and I am familiar with both races."[1] But Schurz's plan in giving self-government to the Philippines was "to make the Philippine Islands neutral territory as Belgium and Switzerland are in Europe."[2] Schurz fortunately did not live to see the guarantee of Belgium's neutrality treated as a mere "scrap of paper," nor did he become disabused of his profound admiration for the German Emperor, Wilhelm

---

[1] Despatch of Dewey to Sec. of Navy, June 27, 1898.
[2] Speech of Oct. 17, 1899. Speeches, etc., vi. 108.

II. "Whether the Emperor of Germany did not at one time wish to acquire the Philippines, I do not know," he said. "But if we offered him the Philippines to-day with our compliments, he would doubtless ask, 'How large an army do you have to employ to subjugate the country?' The answer would be, 'At present 60,000 men; we may need 100,000.' The Emperor would smilingly reply, 'Thank you. Offer this job to someone who is as foolish as you have been.' He would probably be too polite to say so, but he would doubtless think so." [1] At this time a majority of the best informed people in the United States and England believed that Germany would take these islands if she could get them and apply, if need be, the ruthless methods which the Emperor told his troops to employ in China. "Spare nobody," he said, "make no prisoners, use your weapons in a manner to make every Chinaman for a thousand years to come forego the wish to as much as look askance at a German." [2]

The opposition of Senator George F. Hoar was pathetic. A true Republican, he loved McKinley, who, late in 1898, was committed to taking the Philippines. When he saw the President during December of that year and was taken by the hand with the question, "How are you feeling this winter, Mr. Senator?" "Pretty pugnacious, I confess, Mr. President," "The tears came into his eyes and McKinley said, grasping my hand again, 'I shall always love you whatever you do.'" [3] Hoar planted

---

[1] Speech of Sept. 28, 1900, ibid., 248.
[2] July 2, 1900. The Kaiser's Speeches, Wolf von Schierbrand, 260 (1903).
[3] Autobiography, ii. 315.

himself on the Declaration of Independence that "governments derive their just powers from the consent of the governed." He was a true disciple of Charles Sumner "to whom," he said, "the Declaration of Independence was another gospel." [1] We ought to have treated the Philippines as we did Cuba, he affirmed, and had we done so, a government under Aguinaldo and his associates would have been formed as stable as the governments from the United States to Cape Horn. A democracy, he declared, "cannot rule over vassal states as subject people without bringing in the elements of death into its own constitution." [2] This idea was extensively elaborated by Carl Schurz, but it had great force coming from a true American and a loyal Republican like Senator Hoar.

In truth there is something admirable in these three men pleading for the rights of eight million brown people as they had hitherto for four million blacks. It is the old story of the superior taking the part of the inferior, and it involves the subjugation of race pride and putting one's self in the place of the brown or black man.

McKinley had aspirations after culture and was especially fond of college men. He decided to send a Commission to the Philippines, at whose head should be Jacob G. Schurman, President of Cornell University. During January, 1899, Schurman was summoned to Washington and such an invitation was extended to him. He demurred first because he feared that he could not leave the University and then he said, "To be plain, Mr. President, I am opposed to your Philippine policy; I never

---

[1] Speech in the Senate, Jan. 9, 1899; see Senator Lodge's argument on "consent of the governed." Speeches and Addresses, 326.

[2] Senate speech.

wanted the Philippine Islands." "Oh," was the reply, "that need not trouble you; I didn't want the Philippine Islands either; and in the protocol to the treaty I felt myself free not to take them, but in the end there was no alternative." The American people certainly would not consent to leave the Philippines to Spain, the President argued, and, as that was no longer a question, if "American sovereignty were not set up, the peace of the world would be endangered." We, so he implied, certainly owed responsibilities to the world at large. The President desired this Commission to act as an advisory Cabinet and he especially wished to know what sort of political relations it was wise to establish between the United States and eight million [1] brown men of Asia. He desired aid in shaping such a policy and at the same time a tactful coöperation with the naval and military authorities at Manila.[2] Schurman accepted the Presidency of the Commission and McKinley named as his associates Admiral Dewey, General Otis (who was the military commander in the Philippines), Charles Denby and Dean C. Worcester of the University of Michigan.

When Schurman arrived in Manila he found a war in progress which was an interruption to his peaceful errand. The American and Philippine armies had faced each other near Manila for a number of weeks in hostile array. The Americans had bought the sovereignty of the islands from Spain but the Filipinos supposed that in the event

---

[1] The first Commission adopted that figure (15). The Census of 1903 made the population somewhat less. Enc. Brit.; Blount, Amer. Occupation of the Philippines, 567. Williams wrote that the population to the square mile was about 66, to 350 in Java, 290 in Japan, 200 in India. Odyssey of the P. Com., 306.

[2] Schurman, A Retrospect and Outlook, 2.

of American success they were to be granted their independence. The fight which broke out on February 4, 1899, was therefore one between sovereignty and independence. The feeling which became pretty general among the Filipinos may be stated thus: "If the Americans are going to look on us and treat us as the Spaniards have done for three hundred years we do not want them here." [1] Aguinaldo was the head of the Filipinos and he was a Malay of marked ability. A born leader he knew how to consolidate the different factions in the islands. While he was far from being the "George Washington of the Orient," as some of the anti-Imperialists in America called him, he probably conducted as well as possible the war for independence. But it is a question whether he and most of his followers would have opposed the Americans had they known that they came there not to exploit the islands but to assist them in their progress toward civilization. The Filipinos, however, had been fed with promises until they had come to distrust the white man; and the minute blood was shed the sympathy of the mass ran with their brown brothers. The Filipino soldiers were, however, no match for the Americans, and while they had modern rifles they did not know how to use them, so that casualties on their side were large and entirely out of proportion to the losses of the Americans. By the end of 1899 organized resistance to the United States Government came to an end, and thereafter the insurrection took the form of guerilla warfare which, in many cases, degenerated into brigandage. In November of this year Aguinaldo disappeared into the

---

[1] Unofficial Letters of an Official's Wife, Edith Moses (1908), 74.

wilderness and apparently played little or no part in the guerilla warfare.

The Schurman Commission became one of investigation and in their report of January 31, 1900, maintained that the Philippine Islands could not stand alone. To become "self-governing and independent" they needed the "tutelage and protection of the United States." But the "goal of the intelligent Filipinos" was ultimate independence — "independence after an undefined period of American training."[1] "Should our power by any fatality be withdrawn," it said, "the Commission believe that the government of the Philippines would speedily lapse into anarchy, which would excuse, if it did not necessitate, the intervention of other powers and the eventual division of the islands among them."[2]

About ten per cent of the Filipinos were educated men, of high intelligence. They knew Spanish, the civilization and the literature of Spain, but naturally they were not all saints. A goodly proportion of them were office-seekers of the type we know in the United States, and they desired independence in order to hold the purse strings of the nation, while if they were under an American protectorate they would be protected from other Asiatic and European countries by the American Navy, in the event that they should misconduct themselves in foreign affairs. The radicals, whose true leader was Aguinaldo, influenced a majority of this ten per cent and they swayed the mass. All but less than a million were Ro-

[1] Report, 83.
[2] Senate hearings on affairs in the Philippine Islands, 2983. Henry Cabot Lodge was the efficient chairman of the committee before whom the hearings were had.

man Catholic Christians and this religion was imposed
upon them by the Spanish conquest three hundred years
before, and the Spaniards brought to them also Spanish
civilization which proved to be an element of great progress. In one respect at least the Filipinos stood high in
comparison with other Orientals and even Europeans —
in their regard for women. Antedating the Spanish conquest there was an equal inheritance law. Never were
soldiers and officers of the American Army more mistaken than when they called the Filipinos "niggers," as
in all essentials the Filipinos stood far in advance of the
American negro.[1] Really the Filipinos and Americans
should have stood shoulder to shoulder instead of appeal-
ing to force for their varying immediate aims. But as
Carl Schurz sagely remarked, "The best government
will always be unpopular if it is foreign government." [2]

When Storey, Hoar and Schurz opposed the Philippine
policy of the administration on the ground that "governments derive their just powers from the consent of the
governed" they were entirely logical, for the course of
events makes it evident that the Filipinos did not desire
American rule; but it was no more flagrant a case than
the war of the North on the Confederate States, as the
Southern people desired a government of their own with
slavery amply protected. Lincoln conducted the war on
the ground that a majority of the Southern people were
not of the same mind as their leaders, and McKinley,
Root and Taft made war on the Philippine insurgents
with a similar view.

---

[1] As to this see Blount, American Occupation of the Philippines, 365.
[2] Schurz, Speeches, vi. 175.

Portrait by Philip A. de László.

McKinley was a rare judge of men.   When he forced
the resignation of Russell A. Alger as Secretary of War, he
appointed to the position Elihu Root of New York.   The
appointment was made during July, 1899, and Root thus
told the story: "Having just finished the labors of the
year and gone to my country home, I was called to the
telephone and told by one speaking for President
McKinley, 'the President directs me to say to you that
he wishes you to take the position of Secretary of War.'
I answered, 'Thank the President for me, but say that it
is quite absurd.   I know nothing about war.   I know
nothing about the army.'   I was told to hold the wire,
and in a moment there came back the reply, 'President
McKinley directs me to say that he is not looking for
anyone who knows anything about the army; he has got
to have a lawyer to direct the government of those Spanish islands and you are the lawyer he wants.'   Of course,"
proceeded Root, "I had then, on the instant, to determine what kind of a lawyer I wished to be, and there was
but one answer to make, and so I went to perform a lawyer's duty upon the call of the greatest of all our clients,
the government of our country."

Root described his labor: "It was a fascinating work.
It was the work of applying to some ten millions of people
in Cuba and Porto Rico and the Philippines, the principles of American liberty.   They were living under laws
founded upon the customs of their lives, customs drawn
from old Spain and developed in social and industrial
activity quite unlike that of the United States; and the
problem was to apply those principles which are declared
in our constitutions, which embodied the formative idea
of the Declaration of Independence that all men are en-

dowed with inalienable rights, among which are life and
liberty and the pursuit of happiness, to the customs and
the laws of people which had come down from the Spain
of Philip the Second and the Inquisition." [1]

Root's opinion of McKinley after more than two years
of official and personal intercourse may well be cited :
"How wise and skilful he was! how modest and self-
effacing! how deep his insight into the human heart! how
swift the intuitions of his sympathy! how compelling
the charm of his gracious presence! He was so unselfish,
so thoughtful of the happiness of others, so genuine a
lover of his country and kind. And he was the kindest
and tenderest friend who ever grasped another's hand.
Alas that his virtues did plead in vain against cruel
fate!" [2]

As President McKinley was unable to secure the return to the Philippines of his first Commission, he appointed a new one : William H. Taft, Professor Dean C.
Worcester of the University of Michigan, Luke E. Wright
of Tennessee, Henry C. Ide of Vermont and Professor
Bernard Moses of the University of California. It must
be premised that Taft was Judge of the United States
Circuit Court and the height of his ambition was a seat
on the United States Supreme bench. He was desig-
nated as President of the Board and has thus told the
story of his appointment : "It was in February, 1900,
that in the court house in Cincinnati I received from Mr.
McKinley a telegram which read like this, 'If you have
no other engagement, you will do me a great favor by
calling on me in Washington some time next week.' I

---

[1] Military and Colonial Policy, Root, xiv, xv.   [2] Ibid., 112.

did not know of any vacancy existing on the Supreme Court bench but I went to Washington just the same. Arriving at the White House I was ushered into the Cabinet room and there I met the President. 'Judge,' he said, 'I'd like to have you go to the Philippines.' I said, 'Mr. President, what do you mean by going to the Philippines?' He replied, 'We must establish a government there and I would like you to help.' 'But, Mr. President,' I said, 'I am sorry we have got the Philippines. I don't want them and I think you ought to have some man who is more in sympathy with the situation.' 'You don't want them any less than I do,' replied the President, 'but we have got them and in dealing with them I think I can trust the man who didn't want them better than I can the man who did.' You can readily understand," continued Taft, "the feelings of a man whose only object in going to Washington was the hope of finding a vacant cushion on the Supreme Court bench to be asked to go 10,000 miles from home. But after I had talked with Mr. McKinley and with Secretary Root I decided I would go and in a hurry. I went under the influence of Mr. McKinley's personality, the influence he had of making people do what they ought to do in the interest of the public service. Mr. McKinley said he would stand by me in the Philippines and he did." [1]

The instructions to this Commission of April 7, 1900, addressed to the Secretary of War are properly called the magna carta of the Philippines. It is asserted by the editors of the Root volumes [2] that this paper was

---

[1] Speech of President-elect Taft, New York City, Dec. 13, 1908, Boston *Herald*.

[2] Robert Bacon and James Brown Scott.

drafted by Root and with "trifling verbal changes" signed by the President.[1] This is asserted by other writers and so far as I know not contradicted, so it may be recorded as a fact. As the military government was now supreme and it was desirable to avoid any conflict with the Civil Commission, both the general in command and the Commission were directed to report to the Secretary of War. The Commission should at first "devote their attention to the establishment of municipal government, in which the natives of the islands, both in the cities and in the rural communities, shall be afforded the opportunity to manage their own local affairs to the fullest extent of which they are capable, and subject to the least degree of supervision and control, which a careful study of their capacities and observation of the workings of native control show to be consistent with the maintenance of law, order, and loyalty." Next should be the organization of government in the large administrative divisions, the intent being to substitute civil for military control. On September 1, 1900, the legislative authority which had been exercised by the military governor should be transferred to the Civil Commission. "Exercise of this legislative authority," the instructions continued, "will include the making of rules and orders, having the effect of law, for the raising of revenue by taxes, custom duties and imports; the appropriation and expenditure of public funds of the islands; the establishment of an educational system throughout the islands; the establishment of a system to secure an efficient civil service; the organization and establishment of courts; the organization and

---

[1] Military and Colonial Policy, 225.

establishment of municipal and departmental governments, and all other matters of a civil nature. . . . Wherever civil governments are constituted under the directions
of the Commission, such military posts, garrisons and forces
will be continued for the suppression of insurrection and
brigandage and the maintenance of law and order as the
Military Commander shall deem requisite, and the military
forces shall be at all times subject, under his orders, to the
call of the civil authorities for the maintenance of law
and order and the enforcement of their authority."

Natives of the islands should be preferred for the offices
but they must be absolutely and unconditionally loyal
to the United States. The government established is
"not for our satisfaction or for the expression of our theo-
retical views, but for the happiness, peace and prosperity
of the people of the Philippine Islands, and the measures
adopted should be made to conform to their customs,
their habits, and even their prejudices to the fullest extent
consistent with the accomplishment of the indispensable
requisites of just and effective government."

Then followed, substantially, the Bill of Rights of the
American Constitution; but the right to bear arms and
trial by jury were not included in the enumeration of the
safeguards of liberty. Education should be promoted
and extended. This was an easy matter as the desire
for education was almost universal and the wish to learn
English eager. With wisdom the direction to the Commission was: "Instruction should be given in the first
instance in every part of the islands in the language of
the people. In view of the great number of languages
spoken by the different tribes, it is especially important
to the prosperity of the islands that a common medium

of communication may be established, and it is obviously desirable that this medium should be the English language. Especial attention should be at once given to affording full opportunity to all of the islands to acquire the use of the English language." The comprehensive instructions ended with: A "high and sacred obligation rests upon the Government of the United States to give protection for property and life, civil and religious freedom and wise, firm and unselfish guidance in the paths of peace and prosperity to all the people of the Philippine Islands. I," said the President of the United States, "charge this Commission to labor for the full performance of this obligation, which concerns the honor and conscience of their country, in the firm hope that through their labors all the inhabitants of the Philippine Islands may come to look back with gratitude to the day when God gave victory to American arms at Manila and set their land under the sovereignty and the protection of the people of the United States." [1]

The way was paved by the introduction of a bill from the Committee on the Philippines which, although not enacted, offered a statement from Senator Henry Cabot Lodge, who was in full sympathy with our possession of the Philippines. On March 7, 1900, he said: The "President, under the military power, which still controls and must for some time control the islands, could do all that this bill provides. . . . We follow the well-settled precedents of Jefferson and Monroe. . . . We may safely tread in the footsteps of the author of the Declaration of Independence. He saw no contradiction be-

---

[1] Messages and Papers of the President, Supplement, 139.

tween that great instrument and the treaty with
Napoleon." [1]

These instructions were approved by the Spooner
Amendment (March 2, 1901) and by the Philippine Government Act of July 1, 1902. Upon this magna carta
was built the government of the Philippines. The Commission had full power to rule the islands. Root was the
creator and Taft the practical instrument; both were
backed loyally by Presidents McKinley and Roosevelt,
and all wrought together in perfect harmony, furnishing
an example of the wise administration of colonial possessions on a new and original plan. Certainly no government was better served.

The Commission had a guerilla warfare to reckon with.
During 1900 this was kept alive by the hope of Democratic success in the presidential election, as the leaders
assured the masses that, in the event of Bryan's triumph,
their independence would be secured.[2]

During March, 1901, Aguinaldo, who was termed "the
incarnation of the insurrection," was captured, as the
result of a "desperate enterprise" by General Funston
with four American officers, assisted by about eighty Mac-
cabebes, who, though Filipinos, had a long-standing
feud with their brothers, had been loyal to the Spanish
authorities and transferred that loyalty to us. "I take
pride," wrote Theodore Roosevelt to General Funston, "in
this crowning exploit of a career filled with cool courage,
iron endurance and gallant daring, because you have added

[1] Speeches and Addresses, 317 *et seq.*; letter from Senator Lodge, Nov.
15, 1920.
[2] The Americans in the Philippines, Le Roy, ii. 135 *n.*

your name to the honor roll of American worthies." [1]
On April 19 Aguinaldo took the oath of allegiance to
the American Government and has faithfully kept this
oath.[2] He also issued a proclamation in which he said:
"The cause of peace . . . has been joyfully embraced by
a majority of our fellow countrymen who are already
united around the glorious and sovereign banner of the
United States. In this banner they repose their trust,
in the belief that under its protection our people will at-
tain all the promised liberties which they are even now
beginning to enjoy. The country has declared unmis-
takably in favor of peace; so be it. Enough of blood;
enough of tears and desolation. . . . By acknowledging
and accepting the sovereignty of the United States
throughout the entire archipelago, as I now do, without
any reservation whatever, I believe that I am serving
thee, my beloved Country. May happiness be thine." [3]

On September 1, 1900, the Taft Commission entered
upon their legislative work; on July 4, 1901, Taft was
appointed Civil Governor of the islands. By July 4, 1902,
the guerilla warfare was at an end and Root issued this
address to the soldiers: "The President thanks the officers and enlisted men of the army in the Philippines,
both regulars and volunteers, for the courage and forti-
tude, the indomitable spirit and loyal devotion with which
they have put down and ended the great insurrection
which has raged throughout the archipelago against the
lawful sovereignty and just authority of the United
States." When the organized resistance "had been over-

---

[1] Theodore Roosevelt and His Time, Bishop, i. 108.
[2] Blount, American Occupation of the Philippines, 352.
[3] The Philippines, Military Régime, Elliott, 526.

come, they were required to crush out a general system
of guerilla warfare conducted among a people speaking
unknown tongues, from whom it was almost impossible
to obtain the information necessary for successful pursuit or to guard against surprise and ambush." They
"had to do with a population among whom it was impossible to distinguish friend from foe, and who in count-
less instances used a false appearance of friendship for
ambush and assassination. They were obliged to deal
with problems of communication and transportation in
a country without roads and frequently made impassable
by torrential rains. They were weakened by tropical
heat and tropical disease. . . . Under all these adverse
circumstances the army of the Philippines has accomplished its task rapidly and completely. . . . Utilizing
the lessons of the Indian wars it has relentlessly followed
the guerilla bands to their fastnesses in mountain and
jungle and crushed them. . . . Its officers have shown
high qualities of command and its men have shown devotion and discipline." [1]

So far as I know the charges that were made as to the
use of torture by American soldiers consisted in the application of the "Water-cure" to elicit information as to
the whereabouts of hostile bands. A bamboo reed was
placed in the victim's mouth and water was poured down
through it to the disturbance of all the digestive organs.
When the victim was permitted to void the water, the
desired intelligence was frequently procured by the threat
of a renewed application. While very painful this torture was seldom fatal nor permanently damaging.[2] The

[1] Messages and Papers of the Presidents, Supplement, 396.
[2] Blount, The American Occupation of the Philippines, 202.

American soldiers despised the Filipinos and were ready
to practise the principle of "an eye for an eye; a tooth
for a tooth," but in most instances they were restrained
by their officers.[1]

Theodore Roosevelt, who as President was thoroughly
informed, who had a high regard for humanity, who appreciated fully the harm of torture both to the tortured
and to him who inflicts the torture, has written the truth on
this subject in a few words.   "Under the strain of well nigh
intolerable provocation there were shameful instances,
as must happen in all wars, where the soldiers forgot
themselves and retaliated evil for evil. There were one
hundred thousand of our men in the Philippines, a hundred thousand hired for a small sum a month apiece, put
there under conditions that strained their nerves to the
breaking point, and some of the hundred thousand did
what they ought not to have done." [2]

Root fully appreciated the burden which he had assumed. "It concerned the credit and honor of our country that we should succeed in the Philippines," he declared. But he admitted during September, 1902, that
there were moments of despair. "There come always,"
he said, "in every great and difficult undertaking, times
when failure seems possible; times when discourage-

---

[1] The army song signifies the feeling:

"Damn, damn, damn the Filipino
Pock-marked Khakiac ladrone: [Copper-colored thief]
Underneath the starry flag
Civilize him with a Krag.
And return us to our own beloved home,"

sung to the tune of "Tramp, tramp, tramp," Blount, 270.
[2] The Philippines, Mrs. C. Dauncey (1910), 5; see T. Roosevelt and
His Time, Bishop, i. 191; also T. R.'s letter to Bishop Lawrence and address in Arlington Cemetery, ibid.; My Historical Essays, 238.

ments and difficulties and doubts beset the pathway of endeavor."

"As armed resistance ceased," wrote Root, in "island by island, province by province, town by town, civil government was substituted for military government; the bill of rights extended its protection over the people; the writ of habeas corpus became the guaranty of their liberty; elections were held at which the people chose the officers of their own towns and provinces; a native constabulary was organized and proved faithful and effective for the protection of life and property; the people resumed their customary vocations under the protection of law. . . . The personnel of civil government has been brought together under an advanced and comprehensive civil service law which has been rigidly enforced. . . . The Philippine people will follow in the footsteps of the people of Cuba; more slowly indeed because they are not so advanced yet as surely, they will grow in capacity for self-government, and receiving power as they grow in capacity, will come to bear substantially such relations to the people of the United States as do now the people of Cuba, differing in details as conditions and needs differ, but the same in principle and the same in beneficent results." [1]

In those days German opinion in reference to administration was highly regarded. The circular of the German government for 1901, said, "that the American administration of the affairs of the Philippines has, as far as the economic betterment of the country is concerned, already achieved extraordinary success." [2]

---

[1] Milit. and Colonial Policy, Root, 77, 80, 101, 103; 1902, 1904.
[2] Ibid., 78.

The opponents of the policy of the administration maintained that "the Constitution followed the flag," but the United States Supreme Court validated the procedure of the President and of Congress who were sustained by public opinion that denied the inhabitants of the Philippines "equal rights under the Constitution." John H. Latané has written an intelligent chapter analyzing the different decisions in cases relating to Puerto Rico and the Philippines,[1] in which their burden was this subject, and at its close he intimated what has been humorously put by Dooley, "No matter whether the Constitution follows the flag or not th' Supreme Court follows th' illiction returns."[2]

As Root was the creator of the Philippine policy so was William H. Taft its administrator. It was he who by suave and persistent negotiation settled the difficult question of the friars' lands. The friars were Dominicans, Augustinians, Franciscans and Recolectos, held sway in the country and represented the most tyrannical aspect of the Spanish dominion.[3] Making themselves obnoxious to the Philippine people who were, nevertheless, good Catholics, they and their lands must in some way be disposed of, were success to attend the American occupation. To an arrangement which, while maintaining the right of private property, should take away the undoubted grievance of friar ownership, Taft, under authority of an Act of Congress, addressed himself with eminent success. During the progress of the negotiation

---

[1] Chap. viii. America as a World Power.
[2] The Philippines, Military Régime, Elliott, 496 n.
[3] "The people hated the Friars worse than they did the locusts." Odyssey of the P. Com., Williams, 188.

he made a visit to Rome and in the end brought the owners of the lands practically to his terms, finally closing
"the purchase of upward of 410,000 acres at a price of
$7,239,000 gold." He then proposed to dispose of the
lands "to the tenants on contracts of sale with easy pay-
ments for a number of years." This was done. We
did not purchase these lands, he wrote "with a view to a
profitable investment . . . but merely for the purpose of
ridding the administration of the government in the islands of an issue dangerous to the peace and prosperity
of the people." [1] The account which he gave of these
negotiations in his report of November 15, 1903, sub-
stantiated as it is by other sources, stamps him as an unusual colonial administrator. In fact all the glimpses
one gets of his work in the islands are much to his credit.
His unabated energy, his determination to commend
himself to the Filipinos, his smile and hearty handshake,[2]
his tactful speeches, his attendance at dinners and balls,
his excellent dancing thereat [3] — all show his resolution
to make his mission successful. At a meeting in the second city of the islands, an observer wrote, "Taft presided with that cordial good-natured expression which is
one of his greatest charms and which cannot but inspire
confidence and good-will." In another province the
observer was impressed with Taft's master talk. "It
was in detail, yet succinct and clear, fitted to the comprehension of the people." [4]

Personally, he told a Senate Committee in Washington
during February, 1902, "I did not favor going into the

---

[1] Report, Nov. 15, 1903, 44.
[2] Blount, 286.　　[3] Odyssey of the P. Com., Williams, 310.
[4] Ibid., 179, 182.

Philippine Islands. I was sorry at the time that we got
into it. But we are there. . . . I have been called an
optimist; I think the Mark Tapley of this business. It
is true I am an optimist. If I did not believe in the success of what we are attempting to do out there, I would
resign and come home. Certainly no man ever succeeded
who did not believe in the success of what he was doing.
We think we can help these people; we think we can
elevate them to an appreciation of popular government;
and we think that because the experiment has not really
ever been tried before is not reason for saying that the
trial of the experiment may not be a success in this instance." [1]

In truth he had an opportunity to go home. President Roosevelt cabled to him late in 1902: "On January
first there will be a vacancy on the Supreme Court to
which I earnestly desire to appoint you. . . . I feel that
your duty is on the Court unless you have decided not
to adopt a judicial career. I greatly hope you will accept." To this Taft replied: "Great honor deeply appreciated but must decline. Situation here most critical
from economic standpoint. . . . Nothing would satisfy
individual taste more than acceptance. Look forward
to the time when I can accept such an offer but even if
it is certain that it can never be repeated I must now
decline." At the same time he cabled to Secretary Root:
"Chance has thrown every obstacle in the way of our
success but we shall win. I long for a judicial career but
if it must turn on my present decision I am willing to
lose it." Late in November Taft received this letter

[1] Senate Hearings on Affairs in the Philippine Islands, Part i. 346.

from President Roosevelt: "Dear Will, I am disappointed, of course, that the situation is such as to make you feel it unwise to leave, because, exactly as no man can quite do your work in the islands, so no man can quite take your place as the new member of the Court. But, if possible, your refusal on the ground you give makes me admire you and believe in you more than ever." But about one month later President Roosevelt wrote to Taft, the letter being received January 6, 1903: "Dear Will, I am awfully sorry, old man, but after faithful effort for a month to try to arrange matters on the basis you wanted, I find that I shall have to bring you home and put you on the Supreme Court. I am very sorry. I have the greatest confidence in your judgment, but after all, old fellow, if you will permit me to say so, I am President and see the whole field. . . . After the most careful thought, after the most earnest effort as to what you desired and thought best, I have come, irrevocably, to the decision that I shall appoint you to the Supreme Court in the vacancy caused by Judge Shiras' resignation. . . . I am very sorry if what I am doing displeases you, but as I said, old man, this is one of the cases where the President, if he is fit for his position, must take the responsibility."

In answer to this letter Taft sent this cable to the President: "Recognize soldier's duty to obey orders." But "I presume on our personal friendship, even in the face of your letter, to make one more appeal, in which I lay aside wholly my strong personal disinclination to leave work of intense interest half-done." These people are convinced "that I am their friend and stand for a policy of confidence in them and belief in their future and for extension of self-government as they show themselves worthy. . . . Announcement of withdrawal pending settlement of church question, economic crisis, and formative political period when opinions of all parties are being slowly moulded for the better, will, I fear, give impression that change of policy is intended because other reasons for action will not be understood. . . . I feel it is my duty to say this. If your judgment is unshaken I bow to it." To this came a cable from President Roosevelt, "All right, stay where you are. I shall appoint someone else to the Court." [1]

One of the most interesting matters in American history during the first two decades of the twentieth century is the relation between Roosevelt and Taft; to end the Supreme Court incident a violation of chronology in the narrative is needed. We therefore go on to 1906 when Taft was Secretary of War in President Roosevelt's Cabinet. He was again offered a position on the Supreme Court bench but in a personal interview showed unwillingness to accept it. Shortly afterwards, on March 15, 1906, Roosevelt wrote to Taft a letter in which he said: "My dear Will, it is preëminently a matter in which no other man can take the responsibility of deciding for you what is best for you to do. . . . But I appreciate, as every thoughtful man must, the importance of the part to be played by the Supreme Court in the next twenty-five years. . . . There are strong arguments against your taking this justiceship. In the first place, my belief is that, of all the men who have appeared so far, you are the man, who is most likely to receive the Republican nomination,

---

[1] Mrs. W. H. Taft, Recollections, 262 *et seq.*

and who is, I think, the best man to receive it. It is not a light thing to cast aside the chance of the Presidency, even though, of course, it is a chance, however, a good one." Taft considered the offer over four months and then wrote to the President (July 30, 1906) from Murray Bay, Canada, where he was taking his summer vacation, declining the offer, saying: "I would much prefer to go on the Supreme Bench for life than to run for the Presidency. . . . But circumstances seem to me to have imposed something in the nature of a trust to me personally that I should not discharge by now succeeding Justice Brown. In the nature of things the trust must end with this administration and one or two years is short to do much. Yet the next session of Congress may result in much for the benefit of the Filipino and, it seems to me, it is my duty to be in the fight." [1]

While still in the Philippines Taft twice put aside the coveted place and remained in the islands, the climate of which was unsuitable. Before he appeared before the Senate Committee in Washington, on leave for the state of his health, and before these first two offers were made to him of a supreme judgeship, he had submitted to two surgical operations and was in bed for a number of weeks, but maintained "his usual cheerful frame of mind." [2] His wife, too, was debilitated and needed a change to America. Finally, at the end of 1903, he left for Washington to accept the position of Secretary of War. He was popular with the native inhabitants; they loved him and their anxiety when he was ill knew no bounds.

---

[1] J. B. Bishop, Roosevelt and His Time, ii. 99 *et seq.*
[2] Mrs. W. H. Taft, Recollections, 229; Unofficial Letters, Edith Moses, 187.

At the time when President Roosevelt insisted on his acceptance of the second offer of supreme judgeship and it leaked out that Taft was going to leave the Philippines, there was a sincere demonstration in his favor in the city of Manila which was placarded with the sentiment in various languages, "We want Taft." [1] In his farewell speech he declared that the Philippines were for the Filipinos. It need not occasion surprise that President Roosevelt in a review of this colonial administration said that Taft's work in the Philippines is as great as Lord Cromer's in Egypt.

The cost of the Philippines by the end of 1907 is estimated at $300,000,000; besides, the cost per annum of the native scouts and the 12,000 American troops was about 14 millions. [2] The government of the islands is self-supporting, wrote Governor Forbes, and this, according to Blount, is true except for the expense of the scouts and the American soldiers. In February, 1902, Taft told a Senate committee: "I think the intervention of the United States in the Philippine Islands is the best possible thing that could have happened to the Filipino people but . . . for the people of the United States it probably

---

[1] Mrs. W. H. Taft, Recollections, 267.

[2] The American Occupation of the Philippines, Blount, 600. In his report of Dec. 1, 1902, Root wrote: "Since the ending of the insurrection and the complete establishment of civil government in the Philippines, it has been possible to make a farther reduction of the Army and on October 24, 1902, an order was made reducing the enlisted strength to 59,866. . . . The effect of carrying out this order will be to bring the American troops stationed in the Philippines down to an enlisted strength of 13,480." In his report of Dec. 7, 1903, he said, "The American troops, in the Philippines consisted of 843 officers and 14,667 enlisted men. . . . The number can still further be reduced." I have assumed that the number was reduced to 12,000 as Blount was very unfriendly to the American administration.

would be better that chance had not thrown the Filipino people under our guidance and protection." [1]   And during May, 1907, in a speech at St. Louis, he admitted that the islands had been a financial drain. [2]

W. Cameron Forbes, when Vice-Governor, wrote in the *Atlantic Monthly* for February, 1909: "We have completed the separation of Church and State, buying out from the religious orders their large agricultural properties, which are now administered by the government for the benefit of the tenants. We have put the finances on a sound and sensible basis. . . . We have established schools throughout the archipelago, teaching upward of half a million children." And Forbes affirmed that with some natural exceptions it was "safe to travel everywhere throughout the islands without carrying a weapon. We," he continued, "have given the Filipinos almost complete autonomy in their municipalities. . . . The record of the Americans in the Philippines is one of which no American need be ashamed. . . . We are casting off the shackles which held down the laboring classes of the Philippines and, with the laboring classes raised, we are raising all the people to a higher and nobler plane.   We may not as yet have given independence to the Philippines but we are certainly giving independence to the Filipinos." [3]

All the money raised by internal taxation was spent on the islands. There was absolutely no exploitation. "As I look back," wrote Elihu Root in 1916 in a preface

---

[1] Hearings on Affairs in the Philippine Islands, Part 1, 406.
[2] Blount, 357.
[3] Article entitled "A Decade of American Rule in the Philippines." The citations down to "weapon," are made by Blount in his American Occupation of the Philippines.

to Charles B. Elliott's book, "over our American administration in the Philippines . . . . down to the close of
the Taft Administration in the spring of 1913, I think
the American people are entitled to say to themselves
that their work was well done. We maintained in the
islands a very able and honest government which constantly and effectively kept in view the very high standard of purpose with which we began. By limiting this
statement to the end of the Taft Administration I do not
mean to imply that I think any differently of our administration since that time. I simply do not know enough
about it since then to make an assertion one way or the
other. The time during which I knew about the Philippine government covers the first fourteen years, and
as to that time I say that the people of the United States
ought to be proud of their government in the Philippines
and grateful to the men and women who reflected credit
on their country by giving their strength and lives to
that public service." [1]

Root was a broad-minded man as well as a great lawyer. His allusion to "my friend Mr. Schurz" [2] at the
time that Carl Schurz was assailing the Philippine policy
with all the force of his periodic eloquence, shows an absence of partisan spirit. Like Webster, Root earned
the title of "Defender of Peace"; in December, 1913,
he was awarded the Nobel Peace Prize. When Secretary
of State, [3] and James Bryce was Ambassador from Great
Britain, the two by wise diplomacy settled all matters

---

[1] Prefatory note The Philippines, To the End of the Military Régime.
[2] Military and Colonial Policy, Root, 43.
[3] Root was Secretary of War from 1899–1904, Secretary of State from
1905 to Jan. 25, 1909.

of dispute between the two countries. I may parallel
what I wrote of Webster :   The social intercourse between
Root and Bryce while they were at work on these treaties
is one of those international amenities that grace the
history of diplomacy.[1]

It is well now to hear from Archibald C. Coolidge, an
academic man, yet a man of the world, a traveller, an
observer, a thinker, who comprehends thoroughly the
Orient.   "Criticize as we may the details of the present
policy" [in the Philippines], he wrote in 1908, "no impartial observer will deny that since 1898 the Americans
have accomplished a great deal in their task of transform-
ing the islands. Improved means of communication,
public works of all kinds, modern sanitation, justice,
public security, honest and efficient government, popular
participation in the government and a system of general
education form a record to be proud of.   In all this, good
fortune has counted for but little." [2]

---

[1] See my vol. i. 139, 140.   Bryce said in London, July 28, 1920, on the
occasion of unveiling a copy of the Saint-Gaudens statue of Lincoln: "If
I may venture to express what I believe to be the general feeling in America, America looks upon Elihu Root as the greatest Secretary of State
it has had since Daniel Webster.   It was my good fortune to have to negotiate with him in Washington not a few treaties between our two countries, and I have never known in either hemisphere anyone with a wider
range of vision or with a mind more fair and just in handling diplomatic
questions.   He always showed the sincerest wish for perfect concord and
friendly coöperation between our two great countries.   With such a man
it was a pleasure to negotiate, and to listen to such a man is a privilege."
London Daily Telegraph, July 29, 1920; private letter from Elihu Root
Dec. 24, 1920.
[2] The United States as a World Power, 170. The Taft Com. reported
on Nov. 1, 1902 : "By the war and by the rinderpest, chiefly the latter,
the carabaos or water buffalos have been reduced to 10 per cent of their
former number.   The chief food of the common people of these islands
is rice and the carabao is the indispensable instrument of the people in
the cultivation of rice, as they cultivate it, as it is also the chief means of
transportation of the tobacco, hemp and other crops.   The loss of the

James A. Robertson wrote in 1917: The American policy may have resulted in a "loss of efficiency in government. There has been extremely little of 'Woe to the conquered' spirit from Americans, and the slogan 'The Philippines for the Filipinos' has been real. . . . On the whole the result has been better than the most ardent advocates . . . had hoped." The American experiment "has attained valuable results which, notwithstanding the political and anti-Imperialistic diatribes against the sincerity of Americans, has been conducted not without honor." [1] Theodore Roosevelt wrote truly: "The English and Dutch administrators of Malaysia have done admirable work; but the profit to the Europeans in those States has always been one of the chief elements considered; whereas in the Philippines our whole attention was concentrated upon the welfare of the Filipinos themselves, if anything to the neglect of our own interests." [2]

What shall we do with the Philippines, as a large majority of the American people desire to be rid of them if the riddance can be safely and honorably done? Theodore Roosevelt, who, as President for over seven years, gave the subject grave thought, made an answer sound and complete. Thus he wrote in 1913: "We are governing and have been governing the islands in the interests of the Filipinos themselves. If, after due time, the Fili-

---

carabao has reduced the production of rice in the islands 75 per cent and the 25 per cent remaining is in imminent danger from the locusts." Gov. Taft wrote in his report of Nov. 15, 1903: "From the first of January until late in August there was a drought in the islands of unusual length which interfered with the successful reaping of many of the crops, and with the drought a pest of locusts came that bade fair to consume every part of the food supply that grew above the ground."

[1] *American Historical Review*, July, 1917, 817, 830.

[2] Autobiography, 544.

pinos themselves decide that they do not wish to be thus governed, then I trust that we will leave; but when we do leave it must be distinctly understood that we retain no protectorate — and above all that we take part in no joint protectorate — over the islands and give them no guarantee of neutrality or otherwise; that, in short, we are absolutely quit of responsibility for them of every kind and description." [1]

----

[1] Autobiography, 545. Authorities: Dewey's Autobiography; Richardson, x.; McKinley's Messages of Dec. 1899 and 1900; Roosevelt's Message, Dec. 1901, Messages and Papers of the Presidents, Supplement, 1889–1902; Moorfield Storey, Letter to a Friend, Oct. 21, 1899, Secretary Root's Record in the Philippine Warfare (1902), What Shall We Do with Our Dependencies (1903), Before the House Committee on Insular Affairs (1906), Political Pamphlets in Boston Athenæum; George F. Hoar, Speech in U. S. Senate, Jan. 9, 1899, Letter, Our Duty to the Philippines, Jan. 11, 1900, Autobiography, ii., 309; Carl Schurz, Writings, etc., iii., Speeches, etc., vi.; Schurman, Report of Philippine Commission, 1899, A Retrospect and Outlook, Address, 1902; Senate Hearings on Affairs in Philippine Islands, Parts 1, 2, 3, Senate Docs. 23, 24, 25; Reports of Secretary of War, 1900, 1901, 1902, 1903; Reports of Philippine Commission, 1900, 1901, 1902, 1903, House Docs.; Coolidge, The U. S. as a World Power; Elihu Root, Milit. and Colonial Policy; Charles B. Elliott, The Philippines to the End of the Military Régime; ibid., To the End of the Commission Government; James A. Le Roy, The Americans in the Philippines, i. & ii.; Worcester, The Philippines Past and Present, i. & ii.; Blount, The American Occupation of the Philippines; Williams, The Odyssey of the Philippine Commission; Edith Moses, Unofficial Letters of an Official's Wife; The Philippines, Mrs. Campbell Dauncy, Introduction by Theodore Roosevelt; Theodore Roosevelt, Autobiography; Mrs. W. H. Taft, Recollections; Latané, America as a World Power; Olcott, Life of McKinley; Willoughby, Territories and Dependencies; *Scribner's Magazine*, June, 1920.

CHAPTER VIII

On taking the oath of office at the time of McKinley's death Theodore Roosevelt was entirely sincere when he said that "in this hour of deep and terrible bereavement . . . it shall be my aim to continue absolutely unbroken the policy of President McKinley." [September 14.] The student of Roosevelt's seven and one-half years in the White House will fail in their comprehension if he does not believe thoroughly in Roosevelt's sincerity and courage. On the train carrying the late President's body between Buffalo and Washington, Senator Mark Hanna, who must be regarded as the inherited representative of McKinley's policy, said, "Theodore, do not think anything about a second term." That no thought of the sort at this time entered Roosevelt's head is apparent from the remark he made to Joseph B. Bishop on his first day in the White House: "I don't know anything about seven years. But this I do know — I am going to be President for three years and I am going to do my utmost to give the country a good President during that period. . . . I am no second Grover Cleveland. I admire certain of his qualities, but I have no intention of doing with the Republican party what he did with the Democratic party. I intend to work with my party and to make it strong by making it worthy of popular support."[1]

[1] Theodore Roosevelt and His Time, Bishop, i. 150. When hereafter I cite this admirable work I shall refer to it as Bishop.

Theodore Roosevelt

"Wise legislation," declared Roosevelt in seconding McKinley's nomination at the Republican convention in Philadelphia during June, 1900, "is vitally important, but honest administration is even more important." [1] The importance which he gave to administration is apparent from his action during the time that he was President. Believing that a bad colonel makes a bad regiment, he was particular in getting efficiency at the head of departments and in other places where the master gave the cue to his subordinates. He knew McKinley to be a good judge of men and Roosevelt was not of the sort who believed so thoroughly in his own selections that he could not accept those of others. He would take a good man wherever he found him. Root, Hay, Knox and Governor Taft were all chosen by McKinley, yet they became trusted counsellors of Roosevelt. On September 17 he asked all of the members of the Cabinet to remain in office, which they consented to do.[2]

"It is a dreadful thing," he wrote to his friend Senator Lodge, "to come into the Presidency in this way; but it would be a far worse thing to be morbid about it. Here is the task and I have got to do it to the best of my ability, and that is all there is about it." [3]

Continuing "absolutely unbroken the policy of President McKinley" was not the same as continuing the heads of the departments. That Roosevelt meant exactly what he said when he took the oath of office is undoubted, but what he promised was entirely impossible.

---

[1] Official Proceedings, 118.
[2] The reasons for the retirement of Gage, Smith and Long are given by Leupp, The Man Roosevelt, 73 *et seq.*
[3] Bishop, i. 151.

I am, he said, temperamentally more like Cleveland than like McKinley. The legacy which McKinley left to his countrymen in his Buffalo speech was to revise the tariff in the direction of lower duties by means of reciprocity treaties. And there is no doubt that Roosevelt balanced the policy of attacking the tariff first instead of attacking the trusts. Not that he believed that the tariff was the mother of all trusts but he wrote, "As regards political economy I was of course while in college taught the *laissez-faire* doctrines — one of them being free trade — then accepted as canonical." [1] By extreme tariff men he was not regarded as sound on account of this education, as Harvard College was looked upon as devoted to the doctrine of free trade. Although he felt that he could carry a reduction of duties through Congress such a course would divide his party, while in an attack on the Trusts he could carry his party in Congress with him. Therefore during his administration there was no revision of the tariff [2] but his fight against Big Business was one of his keynotes.

Roosevelt endeavored to carry out faithfully what he had said on the day that he took the oath of office. He wrote a cordial letter to Senator Hanna requesting an early conference and received this reply: "There are many important matters to be considered from a political standpoint and I am sure we will agree upon a proper course to pursue. Meantime 'go slow.' You will be be-

---

[1] Charles G. Washburn, Theodore Roosevelt, 112. Autobiography, 30.
[2] Charles G. Washburn, Theodore Roosevelt, 114; see Roosevelt's ideas on The Tariff and Trusts. Speech in Cincinnati, Sept. 20, 1902. Roosevelt, His Life Meaning and Messages, The *Current Lit.* Pub. Co., 1919, 82.

sieged from all sides and I fear in some cases will get the wrong impression. Hear them all patiently but *reserve* your decision." [1]

McKinley's inheritors did not like the position which Roosevelt took towards the large financial interests of the country. He touched upon the subject in his first Annual Message and submitted what he said to Senator Hanna, receiving the advice not to give it so much prominence, but this suggestion he disregarded.[2] His action ought not to have been a surprise to those who had followed his course while Governor of New York and had rated correctly his many public utterances. Nevertheless the announcement of it in the merger of two competing railroads into the Northern Securities Company caused a shock to the financial world.

The Northern Pacific and Great Northern railroads ran from Lake Superior to Puget Sound on the Pacific coast, and on through traffic were competing lines; but for a number of years their relations had been altogether friendly. Both desired a terminal in Chicago which should connect with their St. Paul-Minneapolis lines, and after much discussion and negotiation acquired the Chicago, Burlington and Quincy. James J. Hill, as honest a man as ever lived, whose career from early poverty to superfluous wealth was noted for the confidence other men reposed in him, may be said to be the hero of the merger of the three railroads. He formed a company

---

[1] Oct. 12, 1901. Bishop, i. 154. One cannot fail to be reminded of Polonius's advice to Laertes :

"Give every man thy ear, but few thy voice :
Take each man's censure, but reserve thy judgment." Hamlet, Act i., Sc. 1.

[2] Bishop, i. 159.

called the Northern Securities which was to own the C., B. and Q. property as well as that of the other two. This was a holding company whose officers should manage the three railroads and divide the dividends among the stockholders of the Northern Pacific and Great Northern; the Chicago, Burlington and Quincy stockholders were paid by joint bonds of the two purchasing railroads. Hill's idea in making the merger was for the sake of no vulgar profit but to render the stock of the Northern Securities Company an investment to men and their heirs who would have a greater protection in the event of the death of those now in control. Hill and his attorneys studied the precedents, laws and regulations and especially the decision of the United States Supreme Court in the Knight case, arriving at the conclusion that the Anti-Trust Act of 1890 did not apply to such a merger; they went forward therefore with their plans. And if James J. Hill could have left men who would carry on business as he had carried it on, the merger could not be said to interfere with the public good.

But he had to reckon with Theodore Roosevelt, who was antagonistic to the operations of large financiers and believed that it was incumbent on him as President to protect the public against their operations. While Roosevelt liked Hill, he did not consider J. Pierpont Morgan, who was an active coadjutor with Hill in this enterprise, a good financial adviser. When Morgan heard of the President's opposition to the merger he went to Washington and said to him, "If we have done anything wrong send your man (meaning Attorney-General Knox) to my man (naming one of his lawyers) and they can fix it up." "That can't be done," said the President.

"We don't want to fix it up," added Knox who assisted at this interview, "we want to stop it." Morgan inquired, "Are you going to attack my other interests, the Steel Trust and the others?" "Certainly not," replied the President, "unless we find out that in any case they have done something that we regard as wrong." When Morgan went away Roosevelt expressed his opinion, saying to Knox: "That is a most illuminating illustration of the Wall Street point of view. Mr. Morgan could not help regarding me as a big rival operator, who either intended to ruin all his interests or else could be induced to come to an agreement to ruin none."[1] Roosevelt considered Hill a good financial adviser but said that he had to be on the watch that Hill, in giving him counsel, had not an eye to his own interest. Still Roosevelt appreciated a man who from nothing had amassed a fortune of sixty millions, although he did not rate as the highest ability the acquiring of wealth in this country of enormous resources. His heroes were drawn from another class.

It is interesting to note the conflict between these two honest men. Roosevelt requested an opinion from Attorney-General Knox, who on February 19, 1902, authorized the publication of the following statement: "Sometime ago the President requested an opinion as to the legality of this merger, and I have recently given him one to the effect that, in my judgment, it violates the provisions of the Sherman Act of 1890 (the Anti-Trust Act), whereupon he directed that suitable action should be taken to have the question judicially determined."[2]

---

[1] Bishop, i. 185.
[2] Meyer, History of the Northern Securities Case. Bulletin of the University of Wisconsin, No. 142, 258.

This was a bomb shell in Wall Street and the beginning of the active hostility of the large financial interests to Theodore Roosevelt, who directed the course of his Attorney-General.   Knox knew the ground well, as before McKinley had drawn him from the active practice of his profession, he was a corporation lawyer.   He began suit in the United States Circuit Court in St. Paul on March 10, 1902; and on April 9, 1903, a decision was rendered by four Circuit judges sitting in St. Louis.   This tribunal "decreed that, as the combination known as the Northern Securities Company violated the Anti-Trust Act of 1890, that Company is enjoined from attempting to acquire further stock of the Northern Pacific or Great Northern Railways; it is further enjoined from voting the stock already acquired or attempting to exercise any control whatsoever.   The Northern Pacific and Great Northern are enjoined from permitting any such action on the part of the Securities Company and from paying to that Company any dividends on stock which it now claims to own." [1]

The case went to the United States Supreme Court, the majority opinion of which was written by Justice Harlan (March 14, 1904) which took the ground that the merger was opposed to the Anti-Trust Act of 1890 and therefore illegal; the decree of the lower Court was affirmed.[2]   It was given out that the Court had decided in favor of the Government by 5 : 4 but Justice Brewer, in stating his agreement in the main with the four others, differed in some degree, so that it was jocularly said that

---

[1] 193 U. S. Reports, 255.
[2] This opinion was concurred in by Justices Brown, McKenna and Day. 193 U. S. Reports, 198, 317.

the Government had won by $4\frac{5}{8}$ to $4\frac{3}{8}$.   Many were vitally interested in the decision and the gossip of the day put Justice Holmes, who was appointed by Roosevelt, on the side of the Government.   It was a great surprise therefore that when the decision was known, he should be found on the other side, giving the grounds of his judgment.[1]   Gossip of the day was also concerned with two other judges who were counted against the Government, but as matter of fact concurred with Harlan in his opinion.   This gossip redounded to the majesty of the Court.

Hill's opinion soon after Knox's announcement was given in a private letter.   "It really seems hard," he wrote, "when we look back on what we have done and know that we have led all Western companies in opening the country and carrying at the lowest rates, that we should be compelled to fight for our lives against the political adventurers who have never done anything but pose and draw a salary."[2]   But when the Supreme Court decision, which he thought would be favorable to his enterprise, was rendered, he said, "We must all bow to the law of the land,"[3] and steps were taken to undo the work of combination.   Through the decisions of the Courts, no property was sacrificed, but shares, which had been transferred to the Securities Company, were returned to their original owners; but any such holding company as the Northern Securities was forbidden.

No one who has read carefully the life of Hill can do otherwise than feel sympathy with the man when one of

---

[1] Both Justices Holmes and White delivered dissenting opinions; with them concurred Chief Justice Fuller and Justice Peckham.   193 U. S. Reports, 364, 400.

[2] March, 1902.   Life of Hill, Pyle, ii. 171.

[3] Ibid., 175.

his darling projects was defeated, but as we look at it
now, President Roosevelt was right and the decision of
the Court was sound.   While this combination as directed
by Hill may not have been against the public good, the
mischief lay in the precedent, for, were this merger approved, a few men by successive steps might have controlled the railroad system of the country.   Hill, Morgan and a few of their associates holding the majority of
stock or representing it in the Northern Securities Company, would have controlled the business of the Northern
Pacific, the Great Northern and the Chicago, Burlington
and Quincy Railroads; and by the same token a few men
might have controlled the railroad system of the country.
Roosevelt's idea of the Knight case, which had been decided by the United States Supreme Court in January,
1895, with but one dissenting voice,[1] was that such a
merger as that involved in the Northern Securities case
could be reached only by the action of the States themselves; but by the decision of the same court in the actual (*i. e.* the Northern Securities) case the nation might
act and for this Roosevelt contended.   He thus wrote:
"By a vote of five to four the Supreme Court reversed
its decision in the Knight case, and in the Northern Securities case sustained the Government.   The power to
deal with industrial monopoly and suppress it and to control and regulate combinations, of which the Knight case
had deprived the Federal Government, was thus restored
to it by the Northern Securities case." [2]

---

[1] Chief Justice Fuller delivered the opinion of the Court.   Justice Harlan dissented.   156 U. S. Reports, 1.   The decision was on the 21st.

[2] Autobiography, 469.   I have been much indebted to Meyer's account, *ante.*

From the day of Knox's statement, the line was drawn between Roosevelt and the large financial interests of the country. A goodly part of the history of his administration is due to that conflict, and as Roosevelt was effective as a fighter, he was ready to throw down the gauntlet.

"The Northern Securities Suit," he wrote during August, 1904, "is one of the great achievements of my administration. I look back upon it with great pride for through it we emphasized in signal fashion, as in no other way could be emphasized, the fact that the most powerful men in this country were held to accountability before the law." [1]

Roosevelt had been in the White House only a little over a month when he set tongues to wagging both South and North, among negroes and whites, by having Booker Washington to dinner. His own account of the incident, written in a private letter of November 8, 1901, is an accurate relation: "When I asked Booker T. Washington to dinner I did not devote very much thought to the matter one way or the other. I respect him greatly and believe in the work he has done. I have consulted so much with him it seemed to me that it was natural to ask him to dinner to talk over the work, and the very fact that I felt a moment's qualm on inviting him because of his color made me ashamed of myself and made me hasten to send the invitation. I did not think of its bearing one way or the other, either on my own future or on anything else." [2] Roosevelt was exceedingly hospitable and it was entirely natural for him to invite a man with whom he

---

[1] Bishop, i. 325. [2] Bishop, i. 166.

had business to break bread and eat salt. Washington indeed from his clear comprehension and unselfish advocacy made you forget his color. A North Carolinian, then editor of the *Atlantic Monthly*, had a similar experience. Not having completed his business when luncheon time came, he naturally asked Washington to go along with him and was only reminded of the fact that his guest was a man of color from the attitude of the waiters and the gaze of other patrons in the public restaurant.

Washington was thoroughly tactful, and did his best to avoid having any public mention of the honor which was paid to him, and in fact throughout the whole affair, with one exception, acted the part which his well-wishers might have desired. The dinner incident was on October 18. Five days afterwards Roosevelt and Washington, attending the Bi-Centennial of Yale University, met in the Hyperion theatre at New Haven, the President on the platform where he was to receive the degree of Doctor of Laws and Washington in the body of the theatre as delegate from the Tuskegee Institute. Justice Brewer, an old Yale graduate, delivered the oration and during it said, "Thank God, there have always been in this country college men able to recognize a true Washington whether his first name was George or Booker." [1] Booker was immensely popular in the North. Andrew Carnegie expressed a dominant opinion when he wrote, "We should all take our hats off to the man who not only raised himself from slavery but helped raise millions [?] of his race to a higher stage of civilization." [2] Echoing Justice

---

[1] *Yale Alumni Weekly.*   [2] Autobiography, 276.

Brewer's statement the theatre resounded with applause and Booker Washington got up and bowed. This of course was a jarring incident amid the best of behavior, but he may have been urged to this recognition by someone at his side.

The mischief of Roosevelt's action lay first, in his being looked upon by the negroes as a saviour. President Lincoln had given them political freedom and now President Roosevelt was to raise them to social equality. And second, in its effect on the white people at the South. Their attitude is well expressed by the words of a Southerner living in Tuskegee who was full of praise for Washington's work, "Now when I meet the man who has done all this I can't call him Booker like I would an ordinary nigger, but thunder! I can't call a nigger Mister, so I just say, Professor." A young Southerner said to Leupp: "I love that man [Theodore Roosevelt]; I would do anything in the world for him, follow him anywhere. But the one thing in his career which I shall never get over is the Booker Washington incident. Understand me: I do not disparage Washington's work — I appreciate it as much as you do. I admit all that you say of his personal worth. He has been in my mother's parlor and invited to sit down there. I don't know that I should have had any feeling about the President asking him to lunch or dinner by themselves. But to invite him to the table with ladies — that is what no Southerner can brook!" [1]

At the end of the letter already cited, Roosevelt on November 8, wrote, "As things have turned out I am very

---

[1] The Man Roosevelt, 230. This book has been of much use to me in writing of the Booker Washington incident.

glad that I asked him [Booker Washington], for the clamor aroused by the act makes me feel as if the act was necessary." [1]   This was a note of defiance but his mature opinion afterwards was different.   He said to me that he had made a mistake in asking Booker Washington to dinner; that among the Southerners there was prejudice against such action and, while he could not comprehend their feeling, it was there and had to be reckoned with.   He began his administration with great consideration for the South in the matter of Federal appointments and while, after the Booker Washington incident there was criticism in regard to some of them, on the whole he stood pretty well at the South.   "Half my blood is Southern," he wrote. [2]   It was understood that he did not approve of the policy of forcing negro suffrage upon the Southern States involved in the Reconstruction Acts of Congress and the XV Amendment and he never repeated the Booker Washington incident. [3]   In his Autobiography written in 1913 he made no mention of it.   But his action did not injure him permanently in the South.   When he came before the people for election in 1904 he carried Missouri by a handsome majority, the first time in her history since 1868 when she had voted for the Republican candidates.   The result in Maryland was so close that he was adjudged one electoral vote. [4]

"The year 1902," wrote Bishop, "was one of incessant activity for Roosevelt." [5]   How could it be otherwise with a man of his capacious brain, equal in action and study to that of three men!   Henry Adams, who was on

---

[1] Bishop, i. 166.   [2] Bishop, i. 154.
[3] William R. Thayer's Roosevelt, 284.
[4] A History of the Presidency (1916), Stanwood, ii. 137.   [5] P. 188.

terms of social intimacy, wrote: "Power when wielded by abnormal energy is the most serious of facts and all Roosevelt's friends know that his restless and combative energy was more than abnormal. Roosevelt . . . was pure act." He might wield "unmeasured power with immeasurable energy in the White House." [1] When he opened the South Carolina Interstate and West Indian Exposition in December, 1901, at Charleston it was an expansionist President who hoped "that it may prove of great and lasting benefit to our industries and to our commerce with the West Indies." [2]

"Of the making of expositions there is seemingly no end," wrote James B. Townsend. "The Pan-American at Buffalo had hardly closed its gates in November [1901] when the . . . Charleston Exposition threw open its doors. . . . It is a far cry from Buffalo to Charleston — over a thousand prosaic miles in actual figures but in midwinter seemingly half the globe in climate and surroundings. The traveler who turned his back upon the deserted halls of the Pan-American, swept by the wintry blasts from the North and found himself thirty-six hours later in Charleston, her feet bathed in the almost tideless summer seas, her quaint old buildings recalling the far past, a warm sun making the city beautiful, and the Cherokee roses blooming in its old gardens, felt himself indeed the pleased victim of a transformation carried by magic 'from lands of snow to lands of sun.' " [3] The Exposition opened on December 1, 1901, and continued until June 1, 1902, and on April 9, President Roosevelt

---

[1] Bishop, 152; Education, 417.
[2] Appleton's Annual Cyclopaedia, 1902, 644.
[3] *Cosmopolitan Magazine*, March, 1902, 523.

was in Charleston and addressed the "Men and women of the South, my fellow-citizens of the Union." "Charleston," he said, "is a typical Southern city. . . . All of us, North and South, can glory alike in the valor of the men who wore the blue and of the men who wore the gray. Those were iron times and only iron men could fight to its terrible finish the great struggle between the hosts of Grant and Lee." I nominated as Vice-Governor of the Philippines, he said, an "ex-Confederate, General Luke Wright of Tennessee, who in the Civil War fought with distinction in a uniform of Confederate gray. . . . Of course," he declared in conclusion, "we are proud of the South. . . . I am proud of your great deeds, for you are my people." [1]

June, 1902, found the President attending the Commencement Exercises of Harvard University when his Alma Mater conferred upon him the degree of Doctor of Laws. President Eliot, in one of his famous characterizations, spoke of him as "a true type of the sturdy gentleman and the high-minded public servant of a democracy." [2] After Roosevelt's speech at the Alumni dinner, Eliot said of him, in the hearing of John Hay, who was the recipient of the same honor, "What a man! Genius, force and courage and such evident honesty." [3] In this speech Roosevelt complimented John D. Long and Senator Hoar, and referred to Henry Cabot Lodge as his "closest, stanchest and most loyal personal friend." He spoke highly of Hay, Root, Taft and Leonard Wood,

---

[1] Roosevelt's Presidential Addresses, etc. The *Review of Reviews* Co. (1910), i. 18 *et seq.*
[2] Washburn, 65.
[3] Life of Hay, Thayer, ii. 348; Washburn, 65.

and the talk merited the words which Hay, with becoming modesty, wrote, "It was the speech of a great ruler and a great gentleman." [1] It is an admirable trait in Roosevelt's character that, having accepted his assistants from his predecessor, he stood by them and gave them due credit. He never had any envy of his helpers from which some great men are not free.

> " I could do more to do Antonius good,
> But 'twould offend him," [2]

declared one of Mark Antony's officers.

During the last of August and early in September Roosevelt made a number of speeches in the New England cities, the burden of which was that the general government must be given the power to regulate "great corporations which we rather loosely designate as trusts." [3] It must be remembered that we are now, in the year 1902, before the decision of the United States Supreme Court in the Northern Securities case which was not rendered until March, 1904, and that neither Roosevelt nor the crowds that flocked to hear him were aware what the decision would be, but he was insistent that the general government should be given this power through legislation by Congress. "At present," he declared in Boston, "we have really no efficient control over a big corporation which does business in more than one State." [4] "We must get power first, then use that power fearlessly but with moderation, with sanity, with self-restraint." [5] "So far from being against property," he said during his

---

[1] Life of Hay, Thayer, ii. 349. The speech is printed in the *Review of Reviews*, Pub. 78.

[2] Antony and Cleopatra, iii. 1.

[3] *Current Lit.* Pub., i. 40.

[4] *Current Lit.* Pub., i. 45.   [5] Fitchburg, ibid., 55.

speech in Boston, "when I ask that the question of trusts be taken up, I am acting in the most conservative sense in property's interest.   When a great corporation is sued for violating the Anti-Trust Law, it is not a move against property, it is a move in favor of property, because when we make it evident that all men, great and small alike, have to obey the law, we put the safeguard of the law around all men. . . . I am advocating action to prevent anything revolutionary. . . . The first thing we want is publicity. . . . The publicity itself would cure many evils." [1]

During his tour he enunciated truths which showed that in his pursuit of the so-called trusts he would be actuated by sound principles. "We are passing through a period of great commercial prosperity," he said in Providence, "and such a period is as sure as adversity itself to bring mutterings of discontent. . . . The spirit of envy and jealousy springs up in the breasts of those who, though they may be doing fairly well themselves, see others no more deserving who do better. Wise laws and fearless and upright administration of the laws can give the opportunity for such prosperity as we see about us. But that is all that they can do. . . . It is not true that the poor have grown poorer but some of the rich have grown very much richer." No State government and town can "by some queer patent device supply the lack of individual thrift, energy, enterprise, resolution." "The best laws that the wit of man can devise would not make a community of thriftless and idle men prosperous." [2]

---

[1] *Current Lit.* Pub., i. 43, 47, 48.
[2] *Current Lit.* Pub., i. 31, 33, 57, 91.   The last two citations are from speeches in Dalton, Mass., and in Logansport, Indiana.

While at Pittsfield, Mass., he suffered a severe accident.
A trolley car, going at a high rate of speed, ran into a
carriage, in which he was riding; a secret service man
who sat on the box with the driver was instantly killed;
the President was thrown forty feet and fell upon his
right cheek which with his right leg was badly bruised.
The accident took place on September 3, but nothing
daunted he started on the day following from Oyster
Bay on a speech-making tour through the South and
West.[1]

The most notable speech was made in Chattanooga on
September 8 to the Brotherhood of Locomotive Firemen.
"I believe emphatically in organized labor," he declared;
and then he preached the gospel of work in words to fit
the occasion: "Your work is hard. Do you suppose I
mention that because I pity you? No; not a bit. I
don't pity any man who does hard work worth doing.
I admire him. I pity the creature who doesn't work at
whichever end of the social scale he may regard himself
as being. The law of worthy work well done is the law of
successful American life. I believe in play too — play
and play hard while you play; but don't make the mistake of thinking that that is the main thing. The work
is what counts." [2]

An abscess developing on the injured leg, forced him to
abandon his trip and return to Washington.

---

[1] Bishop, i. 196.
[2] *Current Lit.* Pub., i. 69, 70.

CHAPTER IX

In 1902 President Roosevelt was confronted with a strike in the anthracite coal regions, which until then was the greatest coal strike in American history. After many and futile negotiations the strike was declared on May 15, and this brought out all of the miners of anthracite coal. Three men of various education and walks in life were earnestly in favor of settling the strike, but their efforts, both before and after the declaration, were for a while unavailing. John Mitchell, the President of the miners' union,[1] was one of the three, and he wrote in his book published in 1903: "The average wage earner has made up his mind that he must remain a wage earner. He has given up the hope of a kingdom to come where he himself will be a capitalist and he asks that the reward for his work be given to him as a workingman. Singly, he has been too weak to enforce his just demands and he has sought strength in union and has associated himself into labor organizations. . . . There is no necessary hostility between labor and capital. Neither can do without the other; each has evolved from the other. Capital is labor saved and materialized; the power to labor is in itself a form of capital. There is not even a necessary fundamental antagonism between the laborer and the capitalist. Both are men with the virtues and vices of men and each wishes at times more than his fair share." [2]

---

[1] The official title was United Mine Workers of America.
[2] Organized Labor, Mitchell, ix.

Mark Hanna was another. As owner of bituminous coal mines, he had had a large experience with striking miners. He had tried the old-fashioned lock-out, negotiation with the miners' union and the substitution of green men for the old miners, with the purpose of breaking up a strike or ending a lock-out. He had come to the conclusion that of all of them, negotiation with the miners' union was on the whole the best plan. His business experience was now joined to his political standing and he gave the benefit of both to the public.

Then there was President Roosevelt. With a practical agreement between the three it might have seemed as if a resolution were easy; and they had to deal with only six organizations as through mining and railroad combinations, the whole business of mining anthracite coal may have been said to be centered in these six, chief of whom was George F. Baer, President of the Philadelphia and Reading Coal and Iron Company as well as of the Railroad Company. Baer, a self-made man, a lawyer by profession, seems to have dominated all the rest and even for a time to have prevailed over J. P. Morgan who had great influence with all of the coal operators.

The bituminous coal miners in session at Indianapolis during July, 1902, decided against a sympathetic strike, for the reason that they had a contract with the producers not expiring until the following April; but although living up to their contract, they arranged to give to their brothers in the anthracite region the largest amount possible of material assistance which enabled them to prolong the strike. Thus affairs continued during the summer of 1902. There was a dead-lock between the miners and producers. When September came, the public in eastern Pennsylvania, New Jersey, New York and New England began to be alarmed regarding their supply of anthracite coal, as on that depended practically their domestic use. Much pressure was brought to bear that in some way the matter be settled so that the public should have their usual supply. Of this pressure the greatest amount was on the President, who appreciated thoroughly the gravity of the situation, and on September 27 wrote to Senator Hanna: "What gives me the greatest concern at the moment is the coal famine. Of course we have nothing to do whatever with this coal strike and no earthly responsibility for it. But the public at large will tend to visit on our heads responsibility for the shortage in coal. . . . But I do most earnestly feel that from every consideration of public policy and good morals, the operators should make some slight concession." [1]

No one after the President bore so important a part in this matter as did Mark Hanna. He had temporarily settled the anthracite coal strike of 1900, had now become chairman of the Industrial Department of the Civic Federation,[2] whose object was to prevent strikes and lockouts through trade agreements by means of collective bargaining. This position gave him an added influence with the men. He shared the President's "anxiety in regard to the coal situation." Visiting him at Oyster Bay he went thence to New York City where he saw Mitchell and Morgan. He obtained from Morgan a proposition of settlement which Mitchell, on behalf of

---

[1] Life of Hanna, Croly, 397.
[2] As to Hanna's connection with the Civic Federation see Croly, 390 et seq.

the miners, agreed to accept. "I really felt encouraged," he wrote to the President, "to think that I was about to accomplish a settlement. I went to Philadelphia and saw Mr. Baer and to my surprise he absolutely refused to entertain it." [1]

Apparently at this time Baer was the master of the situation. He maintained that the operators must control their own business and not allow any dictation from a miners' union. To the demand for arbitration their reply was, "We have nothing to arbitrate." Hanna felt that the operators were determined on starving the miners to submission which seemed to him difficult as they were "getting abundant supplies from their fellow-workmen all over the country." [2]

Roosevelt appreciated every point in the situation. On the same day that he wrote to Hanna, he wrote to Senator Lodge. The operators "have said that they are never going to submit again to having their laborers given a triumph over them for political purposes, as Senator Hanna secured the triumph in 1900. They are now repeating with great bitterness that they do not intend to allow Quay to bully them into making any concession for his political ends any more than they would allow Hanna to do it for his." [3]

Roosevelt, however, made up his mind to leave nothing undone. He invited representatives of the operators and miners to meet him in Washington on October 3, and on their assembling, he made them a brief address, telling them that he was impelled to his action by "the urgency and the terrible nature of the catastrophe impending

---

[1] Hanna's letter of Sept. 29, Croly, 398.
[2] Hanna's letter of Sept. 29, Croly, 398.   [3] Bishop, i. 200.

over a large portion of our people in the shape of a winter fuel famine." [1]   The story of the Conference is told by the President in a letter of October 3 to Hanna.   "Well! I have tried and failed," he wrote.   "I feel downhearted over the result both because of the great misery ensuing for the mass of our people and because the attitude of the operators will beyond a doubt double the burden on us who stand between them and socialistic action. . . . At the meeting to-day the operators assumed a fairly hopeless attitude.   None of them appeared to such advantage as Mitchell, whom most of them denounced with such violence and rancor that I felt he did very well to keep his temper.   Between times they insulted me for not preserving order."   Mitchell proposed "that all matters in dispute be submitted to the arbitration of a tribunal selected by the President." [2]   The President continued in his letter to Hanna, "If the operators had acceded to Mitchell's proposition, I intended to put you on the commission or board of arbitration.   But the operators declined to accede to the proposition. . . . A coal famine in the winter is an ugly thing and I fear we shall see terrible suffering and grave disaster." [3]

Now entered upon the scene Grover Cleveland.   He read in the newspaper of October 4 the account of the Conference of the preceding day and in a private letter to the President expressed himself as "especially disturbed and vexed by the tone and substance of the operators' deliverances."   He suggested that for the moment the proprietors and miners sink their present controversy, produce coal sufficient "to serve the necessities of con-

[1] Bishop, i. 203.   [2] Organized Labor, Mitchell, 387.
[3] Croly, 398.

sumers" and afterwards "take up the fight again where they left off 'without prejudice.'" Roosevelt was glad to receive such a letter; he had been studying Cleveland's and Olney's action in the Pullman car strike [1] and he expected to act with the same firmness that they had shown. Now he told Cleveland that the operators "refused point blank" to consider Mitchell's proposition of arbitration, and he had substantially adopted the suggestion of the letter. On October 6 the President proposed that if the men would go to work, he would appoint a commission to determine matters in dispute promising to do all in his power to have what legislation they proposed enacted. This offer was refused by Mitchell for what he deemed good and sufficient reasons.[2]

The President was not especially pleased that his plan to settle the trouble was thus rejected by Mitchell but this feeling was soon overcome by his irritation at the standpoint of the operators; he now proposed to ask Carroll D. Wright, United States Commissioner of Labor, and two eminent men to make a thorough investigation and to say how the dispute should be settled. He earnestly begged Cleveland to be one of the three. Receiving the Ex-President's assent on October 13, he "immediately wrote to a certain Federal judge asking him to be the third member of the Commission." As the investigation would consume considerable time, the President determined that operations should begin at once, so he arranged with Senator Quay to have the governor of Pennsylvania notify him that he could not keep order in the coal regions without Federal interference. Then

---

[1] See viii. 424.   [2] Organized Labor, 388.

Roosevelt decided to send thither Lieutenant-General John M. Schofield, who was on the retired list of the army, with a sufficient number of regular troops; he should act as receiver, put down all violence, take full charge of the mines and operate them to supply the present demand. Secretaries Root and Knox, both being excellent lawyers, would not have advised this straining of the Constitution; nevertheless they supported the President loyally.[1]

There was considerable violence in the coal regions but where the fault lay it was bootless to inquire. Certainly Mitchell's advice was against anything of the sort and the President who knew all of the facts in the case, stated in a private letter to Bishop on October 13, the matter fairly: "I have been told, on excellent authority, that the disorder has been very great and of very evil kind. On equally good authority I am told the exact contrary. . . . I stand against socialism, against anarchic disorder." [2] Soon after the conference of October 3, all of the national guard of Pennsylvania was sent to the coal regions to act toward the preservation of peace. It was frequently stated by the operators that, if men were properly protected, enough could be secured to man the mines, but this did not prove to be the case.[3]

The President saw accurately the probable course of things, writing thus to Robert Bacon: "The situation is bad, especially because it is possible it may grow in-

---

[1] On Aug. 6, 1908, Roosevelt wrote a letter to the *Outlook* in which he gave a large part of the Cleveland correspondence. The *Outlook*, Aug. 22, 1908, 881. It is also printed by Bishop, i. 204 *et seq.* For the Schofield incident, Bishop, i. 211. T. Roosevelt, An Autobiography, 514; Private Conversation with the President, Nov. 16, 1905.

[2] Bishop, i. 208.   [3] See Mitchell, Organized Labor, 389.

finitely worse. If when the severe weather comes on
there is a coal famine I dread to think of the suffering,
in parts of our great cities especially, and I fear there will
be fuel riots of as bad a type as any bread riots we have
ever seen. Of course, once the rioting has begun, once
there is a resort to mob violence, the only thing to do is
to maintain order." [1]

Before adopting the drastic plan of making General
Schofield a receiver of the mining companies, the President again tried persuasion. By this time the operators,
for some reason not disclosed, had become more placa-
ble. Roosevelt requested Secretary Root to go to New
York to see if he could not get Morgan to agree upon
some plan of arbitration. Root spent the better part of
a day with J. P. Morgan on his yacht *Corsair* and during
this interview, so Root wrote to the President, "we
drafted an agreement of arbitration for a commission
to be appointed by you. Mr. Morgan got the signatures
of the operators to this paper with a single modification.
The modification required that the arbitrators appointed
by you should belong to certain specified classes — an
army engineer, a business man familiar with the coal business, a judge of the locality, a sociologist, etc. When
this paper was presented to the miners, they in turn wished
for some modification of the proposal and it appeared
they would be satisfied to enter into the agreement if
Bishop Spalding [the Roman Catholic bishop of Peoria,
Illinois] could be added to the list of arbitrators and Mr.
Clark could be appointed to the place which called for
a sociologist." [2] The President was in constant consulta-

[1] Oct. 5, Bishop, i. 208.

[2] Letter of Root to the President, June 23, 1903, Bishop, i. 212.

tion with Hanna and learned from him that he had sent a telegram to Mitchell assuring him that the miners "could depend on *absolute* fairness" at Roosevelt's hands.[1]

To clinch the business so that there could be no misunderstanding, Root desired that a member of Morgan's firm should come to Washington and confer with the President. Thereupon, two of the prominent partners came. The interview, which took place on October 15, is best described in a private letter of the President to Senator Lodge: "The operators had limited me down by a full proviso to five different types of men, including an 'eminent sociologist.' . . . The miners, on the other hand, wanted me to appoint at least two extra members myself, or in some fashion to get Bishop Spalding (whom I myself, wanted) and the labor union man on the commission. . . . The operators refused point blank to have another man added. . . . Finally it developed that what they meant was that no extra man should be added if he was a representative of organized labor. . . . It took me about two hours before I at last grasped the fact that the mighty brains of these captains of industry had formulated the theory that they would rather have anarchy than tweedledum, but if I would use the word tweedledee they would hail it as meaning peace. In other words, that they had not the slightest objection to my appointing a labor man as an 'eminent sociologist' and adding Bishop Spalding on my own account, but they preferred to see the Red Commune come rather than to have me make Bishop Spalding or anyone else 'the eminent sociologist,' and add the labor man. I instantly told them that

---

[1] Life of Hanna, Croly, 399.

I had not the slightest objection whatever to doing an absurd thing when it was necessary to meet the objection of an absurd mind on some vital point, and that I would cheerfully appoint my labor man as the 'eminent sociologist.' It was almost impossible for me to appreciate the instant and tremendous relief this gave them. They saw nothing offensive in my language and nothing ridiculous in the proposition, and Pierpont Morgan and Baer, when called up by telephone, eagerly ratified the absurdity; and accordingly at this utterly unimportant price we bid fair to come out of as dangerous a situation as I ever dealt with." [1]

Roosevelt desired to appoint Grover Cleveland on the Commission in lieu of the army engineer, but to this the operators would not agree. In 1915 Roosevelt wrote to Charles Washburn, "I think the settlement of the coal strike was much the most important thing I did about labor from every standpoint." [2] The President wrote to Senator Hanna: "Last night when it became evident that we were going to get a Commission which would be accepted by both sides, I remarked, 'Well, Uncle Mark's work has borne fruit,' and everybody said 'yes.' The solution came because so many of us have for so long hammered at the matter until at last things got into shape which made the present outcome possible." [3] In effecting such a compromise the personality of men counted for much and Roosevelt and Hanna seemed the men of all men to bring about such a result.

---

[1] Bishop, i. 214; Private Conversation with the President, Nov. 16, 1905.

[2] Roosevelt, Thayer, 246; Charles G. Washburn, 82.

[3] Oct. 16, Life of Hanna, Croly, 400.

The Commission was: Brigadier-General John M. Wilson, retired, formerly Chief of Engineers, U. S. A.; E. W. Parker, expert mining engineer, chief statistician of the coal division of the U. S. Geological Survey and editor of the *Engineering and Mining Journal;* George Gray, Judge of the United States Circuit Court, Delaware; E. E. Clark, Chief of the Order of Railway Conductors, sociologist; Thomas H. Watkins, practically connected with the mining and selling of coal; Bishop John L. Spalding of Illinois; Carroll D. Wright, U. S. Commissioner of Labor, Recorder of the Commission.[1] "Most of the miners were Roman Catholics" and "Mitchell and the other leaders of the miners had urged me to appoint some high Catholic ecclesiastic." Bishop Spalding was "one of the very best men to be found in the entire country." [2] Judge Gray was chosen chairman of the Commission.

The miners at once went to work. The relief felt in the eastern part of the country was very great. The well-to-do were spared much hardship, the poor, freezing. Coal, of which there was still a small stock, had advanced to fabulous prices. Now normal conditions obtained. Many homes accustomed to genial warmth blessed Roosevelt because he had used the high office of President to give them comfort.

In five months the Commission made their report to the President, with their different awards. They adjudged that the miners should have an increase of ten per cent in their wages; that there should be no discrimination against union or non-union laborers; a slid-

---

[1] Bishop, i. 217.
[2] Roosevelt, Autobiography, 507, 509.

ing scale of wages was fixed which should increase the pay of the miners with any advance in the price of coal; the award should continue for three years. The Commission further adjudged that any differences of opinion should be referred to a permanent joint committee to be called a Board of Conciliation, to consist of six persons, three of whom should be named by the mine workers and three by the operators. In the event that the six could not agree, the umpire should be "one of the circuit judges of the third judicial circuit of the United States, whose decision shall be final and binding in the premises."[1] John Mitchell maintained that the Commission indirectly acknowledged the miners' union, writing, "While disclaiming the wish to compel the recognition of the United Mine Workers of America, the Commission in actual practice made that recognition inevitable and immediate."[2]

"Time," wrote Joseph B. Bishop in 1920, "has completely justified the President's course. Not only did the findings of the Commission secure peace in the anthracite mines during the three stipulated years, but permanently, for since 1902 there has been no strike there and no serious labor trouble."[3]

Germans living in Venezuela had claims against her which were assumed by the German Government; there were also British and Italian claims which had been assumed respectively by Great Britain and Italy so that the question of indemnity became one between governments. For our purpose, Italy may be left out of con-

---

[1] Report of Anthracite Coal Commission, 80 *et seq.*
[2] Organized Labor, 394.   [3] Vol. i. 219.

sideration and our attention directed to Germany and Great Britain, between which the printed records of Foreign Relations show a community of interest and feeling. In 1901 these two powers offered a number of times to submit the dispute to arbitration and especially by the note of the German Government of July 16, 1901,[1] but Venezuela refused such an offer. In 1902 Germany and Great Britain had a squadron of war-vessels off the Venezuelan coast for the purpose of collecting what was due their citizens. The story would be no other than one of shiftiness on the part of a South American power in her diplomacy and action were it not that the proceeding of the German Government in 1902 gave the occasion of a bout between the President and the Kaiser. In December, 1902, Venezuela desired arbitration, which now Germany did not want, and the suspicion of Roosevelt became aroused that she "intended to seize some Venezuelan harbor and turn it into a strongly fortified place of arms on the model of Kiauchau [Kiaochow] [2] with a view to exercising some degree of control over the future Isthmian Canal, and over South American affairs generally."

England and Germany at this time threatened a blockade and on December 9, 1902, captured all of the Venezuelan war-vessels in the port of Caracas, her capital; and four days later, the united fleets bombarded the forts

---

[1] Foreign Relations, 1904, 507.

[2] Kiaochow Bay, a large inlet in China, "was seized in November, 1897, by the German fleet. . . . The bay and land on both sides of the entrance were leased to Germany for 99 years. During the continuance of the lease Germany exercises all the rights to territorial sovereignty, including the right to erect fortifications." Encyclopædia Britannica, xv. 783.

of the town of Puerto Cabello, the cause being an alleged insult to the British flag on a British merchant vessel.[1] Germany favored a "pacific blockade" while Great Britain did not believe there could be such a thing. "Has war been declared?" the Prime Minister, Mr. Balfour, was asked in the House of Commons, and he replied, "Does the honorable and learned gentleman suppose that without a state of war you can take the ships of another power and blockade its ports?"[2]

In October, 1915, William Roscoe Thayer writing a chapter, "The German Menace Looms Up," in his "Life of John Hay," gave the inside of Germany's ulterior purpose; this history aroused great interest. Roosevelt on August 21, 1916, wrote a letter to Thayer in which he told the whole story,[3] confirming what Thayer had already written and elaborating the incident. In his Message to Congress of December, 1901, the President had said, "The Monroe Doctrine is a declaration that there must be no territorial aggrandizement by any non-American power at the expense of any American power on American soil." To Roosevelt it seemed that the result of Germany's action would be a violation of the Monroe Doctrine and, if she refused to arbitrate the whole question, she would wage war against Venezuela and take possession of a seaport. "Germany," he wrote, "declined to agree to arbitrate the question at issue between her and Venezuela and declined to say that she would not take possession of Venezuelan territory, merely saying that such possession would be 'temporary.'"

---

[1] Foreign Relations, 1903, 790, 797.
[2] Dec. 17, 1902, Foreign Relations, 1903, 455.
[3] Thayer printed this letter as an appendix to his second edition.

The attitude of England was different. Henry White heard on December 16 Lord Lansdowne, the Foreign Minister, say in the House of Lords, "It is not intended to land a British force and still less to occupy Venezuelan territory." [1]   The correspondence with Great Britain was conducted by Henry White, the first Secretary of Legation, who, seeing his own country's side with persistency could present it to a foreign power with the courtesy that obtains in diplomatic transactions — "the most useful man in the entire diplomatic service during my presidency, and for many years before was Henry White," [2] said Roosevelt. "I speedily became convinced," wrote Roosevelt, "that Germany was the leader and the really formidable party in the transaction and that England was merely following Germany's lead in rather half-hearted fashion."

"I saw the Ambassador" [Holleben, of Germany] related Roosevelt, "and explained that in view of the German squadron on the Venezuelan coast I could not permit longer delay in answering my request for an arbitration and that I could not acquiesce in any seizure of Venezuelan territory. The Ambassador responded that his government could not agree to arbitrate and that there was no intention to take 'permanent' possession of Venezuelan territory. I answered that Kiauchau was not a permanent possession of Germany — that I understood it was merely held by a 99 years' lease and that I did not intend to have another Kiauchau, held by similar tenure, on the approach to the Isthmian Ca-

---

[1] Foreign Relations, 1903, 453.
[2] Theodore Roosevelt, Autobiography, 388.

nal." The President further said that if he did not re-
ceive a favorable reply within ten days, he should order
Dewey and his fleet thither to resist any attempt of the
Germans to take possession of Venezuelan territory.

Roosevelt was aware that he could back up the threat.
Paying much attention to naval matters he knew that
our Navy was in efficient condition. Dewey was at Culebra, Puerto Rico, "in command of a fleet consisting of
over fifty ships, including every battle-ship and every
torpedo boat that we had, with orders from Washington to
hold the fleet in hand and be ready to move at a moment's
notice."

A few days afterwards Holleben came to see the President but said nothing in reference to Venezuela, and when
he rose to go he was asked if he had heard anything from
his government regarding the matter in dispute. The
answer was no, whereupon the President said he would
advance the time he had proposed and order Dewey to
sail twenty-four hours previous to the expiration of the
ten days. But before the President found it necessary
to cable to Dewey, Holleben informed him that the German
Emperor would consent to an arbitration and desired
that Roosevelt should be arbitrator. This, after due
consideration, was declined and the case went to the
Hague Tribunal.[1]

This account is confirmed by a letter of President
Roosevelt to Henry White dated August 14, 1906: "At
the time of the Venezuela business I saw the German
Ambassador privately myself; told him to tell the Kaiser
that I had put Dewey in charge of our fleet to maneuver

---

[1] Thayer, Life of Hay, ii. Appendix.

in West Indian waters; that the world at large should know this merely as a maneuver and we should strive in every way to appear simply as coöperating with the Germans; but that I regretted to say that the popular feeling was such that I should be obliged to interfere, by force if necessary, if the Germans took any action which looked like the acquisition of territory there or elsewhere along the Caribbean; that this was not in any way intended as a threat, but as the position on the part of the Government which the American people would demand, and that I wanted him to understand it before the two nations drifted into such a position that trouble might come. I do not know whether it was a case of *post hoc* or *propter hoc*, but immediately afterward the Kaiser made to me the proposition that I should arbitrate myself, which I finally got him to modify so that it was sent to The Hague."

My authority for this bout between the President and the Kaiser is Thayer's account and Roosevelt's letters of August, 1906 and 1916. There seems to be no opposition between them and the printed diplomatic correspondence, Roosevelt's speech of April 2, 1903, cited by John Bassett Moore in his Review of Thayer's Life of Hay,[1] and the President's Message to Congress of December, 1903. It is well known that much diplomatic work is not set down in the printed Foreign Relations. Charles Francis Adams, who had occasion to investigate some phases of English diplomacy, was insistent on the part that private letters played in certain negotiations; and in our own country the daily talk and telephone communications must be considered. Therefore Roosevelt's recollection of this

---

[1] *Political Science Quarterly*, March, 1917, 119.

episode, although not given to the world until 1915 and 1916, seems to me good historical evidence. In no way does the printed record contravene it. In fact, in a study of the correspondence with Germany one may well be convinced that the whole story is not therein told, as many of the despatches are simply given in "paraphrase." The differences regarding arbitration between Great Britain and Germany may be detected and it is easy to believe that Germany was forced in 1902 to an arbitration of the dispute.

After the controversy with the Kaiser had ended with his submission, affairs proceeded smoothly. Both Great Britain and Germany made certain reservations that should not be submitted to the Tribunal. Both countries blockaded the Venezuela ports from December 20, 1902, to February 16, 1903, during which time negotiations went on which resulted in the arbitration. Both of these circumstances were apparently with the consent of President Roosevelt. The Hague Tribunal made its award on February 22, 1904.[1]

President Roosevelt's action toward another European power demands attention. "I feel," he wrote to Finley Peter Dunne [Dooley] "a sincere friendliness for England; but you may notice that I do not slop over about it, and that I do not in the least misunderstand England's attitude." [2] "I think more of England than of any other foreign country," the President said a year later. "She is more sincerely our friend. I detest the Anglophobists. Sometimes when discussing matters with the Irish I am tempted to become an Anglomaniac." [3] For an om-

---

[1] Foreign Relations, 1904, 506.　　[2] November 1904, Bishop, i. 348.
[3] Conversation with President Roosevelt, November 17, 1905.

nivorous reader, as was Roosevelt, no other feeling was possible. The majority of the many books that he read were by English writers. He thoroughly believed in the high civilization expressed in her literature. To him that the two nations possessed the common language of Shakespeare and Milton was no unmeaning talk; it was indeed ingrained in the fibre of his being and he was always ready to acknowledge England as the predominant partner. One may see into his very thought in reading his letter to John Morley [Jan. 17, 1904] wherein he says, "Personally I feel that with all their faults Gibbon and Macaulay are the two great English historians."[1] This feeling toward England must therefore be taken into account in considering the Alaska boundary dispute.

Every British map until 1884 shows the disputed Alaskan territory belonging either to Russia or to the United States according to which had dominion, and no claim was made by Canada to this territory until 1898 when Lord Herschell, at the head of the Joint High Commission, appointed to consider twelve subjects of difference between Canada and the United States, asserted it, eliciting this comment from John Hay, then Secretary of State. On January 3, 1899, he thus wrote to Henry White: "In the case of Alaska it is hard to treat with patience the claim set up by Lord Herschell, that virtually the whole coast belongs to England, leaving us only a few jutting promontories without communication with each other. Without going into the historical or legal argument, as a mere matter of common sense it is impossible that any nation should ever have conceded, or any other nation have accepted,

---

[1] Bishop, i. 269.

the cession of such a ridiculous and preposterous boundary line. We are absolutely driven to the conclusion that Lord Herschell put forward a claim that he had no belief or confidence in, for the mere purpose of trading it off for something substantial. And yet the slightest suggestion that his claim is unfounded throws him into a fury." [1]

It was not only, indeed I think not chiefly, due to the belief that the contested region might be gold-bearing, but rather to the desire to get ports contiguous to the Klondike. This was especially true of Skagway at the head of the Lynn Canal. It was the chief port for the Klondike and under the Canadian claim would be British territory.

The reason of this claim is not far to seek. In 1896 gold was discovered in the Klondike. British Columbia and Alaska went wild over the discovery. Gold might exist in this disputed territory so that it might be of value to either country. Herschell and the British members of the Commission would settle no other question unless the Alaska boundary was first determined, and as the Joint High Commission could not agree on that, they adjourned without arriving at any conclusion. It was therefore one of the foreign matters bequeathed to the Roosevelt administration.

Then came the South African War [1899–1902] and out of friendship to England, the President did not want to press the matter; he was indeed in no hurry but, if gold were discovered, he intended to occupy the territory. The English proposed arbitration. Our Ambassador favored that disposition of the matter and possibly so

---

[1] Life of Hay, Thayer, ii. 205.

did our Secretary of State. But the President said, no. It is no question for arbitration. Roosevelt indeed distrusted the opinion of our Ambassadors to England; they were prone to see the English side of any question.[1] James Bryce wrote in 1888: "Even in these days of vigilant and exacting constituencies one sees many members of the House of Commons, the democratic robustness or provincial crudity of whose ideas melts like wax under the influence of fashionable dinner-parties and club smoking rooms."[2] Educated men know the charm of English society and can appreciate how our official representatives, recipients as they are of manifold attentions, fall victims to that charm.

The President was firm. The result was the Convention of January 24, 1903, which constituted a Tribunal of "six important jurists of repute," to determine the boundary line between Alaska and British Columbia. Three members were to be appointed by the President; three by his Britannic Majesty. A majority should determine the award.[3] The President named Henry Cabot Lodge, Senator from Massachusetts, Elihu Root, Secretary of War, and George Turner, ex-Senator from Washington. Before these were definitely appointed the President endeavored to get a Justice of the Supreme Court, but he declined on the ground that the post was not in line with his duties. Another Justice was approached with a like result.[4] The selections of the Presi-

---

[1] Conversation with the President, Nov. 17, 1905; Life of Hay, Thayer, ii. 207, 208; Life of Roosevelt, Thayer, 174. But see Life of Choate, Martin, ii. 228, 235, 237, 238.

[2] American Commonwealth, ii. 230.

[3] Foreign Relations, 1903, 488.

[4] Diplomatic Memoirs, John W. Foster, ii. 199.

dent were criticised, both in Canada and the United States, as not being according to the Treaty which called for "impartial jurists of repute." The editor of Hall's International Law (ed. 1904) spoke of the choice of the American members as a "serious blot on the proceedings." But the British government did not officially make any complaint. They named as members, Baron Alverstone, Lord Chief Justice of England, Louis A. Jetté, Lieutenant-Governor of Quebec, and A. B. Aylesworth of the Toronto bar.[1]   London was selected as the place for the sitting of the Tribunal.

After the appointment of the Tribunal and before its decision, the President wrote to Justice Holmes a letter [July 25, 1903], which he might show "privately and unofficially" to Joseph Chamberlain, the Colonial Secretary. He also wrote one of similar import to Henry White which as desired was shown to Arthur Balfour, Prime Minister. In the letter to Justice Holmes the President said: "Nothing but my very earnest desire to get on well with England and my reluctance to a break made me consent to this appointment of a Joint Commission [officially a Tribunal] in this case; for I regard the attitude of Canada which England has backed, as having the scantest possible warrant in justice. However, there were but two alternatives. Either I could appoint a commission and give a chance for agreement; or I could do as I shall of course do in case this Commission fails and request Congress to make an appropriation which will enable me to run the boundary on my own hook. . . . The claim of the Canadians for access to deep

---

[1] Diplomatic Memoirs, J. W. Foster, ii. 198.

water along any part of the Canadian [Alaskan] coast is just exactly as indefensible as if they should now suddenly claim the island of Nantucket. There is not a man fit to go on the Commission in all the United States, who would treat this claim any more respectfully than he would treat a claim to Nantucket. . . . But there are points which the Commission can genuinely consider. There is room for argument about the islands in the mouth of the Portland Channel. . . . The objection raised by certain Canadian authorities to Lodge, Root and Turner, and especially to Lodge and Root, was that they had committed themselves on the general proposition. No man in public life in any position of prominence could have possibly avoided committing himself on the proposition. . . . Let me add that I earnestly hope that the English understand my purpose. I wish to make one last effort to bring about an agreement through the Commission which will enable the people of both countries to say that the result represents the feeling of the representatives of both countries. But if there is a disagreement I wish it distinctly understood, not only that there will be no arbitration of the matter, but that in my Message to Congress I shall take a position which will prevent any possibility of arbitration hereafter; a position, I am inclined to believe, which will render it necessary for Congress to give me the authority to run the line as we claim it, by our own people without any further regard to the attitude of England and Canada." [1] And Hay wrote to Foster on September 20, 1903: "I hear the usual pessimistic forecasts — some

---

[1] Bishop, i. 259; Thayer, Life of Roosevelt, 176.

from London — some from this side. But I shall not believe, until I am forced to, that Lord Alverstone can so shut his eyes to law and evidence as to give a verdict against us, especially as he must know that this is the last chance for an honorable and graceful retreat from an absolutely untenable position. I am sincerely sorry they have got themselves into such a fix; but it is their own fault and they will make a fatal mistake if they refuse to avail themselves of the opportunity we have given them to get out." [1]

The decision of the Tribunal was made October 20, 1903, and fixed the land boundary well back of all the inlets, as was the chief contention of the United States. This was done by a vote of four to two, Lord Alverstone siding with the Americans and the two Canadian members dissenting. The Tribunal was unanimous in giving to Canada two of the four uninhabited islands.[2] The two Canadian members not only did not sign the award but gave to the press "a carefully prepared interview in which they declared that the decision was not judicial in its character." John W. Foster, who criticised the appeal to the press by the Canadian members, did not share the censure meted out to them for their failure to sign the award. He wrote with the impartiality which distinguishes his work: "A similar precedent is to be found in the Halifax Fisheries Arbitration of 1877, when the American member not only refused to sign the award but questioned its validity. A better practice was observed in the Fur-Seal Arbitration at Paris in 1893. The two American members, Justice Harlan and Senator Morgan, were outvoted on almost every one of the six

---

[1] Diplomatic Memoirs, John W. Foster, ii. 206.
[2] Foreign Relations, 1903, 543; Foster, Diplomatic Memoirs, ii. 203.

points submitted to the Tribunal; but, without with-drawing their votes they cheerfully united with their colleagues in signing the award." Foster went on to say, "The people of the United States were very angry at the Halifax award and were by no means pleased with the result of the Fur-Seal Arbitration at Paris."[1]

On June 8, 1911, Roosevelt wrote to Admiral Mahan: "The settlement of the Alaskan boundary settled the last serious trouble between the British Empire and our-selves as everything else could be arbitrated. . . . I feel very differently towards England from the way I feel towards Germany."[2]

Roosevelt, shortly before his death [January 6, 1919], wrote to Mahan a letter that may be taken as his legacy to his countrymen: "I regard the British Navy as prob-ably the most potent instrumentality for peace in the world. I do not believe we should try to build a navy in rivalry to it but I do believe we should have the second navy in the world. Moreover I am prepared to say what five years ago I would not have said, I think the time has come when the United States and the British Empire can agree to a universal arbitration treaty. In other words I believe the time has come when we should say that under no circumstances shall there ever be a resort to war between the United States and the British Empire, and that no question can arise between them that cannot be settled in judicial fashion."[3]

---

[1] Diplomatic Memoirs, ii. 204.   [2] Life of Mahan, Taylor, 203.
[3] Life of Mahan, Taylor, 224. In this account I have also consulted J. W. Foster's Article on the Alaskan Boundary, *National Geographic Magazine*, Nov. 1899, printed as Doc. No. 2, 58th Cong., Special Session; The Case of the U. S.; The Argument of the U. S., both of which are printed by the Gov't Printing Office.

CHAPTER X

"By far the most important action I took in foreign affairs during the time I was President," wrote Roosevelt, "relates to the Panama Canal."[1] At the time Hay became Secretary of State there was a feeling in the country decidedly in favor of joining the two oceans by a canal. Long existent, the feeling had been fostered by the events of the Spanish-American War and especially by the voyage of the *Oregon* around Cape Horn. As she was desired to reinforce the Atlantic fleet, it could not be ignored how much sooner she would have made the junction had there been a canal from the Pacific to the Atlantic. The Clayton-Bulwer Treaty with England, made in 1850,[2] stood in the way. Hay set to work to supersede this and negotiated a Treaty which was signed by him and Lord Pauncefote, the British Ambassador, on February 5, 1900. Roosevelt, who was then Governor of New York, in a friendly letter to Hay criticised severely two points in the Treaty: the first was the prohibition of fortifying the canal, and the second was a virtual invitation to foreign powers to a joint guarantee that in his view would tend to invalidate the Monroe Doctrine.[3]

Hay was irritated that the Senate did not ratify the Treaty; he deemed it an "irreparable mistake of our Constitution" which put it into "the power of one-third +1 of the Senate to meet with a categorical veto any treaty negotiated by the President."[4] He spoke against

---

[1] Autobiography, 553.   [2] Vol. i. 199.
[3] Life of Hay, Thayer, ii. 339.   [4] To Choate, ibid., 219.

the Senate "almost with ferocity."[1]　His sayings reported by tale bearers did not help his cause with the senators and he was never popular with the Senate.　Yet much more than anything of the sort, the ideas which lay at the bottom of Roosevelt's friendly criticism affected the Senate's action in regard to the Treaty and they made amendments to it which embodied tacitly these objections.　The British Government did not accept the amendments.　Hay resigned his position as Secretary of State in the following words: "Dear Mr. President: The action of the Senate indicates views so widely divergent from mine in matters affecting, as I think, the national welfare and honor, that I fear my power to serve you in business requiring the concurrence of that body is at an end.　I cannot help fearing also that the newspaper attacks upon the State Department, which have so strongly influenced the Senate, may be an injury to you if I remain in the Cabinet."　McKinley, in a very manly letter, refused to accept his resignation.[2]

Hay did not let his irritation prevent his going ahead with the project, and he took steps toward the negotiation of a new Treaty.　Meanwhile Roosevelt had become President and the new Treaty, which is known as the second Hay-Pauncefote Treaty, was signed by Hay and Pauncefote on November 18, 1901, was ratified by the Senate on December 16 by 72 : 6 and concurred in by the British Government.　Under this Treaty, the canal was built.　It provided that it should supersede the convention of 1850 and that the canal might be constructed

---

[1] Life of Hay, Thayer, ii. 233.
[2] Ibid., ii. 226.

either by the United States or by corporations that it
might aid.[1] A clear statement of its meaning on one
disputed point is given by Shelby M. Cullom, who was
then a member and soon to become chairman of the
Committee on Foreign Relations. "The first and second
Hay-Pauncefote treaties must be construed together;
the first Hay-Pauncefote Treaty contained a prohibition against fortifications; the second Hay-Pauncefote
Treaty neither prohibited nor in terms agreed to fortifications, but was silent on the subject; therefore, the legal
construction would be that Great Britain had receded
from the position that the canal should not be fortified." [2]

The canal was fortified. James Bryce wrote: "The
visitor who sees the slopes where these forts and batteries
are to be placed, asks who are the enemies whom it is
desired to repel. Where is the great naval power that
has any motive either of national enmity or of self-
interest sufficient to induce it to face the risks of a war with
a country so populous, so wealthy and so vigorous as
the United States?"[3] The peace-loving American who
gazes at the forts on the cliffs of Gibraltar might put *pari
passu* the same question.

Public sentiment had decided that there should be an
inter-oceanic canal and that it should be constructed
by the United States. The question was should it go
by Nicaragua or across the Isthmus of Panama? When
Hay wrote on January 15, 1900, "The canal is going to
be built, probably by the Nicaragua route,"[4] he expressed

---

[1] Digest of International Law. John Bassett Moore, iii. 219. The
Treaty is printed in full and the first Hay-Pauncefote Treaty is given
on p. 210.
[2] Fifty Years of Public Service, 381.   [3] South America, 32.
[4] Life of Hay, Thayer, ii. 222.

the popular opinion. The Nicaragua canal "has become a sentiment," said Senator Hanna in his great speech advocating the Panama route. Three commissions had decided in favor of it. "I want to confess," declared Hanna, "that in common with all my fellow citizens I shared in that feeling and belief and, as the necessity seemed to grow and demand an isthmian canal [through Nicaragua], I would have been prepared, under the influences which then existed, to give my hearty support to that project."

The advantage of Panama over Nicaragua was well put forward by Hanna in this speech. "The Panama Canal route," he said, "is 49 miles long as against 183 miles of the Nicaraguan route." The New Panama Canal Company (French) which had previously offered to sell its plant, rights, privileges, franchises and concessions for 109 millions had now come down to 40 millions.[1] Included in this offer were all of the existing shares of the Panama railway except about 1100; the total was 70,000 shares. The last Commission had, on receiving the new offer of the French company, made a supplementary report (January 18, 1902) recommending the Panama route. The question of earthquakes, volcanic eruptions, of the cost of construction and operation was all in favor of the canal by way of Panama.[2]

This was Hanna's greatest effort in the Senate. According to Senator George F. Hoar, no mean judge, he was eloquent as he discussed the question in all of its

---

[1] Jan. 9, 1902.

[2] Hanna's speech was made June 5 and 6, 1902, is reported in the Congressional Record, 6317 et seq.; see also Life of Hanna, Croly, 379 et seq.

bearings. "He changed the whole attitude of the Senate," wrote Cullom, "concerning the route for an interoceanic canal. We all generally favored the Nicaraguan route. Senator Hanna became convinced that the Panama route was best and he soon carried everything before him to the end that the Panama route was selected."[1]

A bill providing for the construction of the Nicaraguan canal had passed the House almost unanimously and to the bill as it came to the Senate, Spooner had added an amendment providing for the purchase of the rights, privileges, franchises, concessions, right of way, unfinished work, plants and property of the New Panama Canal Company of France for 40 millions, and the construction of the canal across the Isthmus of Panama, but if "the President be unable to obtain for the United States a satisfactory title to the property of the New Panama Canal Company and the control of the necessary territory of the Republic of Colombia within a reasonable time and upon reasonable terms," then the President

---

[1] Fifty Years of Public Service, 281. "The United States had been committed for thirty years to an isthmian canal by the Nicaragua route. It came to be considered as 'the American line.' The resolution in its favor had passed the House. Senator Hanna gave to the study of the question, which was purely a business one, a mind long trained in construction contracts. He came to the conclusion that we should build on the Panama route. . . . He accomplished that rarest of triumphs, the command of a listening Senate." — Senator C. M. Depew. Senator Charles Dick who succeeded Hanna in the Senate said: "His greatest achievement in this body was in converting a hostile majority to favor the route for an isthmian canal which his judgment declared was the best. He came to this conclusion only after most thorough investigation. When he entered upon this contest few of the Members of Congress agreed with him. . . . He was told that his efforts would be futile. He entered upon the contest with all the zeal and energy of his strong nature. By personal appeals, by labors in committee and on this floor he urged his views." Memorial addresses, 104, 131.

"might fall back to the Nicaragua route." [1] This passed the Senate by 42 to 34,[2] was accepted by the House, signed by the President and was entirely satisfactory to public opinion.

On the basis of this act Hay negotiated what is known as the Hay-Herran Treaty, signed January 22, 1903. Dr. Herran was the chargé d'affaires of Colombia in Washington. Colombia's executive officer was Marroquin, a usurper who had been Vice-President and now assumed to be acting President. He was called a dictator by Roosevelt and those who supported his action, but his word was far from being law. At first really in favor of the Treaty, he succumbed to a popular sentiment, which was excited by the Finance Minister and the press of Bogotá, and did not advocate strongly the Treaty before the Colombia Congress as Roosevelt and Hay thought he should have done. The Treaty was not valid unless approved by the Colombia Congress and the popular feeling, at least in Bogotá, the capital, was that the ten million bonus and the $250,000 per year after nine years, which was what the United States had agreed to pay by the Hay-Herran Treaty, was not sufficient compensation for that which Colombia was conceding to the United States. It was thought that the provision of the Spooner Act that, unless proper arrangements could be made with the Republic of Colombia and the French Canal Company, the United States was empowered to construct the Nicaraguan Canal, was a mere bluff to make better terms with Colombia which looked upon the Isth-

[1] Acts of Congress relating to the Panama Canal, 27. This included 68,863 shares of the Panama Railroad Company out of a total of 70,000 shares.

[2] Life of Hanna, Croly, 384.

mus of Panama "as a financial cow to be milked for the benefit of the country at large."[1]   Therefore the Senate of Colombia in two different sessions, as a response to popular sentiment aroused largely by the press of Bogotá, rejected the Treaty in August and postponed the consideration of it indefinitely in October.[2]

Unquestionably the Hay–Herran Treaty should have been ratified. The arguments of Roosevelt and Hay in its favor are unanswerable, but the idea of the Bogotá press and the Colombia Senate was that more money might be had. General Reyes, who was really a friend to a fair composition between the two countries, thought that ten millions from the French Company and an increase of five millions from the United States would insure the ratification of the Treaty.[3] The more radical pretended that the French concession expired in 1904 and, if ratification were postponed, Colombia might receive the whole forty millions which the United States had agreed to pay to the French Company. But this concession to the French Company had been extended to 1910, and to repudiate such a plain contract would hardly have been done even by a country so regardless of plighted faith as was Colombia. Take it all in all, the action of Colombia was blackmail and aroused all the fighting qualities in Roosevelt's nature. A true convert to the Panama Canal, he determined that the canal should there be built.

Events now moved swiftly. Hay telegraphed on July 13 to Beaupré, our Minister at Bogotá: "Neither of the

---

[1] Life of Hay, Thayer, ii. 304.

[2] August 12, October 30.   As the Senate rejected it the House did not pass upon it.   [3] July 9, Foreign Relations, 1903, 163.

proposed amendments mentioned in your telegram [Reyes's suggestion *ante*] received to-day would stand any chance of acceptance by the Senate of the United States, while any amendment whatever or unnecessary delay in the ratification of the Treaty would greatly imperil its consummation." [1]

It was bruited about in Bogotá that, in the event of non-ratification of the Treaty, Panama would secede from Colombia, get the ten million bonus and the annual stipend herself, but as to that the Colombia Senate, backed by popular sentiment, was willing to take the chance. Colombia had a population of five millions divided into nine departments of which Panama was one, and the number of its inhabitants was about 250,000. The Colombian army consisted of 10,000.[2]

Now appeared upon the scene Philippe Bunau-Varilla, a celebrated French engineer, who had been connected with the French Canal enterprise and was now much concerned in having the Panama route adopted and the French Company receiving actually the forty millions without any deduction in favor of the "corruptionists" of Bogotá; he therefore fomented with great skill a revolution in Panama.   It was practically a bloodless [3] revolution and resulted in a Treaty between the Republic of Panama and the United States, providing for the construction of the canal.   While neither President Roosevelt nor Secretary Hay connived at the revolution, they sympathized with it.   "No one," declared President Roosevelt

---

[1] Foreign Relations, 1903, 164.
[2] Reyes, Foreign Relations, 288.
[3] One Chinaman was killed. Despatch of Ehrman to Hay, Nov. 4. Ehrman was Consul-General in Panama. Foreign Relations, 1903, 232.

in his Message of January 4, 1904, "connected with this Government had any part in preparing, inciting, or encouraging the late revolution on the Isthmus of Panama, and that, save from the reports of our military and naval officers, no one connected with this Government had any previous knowledge of the revolution except such as was accessible to any person of ordinary intelligence who read the newspapers and kept up a current acquaintance with public affairs." [1]   In August, wrote Roosevelt, "it began to appear probable that the Colombian legislature would not ratify the treaty. . . . Everyone knew that the revolution was a possibility but it was not until toward the end of October that it appeared to be an imminent probability. Although the Administration, of course, had special means of knowledge, no such means were necessary in order to appreciate the possibility and toward the end the likelihood, of such a revolutionary outbreak and of its success." [2]   As Roosevelt said to William R. Thayer many years later, "The other fellows in Paris and New York had taken all the risk and were doing all the work. Instead of trying to run a parallel conspiracy I had only to sit still and profit by their plot — if it succeeded." [3]

The President ordered naval ships to Colon (the port of Panama on the Caribbean Sea which was an arm of the Atlantic) and thus prevented the landing of a reinforcement of Colombian troops that would have suppressed the revolution. How much the revolutionists

---

[1] Foreign Relations, 1903, 272. Also Hay, ibid., 295, 310; T. Roosevelt, Autobiography (1913), 564.
[2] Message of January, 1904. Foreign Relations, 1903, 263, 264.
[3] Roosevelt, 190.

were dependent on the United States is seen by a citation from Bunau-Varilla's book. "From the morning of the 2d November (1903)," he wrote, "all the inhabitants of Colon were looking towards Kingston, hoping for the appearance of the ship symbolizing American protection. As the hours passed, disappointment gradually invaded all hearts. Towards nightfall despair was general, when suddenly a light smoke arose in the direction of the northeast. This was a ray of hope! If it were the liberator! Little by little, the smoke thickened, the ship emerged above the horizon and soon the Star-Spangled Banner dominated the Bay of Colon. A burst of delirious enthusiasm shook the whole Isthmus. It was really true! Bunau-Varilla had effectually obtained for the unfortunate country the protection of the powerful Republic! At this moment, without one word having been uttered the revolution was accomplished in the hearts of all. . . . In the morning of the 3d of November General Tovar (of Colombia) arrived quietly with about 500 soldiers. . . . If these troops had arrived twenty-four hours earlier nobody would have made a move. . . . The Independent Republic of Panama was proclaimed. The revolution had been made without shedding a drop of blood." [1] The ship which arrived so opportunely for Bunau-Varilla's scheme was the *Nashville*. It may therefore be said that unless President Roosevelt had ordered our vessels-of-war to Colon the Panama revolution would

---

[1] Panama, Bunau-Varilla, 335. The incident is repeated in The Great Adventure of Panama (1920) in which Bunau-Varilla also states, "All is saved [by the arrival of the *Nashville*]. . . . Colombia can say to-day that the Republic of Panama was born owing to American protection." 243, 247.

have been suppressed.[1] "I simply lifted my foot," affirmed Roosevelt. "Oh, Mr. President," said Attorney-General Knox in Cabinet meeting, "do not let so great an achievement suffer from any taint of legality." [2]

It is probable that Roosevelt had better have exercised the virtue of patience as he was so advised by Senator Hanna.[3] Many things might have happened without the secession of Panama. Popular sentiment in the United States was now in favor of the Panama route. Senator John T. Morgan of Alabama, who although a Democrat had been made chairman of the Inter-Oceanic Canal Committee by a Republican Senate, on account of his enthusiasm for an Inter-Oceanic Canal, had made the Senate majority report in favor of the Nicaragua route. But Hanna was the "instigator of the minority report and became the leader in the Senate of the pro-Panama party," [4] and the successor of Morgan as the chairman of the committee. He was as enthusiastic for Panama as was Roosevelt, and could probably have influenced the Senate in its favor, despite the backing-down of Colombia. The eruption of Mont Pelée in Martinique during May, 1902, costing about 40,000 lives, was a powerful argument in favor of Panama, as it was well understood that the danger from volcanoes and earthquakes was greater by the Nicaragua route. "Volcanoes and earthquakes," said Hanna in the Senate, "seem to be a burning question just now while Mount Pelée is discharging its fire, and they have led to a more careful consideration of that matter." [5]

---

[1] For the disposition of the vessels reinforcing the *Nashville*, see Roosevelt in Foreign Relations, 1903, 266.

[2] Impressions, Abbott, 139, 140.

[3] Bishop, i. 278.   [4] Life of Hanna, Croly, 380.   [5] Record, 6319.

A mischief in Roosevelt's action was that it aggravated the suspicions of the Central and South American republics of the United States and led them to believe that the doctrine of might makes right prevailed in Yankeedom; so that if exercising the virtue of patience involved a delay of only twelve months, it better have been exercised. Moreover it may have been wise to nurse a coterie in the Republic of Colombia in the hope that the violent public sentiment of Bogotá might pass away. Marroquin, unpopular as he was in Bogotá, had appointed as governor of Panama Senator Obaldia. "Obaldia's separatist tendencies," wrote our Minister Beaupré to Hay, "are well known and he is reported to have said that, should the canal treaty not pass, the department of Panama would declare its independence and would be right in doing so. That these are his opinions there is of course no doubt." [1] Reyes, the probable and actual successor of Marroquin, was well worth cultivating and his dignified correspondence with Secretary Hay during December, 1903, and January, 1904, manifest a man with whom one could bargain.

"Such a scheme" [that of the secession of Panama and its annexation to the United States], wrote Adee, Assistant-Secretary of State to Hay, "could, of course, have no countenance from us — our policy before the world should stand like Mrs. Cæsar, without suspicion." [2] That the policy determined on was not above suspicion is evident from Moorfield Storey's address at the Massachusetts Reform Club during December, 1903; from Daniel H. Chamberlain's "Open letter to John Hay" in the New

---

[1] Foreign Relations, 1903, 193.
[2] Life of Hay, Thayer, ii. 313.

York *Times* of October 2, 1904; from James C. Carter's criticism; from George L. Fox's brochure of 1904, entitled "President Roosevelt's Coup d'État"; from Leander T. Chamberlain's article entitled "A Chapter of National Dishonor," reprinted from the *North American Review* of February, 1912, as a Senate document; and from George L. Fox's letter to the New York *Nation* of February 24, 1916, reprinting the protest of many Yale professors of December 24, 1903, against the treatment of Colombia.[1]

Saddest of all was the attitude of Senator George F. Hoar. In a speech in the Senate on December 17, 1903, he said: "No man in this country desires more eagerly than I do to support the Administration and to act with my Republican associates in this matter. I desire the building of the canal. It is one of the great landmarks, rarely found once in a century, in the progress of humanity, bringing nations together and making the whole world kin. I hope that it is a laudable ambition that this may be accomplished in my time by the party with which I have acted from my youth, and by the Administration of my choice. Nothing can be more delightful to me than that it shall be accomplished by the President of whom I have supposed I had the right to speak as an honored and valued personal friend. . . . Before the revolution broke out our Government instructed its man-of-war to prevent the Government of Colombia from doing anything in anticipation of the revolution to prevent it. . . . Colombia was a friendly nation. . . . It is said that she

---

[1] The address of Storey and article of D. H. Chamberlain are preserved as pamphlets in the Boston Athenæum. The article of L. T. Chamberlain is in a bound volume of "Tracts." In regard to James C. Carter see Life of Hay, Thayer, ii. 324.

negotiated a treaty with us by her Executive, and then that her Executive took no steps to persuade her Congress to ratify it.   Indeed she did exactly what we did with Denmark thirty years ago in the case of St. Thomas, what we have done lately with several commercial treaties and what the present Administration did with Great Britain within a year in the matter of the Newfoundland fishery treaty." [1]

Senator Shelby M. Cullom was present at an interview between President Roosevelt and Senator George F. Hoar and has thus related the incident : "The President wanted the Senator to read a Message which he had already prepared in reference to Colombia's action . . . [probably the Message of January 4, 1904]. The President was sitting on the table, first at one side of Senator Hoar and then on the other, talking in his usual vigorous fashion, trying to get the Senator's attention to the Message. Senator Hoar seemed averse to reading it but finally sat down, and without seeming to pay any particular attention to what he was perusing, remained for a minute or two, then arose and said 'I hope I may never live to see the day when the interests of my country are placed above its honor.'   He at once retired from the room without uttering another word." [2]

It must not be forgotten however, that Roosevelt, Hay and Root who was Secretary of War at the time of taking Panama, are a powerful trio to combat.   Roosevelt and Hay represented a common-sense view while Root's legal analysis is very strong.[3]   Their action was

---

[1] Record, 316 *et seq.*
[2] Fifty Years of Public Service, 212.
[3] Bishop, i. 301 *et seq.*

in no way for self-aggrandizement but solely in the interest of the country that they represented. "The canal would not have been built at all save for the action I took," declared Roosevelt in 1913.[1] There is no question that he believed this sincerely to the day of his death, but for the moment in this statement he indulged in prophecy forgetting Hosea Biglow's remark, "Don't never prophesy — onless ye know."

A Junta of the provisional government of Panama appointed Philippe Bunau-Varilla "Envoy Extraordinary and Minister Plenipotentiary near the Government of the United States with full powers for political and financial negotiations." On November 13 the Republic of Panama was recognized by the United States. This action was followed by like recognition of France, Germany, Denmark, Russia, Sweden and Norway, Nicaragua, Peru, China, Cuba, Great Britain, Italy, Costa Rica, Japan and Austria-Hungary.[2] On November 18 Hay and Bunau-Varilla signed the Treaty which goes under their names. It was soon ratified by Panama.[3] The United States Senate ratified it on February 23, 1904, by a vote of 66 : 14. Under it the canal was built.

"We were able to make with Panama a much more satisfactory treaty than we had with Colombia," wrote Cullom.[4] The United States guaranteed the independence of Panama. Panama granted to the United States a zone of land ten miles wide from which the cities of Panama and Colon (the Pacific and Caribbean seaports)

---

[1] Autobiography, 569; see also Fear God and Take Your Own Part, written in 1916, 305.
[2] Roosevelt, January 4, 1904. Foreign Relations, 276.
[3] Panama, P. Bunau-Varilla, 349, 364, 367, 372, 384.
[4] Fifty Years of Public Service, 383.

were excepted, but the United States was given full power to enforce the sanitation and public order of those two cities. The United States was to pay to Panama ten millions in gold coin and, beginning nine years after the ratification of the treaty, an annual payment of $250,000. Panama granted to the United States authority to fortify the canal and "if it should become necessary at any time," to employ its land and naval forces at its discretion.[1]

"After paying $40,000,000 to J. P. Morgan & Co. for their subsequent transfer to the new company," so wrote Bunau-Varilla, "the American Government resumed on the 4th of May 1904, the work of completion of the great French undertaking after fifteen years, four months and twenty days practical suspension of activity." [2]

James Bryce wrote about the canal in a manner to gratify the American heart, when the source is considered. "In these forty miles of canal," he said, "(or fifty if we reckon from deep water to deep water) the two most remarkable pieces of engineering work are the gigantic dam (with its locks) at Gatun and the gigantic cutting at Culebra, each the hugest of its kind that the world has to shew. . . . Nothing less than an earthquake will

---

[1] Treaties relating to the Panama Canal, 13.

[2] Panama, 430. I have used Foreign Relations, 1903, more than the citations to them seem to warrant. All the despatches of our competent minister to Colombia, Beaupré, are well worth reading. Theodore Roosevelt, Autobiography; Life of Hay, Thayer, ii.; do. Roosevelt; Bishop; Life of Hanna, Croly; Panama, Bunau-Varilla; do. The Great Adventure of Panama. I have also used Roosevelt, Fear God and Take Your Own Part; Life of Roosevelt, Leupp; do. Lewis; The Panama Gateway, Bishop; Life of Foraker, ii.; Encyclopædia Britannica; Senate debate on Treaty with Columbia, open executive session, April, 1921, especially speeches of Senators Lodge, Kellogg, Knox, Borah and Johnson.

affect them and of earthquakes there is no record in this region though they are frequent in Costa Rica, two hundred miles away. . . .   There is something in the magnitude and the methods of this enterprise which a poet might take as his theme.   Never before on our planet has so much labor, so much scientific knowledge, and so much executive skill been concentrated on a work designed to bring the nations nearer to one another and serve the interests of all mankind. . . .   The chief engineer, Colonel Goethals, is the head not only of the whole scheme of construction but of the whole administration, and his energy, judgment and power of swift decision are recognized to have been a prime factor in the progress of the work and the excellence of the administrative details.   The houses erected by the United States government are each of them surrounded on every floor by a fine wire netting which, while freely admitting the air, excludes winged insects.   All the hospitals have been netted so carefully that no insect can enter to carry out infection from a patient. . . .   The discovery, made while the United States troops were occupying Cuba after the war of 1898, that yellow fever is due to the bite of the Stegomyia, carrying infection from a patient to a healthy person, and that intermittent fevers are due to the bite of the Anopheles, similarly bearing poison from the sick to the sound, made it possible to enter on a campaign for the prevention of these diseases among the workers on the Isthmus. . . .   One may be for days and nights on the Isthmus and neither see nor hear nor feel a mosquito.   To have made one of the pest houses of the world . . . as healthy as Boston or London is an achievement of which the American medical staff and their country

for them, may well be proud; [1] and the name of Colonel
Gorgas, the head of that medical staff to whose unwea-
ried zeal and care this achievement is largely due, deserves
to stand on the roll of fame beside that of Colonel Goethals, the chief engineer and chairman of the Commission, who has directed and is bringing to its successful
issue, this whole great enterprise. . . . It is expected that
the construction of the canal will be found, when it is
finished, to have cost nearly $400,000,000." [2]

Bryce in 1921 disposes of what was at the time a
mooted question. " It deserves to be noted," writes
Bryce, "as a mark of Roosevelt's good sense and dis-
cernment that he had, at an early stage in the long debates
over the canal project, made up his mind that a sea level
canal was practically out of the question. There was
a grandiosity about the idea of an ocean highway with no
locks which might have been expected to attract him.
But his gift for weighing arguments and reaching the
correct conclusion made him grasp and hold fast to the
decision [that of a lock canal] which experience has abundantly approved." [3]

---

[1] For a striking article on the sanitation of the Isthmus see Charles F.
Adams, Massachusetts Historical Society, May 1911, 610.

[2] South America, 23 *et seq*. The cost up to 1916 according to
Theodore Roosevelt was $375,000,000, Fear God and Take Your Own
Part, 311.

Up to June 30, 1920, $467,431,257.41 had been appropriated for the
canal. Of this $379,840,741.92 was appropriated for the construction of
the canal and its immediate adjuncts. The rest went to: fortifications,
$34,658,400.81; nine annual payments to Panama, $2,250,000; for operation and maintenance, $50,511,914.68. Up to the same date $7,215,288.68
had been repaid on the cost of construction; $33,303,581.67 had been
collected in tolls. Other receipts besides those two make the total receipts to June 30, 1920, $42,176,261.22. — Report of Governor of the Pan-
ama Canal, 1920, 155, 156.

[3] Review of J. B. Bishop's Roosevelt. The *Literary Review*, N. Y. *Eve.
Post*, Feb. 19, 1921.

CHAPTER XI

HENRY WHITE wrote in a private letter, "Roosevelt was the only man I have ever met who combined the qualities of an able politician at home with those of an equally good diplomatist abroad." We have seen something of his work as diplomatist in Chapter IX and shall see more as the history goes on; he was now to measure himself against the ablest politician in the United States, unless he himself were entitled to that designation, Mark Hanna. The stake was the Republican nomination for the presidency in 1904. Hanna did not approve of Roosevelt's action toward the large financial interests of the country, yet feeling that Roosevelt might have the country at his back did not act openly in opposition. On the contrary, to a certain extent, he worked with him and the President was grateful for his assistance. Writing to Taft, then Civil Governor of the Philippines, under date of March 13, 1903, he said, "With both Hanna and Aldrich I had to have a regular stand-up fight before I could get them to accept any trust legislation, but when I once got them to say they would give in, they kept their promise in good faith and it was far more satisfactory to work with them than to try to work with the alleged radical reformers." [1]

Under this seeming harmony there was, however, a quiet opposition. Hanna had the support of the financial and business interests of the country but he was

---

[1] Bishop, i. 237.

keen enough to know that something beside the backing of Wall Street and associated interests was necessary to the man who had political aspirations. He secured the support of the Labor Unions. During August, 1902, he declared: "The natural tendency in this country, ay, and in the world over, has been the selfish appropriation of the larger share by capital. As long as labor was in a situation which forced it to submit, that condition would to a very large degree continue. If labor had some grievance and each laborer in his individual capacity went to his employer and asked for consideration, how much would be shown to him? Not much. Therefore when they banded together in an organization for their own benefit which would give them power, if necessary, to demand a remedy, I say organized labor was justified. . . . It is truly astonishing to consider what trivial disagreements have occasioned some of the most serious strikes. I have seen two parties stand apart, each with a chip on his shoulder, defying his opponent to knock it off. . . . While labor unions may have proved a curse to England, I believe that they will prove a boon to our own country. . . . Two factors contributed to the prosperity of our nation — the man who works with his hands and the man who works with his head — partners in toil who ought to be partners in the profit of that toil." And again in May, 1903, "I believe in organized labor and I believe in organized capital as an auxiliary." [1]

Collective bargaining was Hanna's remedy for labor troubles and this doctrine he thoroughly elaborated. By his famous "stand pat" speech at Akron during September, 1902,[2] he won the support of manufacturers and busi-

---

[1] Croly, 405 et seq.   [2] See Croly, 417, for a full account of it.

ness men who did not want the present tariff disturbed. That Roosevelt and Hanna seemed to be drifting apart troubled a supporter of Roosevelt who was likewise a thorough-going Republican; together, he said, their power among Republicans was immense; should they openly differ and put up a fight they could smash the party. This was reported to Hanna who looked grave but said nothing. To a further remark that he seemed to have with him two inconsistent influences, the financial interests and organized labor, he said simply, I have the support of both. Hanna had likewise the backing of the Roman Catholic Church and of the Salvation Army, so that he was not an opponent to be despised and he was not in any respect thought slightingly of by Roosevelt.

The opposition between the two became public during May, 1903, and the occasion was the Republican State Convention of Ohio which met in June. Roosevelt desired ardently the presidential nomination; he was popular throughout the country evidenced by many official declarations in his favor. He kept himself before the public, travelling about the country, speaking constantly and was in the far West when this threatened disturbance in the relations between Roosevelt and Hanna became known. Foraker, who was senior Senator from Ohio, belonged to a different section of the party from the Hanna-McKinley section and felt that he had not received his share of the patronage under the McKinley administration. For this and from the antagonism that had grown up between him and Senator Hanna, he was willing to widen the breach between the President and the Senator. Prompted as he affirmed, by expressions from Hanna's henchmen, he gave out during the last of May, 1903, an interview in which he declared: "Roosevelt has made a good President. He has been alert, aggressive and brilliant and with it all he has been successful. . . . He is to-day the best known and the most popular man in the United States. . . . Many States indorsed and declared last year in favor of him as our candidate for 1904. Nearly all the Northern States will make similar declarations this year. I do not know of any reason why Ohio should not also declare in favor of him. . . . I think it would be very wise for the Republicans of Ohio at the approaching State convention not only to indorse the administration of President Roosevelt, but also to declare their intention to support him next year as our candidate for the Presidency." [1] On May 24 Hanna replied to this in a statement which was given to the press. "I am not, and will not be, a candidate for the Presidential nomination. On account of my position as Chairman of the Republican National Committee and the further fact that this year I am supposed to have a vital interest in the results in Ohio as bearing upon my reëlection to the United States Senate, it would be presumed that I might have some influence as to the policy or action of the State convention this year in national affairs. In that connection, it would seem apparent that whatever that influence might be it had been exerted in a direction which would cause just criticism on the part of any other person who might aspire to be a candidate for the Republican nomination for President in 1904. For these reasons I am opposed to the adoption of such a resolution."

---

[1] Notes of a Busy Life, Foraker, ii. 110.

On the same day Hanna telegraphed to the President who was at Seattle, Washington: "The issue that has been forced upon me in the matter of our State convention this year indorsing you for Republican nomination next year has come in a way which makes it necessary for me to oppose such a resolution. When you know all the facts I am sure that you will approve my course." Roosevelt replied on the same day: "Your telegram received. I have not asked any man for his support. I have nothing whatever to do with raising this issue. Inasmuch as it has been raised, of course, those who favor my administration and my nomination will favor indorsing both, and those who do not will oppose." This brought from Hanna the rejoinder on May 26: "Your telegram of the 23d received. In view of the sentiment expressed I shall not oppose the indorsement of your administration and candidacy by our State convention. I have given the substance of this to the Associated Press." On May 29 in reply to a letter from Hanna Roosevelt wrote from Ogden, Utah: "Your interview was everywhere accepted as the first open attack on me, and it gave heart, curiously enough, not only to my opponents but to all the men who lump you and me together as improperly friendly to organized labor and to the working men generally. . . . The general belief was that this was not your move save indirectly; but that it was really an attack by the so-called Wall Street forces on me, to which you had been led to give a reluctant acquiescence. . . . After thinking the matter carefully over I became sure that I had to take a definite stand myself. I hated to do it, because you have shown such generosity and straightforwardness in all your dealings with me that it was peculiarly painful to me to be put, even temporarily, in a position of seeming antagonism to you. No one but a really big man — a man above all petty considerations — could have treated me as you have done during the year and a half since President McKinley's death. I have consulted you and relied on your judgment more than I have done with any other man." [1] Two days previously Roosevelt wrote confidentially to Senator Lodge: "I decided that the time had come to stop shilly-shallying and let Hanna know definitely that I did not intend to assume the position, at least passively, of a suppliant to whom he might give the nomination as a boon. . . . I rather expected Hanna to fight, but made up my mind that it was better to have a fight in the open at once than to run the risk of being knifed secretly. . . . I am pleased at the outcome and it simplifies things all round, for in my judgment, Hanna was my only formidable opponent so far as the nomination is concerned." [2]

There can be no question that the President gained in this controversy. The adroit cartoonist of the *New York Herald* illustrated this in a picture of Hanna shaking his fist at Foraker and with not the best grace in the world, handing a bouquet, labelled "endorsement" to Roosevelt who expressed himself as "delighted." [3] But no change in their personal relations followed. On June 10 the President attended the marriage of Hanna's daughter Ruth to Joseph Medill McCormick, addressing in his hearty manner the Senator who met him at the railway station as "Uncle Mark." The Senator made

---

[1] Croly, 424 *et seq.*
[2] Bishop, i. 245.
[3] A Cartoon History of Roosevelt's Career, Albert Shaw, 95.

the wedding a festive occasion and gathered together a number of personal and political friends.

Mark Hanna's eye was on the Ohio political campaign of 1903 when the issue was fairly made. Should he be reëlected to the senatorship over his Democratic opponent? His party had carried Ohio the previous year by an immense majority but a strict personal issue was absent. It may be said that he now [i. e., in 1903] dominated the campaign, carrying the State by over 100,000 for the Republican nominee for governor, Myron T. Herrick, and with a Republican majority on the joint ballot of 91 in the legislature, a very gratifying result which put Mark Hanna to the fore again as a candidate for the presidential nomination.

In the meantime the President had lost the support of a part at least of organized labor. On May 19, the Public Printer discharged William A. Miller; the real reason was his expulsion from a local union. Miller contested his dismissal and carried the case to the Civil Service Commission that reported in his favor, whereupon the President ordered him to be reinstated. The American Federation of Labor took up the case and decided the action of the President unfriendly. Roosevelt gave their Executive Council, at the head of which was Samuel Gompers, their President, an interview in which he justified his action, writing in a private letter somewhat before his talk to the labor representatives: "It is a sheer waste of time for those people, through such resolutions as those of the unions you quote, to threaten me with defeat for the Presidency next year. Nothing would hire me even to accept the Presidency if I had to take it on terms which would mean a forfeiting of self-

respect. . . . . I should refuse to take it at the cost of un-
doing what I did in the matter of Miller and the Labor
Union. The labor unions and the trust magnates may
perhaps unite against me. If so, I shall do my level best
to make the fight an open one and beat them — and I
think I run a good chance of winning; and if I fail I shall
not regret the policy I have pursued." [1] The President
thought that he had at his back the "one-suspender men,"
otherwise called by a sturdy democrat, "the dinner-pail
men," the small shopkeepers and a large proportion of
the farmers.

The Wall Street men and Hanna are working together
to prevent my nomination in Chicago, said the President.
So far as Wall Street was concerned he was right. The
financial interests were opposed to Roosevelt and they
believed that anything to beat him was the correct policy.
A reasonable amount of money could be raised to secure
for Hanna the nomination and election, and they and
certain politicians were at one in the conviction that
Roosevelt if nominated could not be elected. But Hanna
would give them no countenance, nor would he declare
for Roosevelt. The breach widened. George B. Cortelyou,
who had been McKinley's and Roosevelt's private secretary and was now Secretary of the new Department
of Commerce and Labor, made an attempt to bring the
two together. He went to see the Senator, who declared
that "he was not a candidate, that he had never been
nor would be a candidate." So he had assured Roosevelt
but he was tired, he said, "of going to the White House
every day, of putting his hand on his heart and being

---

[1] Bishop, i. 251. As regards the Miller case, ibid., 249 *et seq.*; Roosevelt, Messages, *Current Lit.* Pub. Co., i. 159 *et seq.*

sworn in." Somewhat later Cortelyou went to see the President and found him in conference with three friends, one of whom was a member of the Cabinet and another a Senator. The President said in his emphatic way, "Yes, Mr. Hanna ought to make an unequivocal public statement of his position," when Cortelyou assured the President and his friends that "Mr. Hanna has no intention of being a candidate for President." [1]

Thus affairs continued during December, 1903, and January, 1904. It is not difficult to understand Hanna's position. He did not believe in Roosevelt's policy toward the financial and business interests of the country and Hanna knew that he had their backing and also that of the Labor Unions; had he been ten years younger and in good health he would probably have made a fight against Roosevelt for the Republican nomination. But his health was poor, he was 66, he knew the power which the national administration could exert for the nomination and he hesitated to take up the contest. With design therefore, he let the golden moment slip when he was present at Columbus, making a brief speech of thanks to the Ohio legislature for the senatorship and failing to announce his candidacy for the presidential nomination. Late that month Cornelius N. Bliss said that Hanna had wittingly let pass the nick of time; had he eighteen days previously declared himself a candidate, he and Roosevelt would have been competitors for the nomination.[2]

Some of Hanna's advocates were determined to force

---

[1] Croly, 437. According to Croly, James R. Garfield, then Commissioner of Corporations, and Theodore E. Burton, representative from the Cleveland district, were effective in preventing the breach from widening. See also letter of O. H. Platt, cited by Croly, 441.

[2] The address in Columbus was Jan. 12, 1904; the talk of Bliss, Jan. 30.

the nomination upon him and argued that, as the call of States was in alphabetical order, Alabama and Arkansas would first be called, would vote for Hanna whence there would come a tidal wave that would result in his nomination. Charles G. Washburn, a friend and college classmate of Roosevelt, wrote: "I was a delegate to the Convention that nominated Roosevelt for President in 1904. A portrait, of heroic size, of Mark Hanna, hung over the platform. I said to a man who sat next to me 'What would happen if Hanna were living?' He said in reply, 'He would be nominated here to-day.'" [1]

By the end of January, 1904, Roosevelt was confident, writing thus to Shaw: "In confidence I can tell you that outside all the Southern States I am now as certain as I well can be that if Hanna made the fight (for the nomination) and with all the money of Wall Street behind him, he would get the majority of the delegations from no State excepting Ohio; and from the South I should have from a third to a half of the delegates, and most of the remainder would have been pledged to me and would have to be purchased outright against me. I believe that the best advisers among my opponents themselves see this and have very nearly made up their minds to give up the contest. In a few weeks I think that most of the Wall Street Republicans will have concluded that they have to, however grudgingly, support me. . . . My nomination has become assured, in my judgment, before they give up the contest." [2]

Hanna was capable of a high aspiration and this took the form with him of a reconcilement between capital

---

[1] Roosevelt, 53.   [2] Bishop, i. 314.

and labor to which he was willing to devote his business experience and political standing. Unquestionably he as leading Senator and Roosevelt as President might have accomplished much; both loved their country and would make personal sacrifices for it; both had personal morals above reproach; both had a high idea of service; but the two could not work sympathetically together. Shakespeare told why, "An two men ride of a horse, one must ride behind." [1]

Now entered upon the scene the King of Terrors. Hanna died on February 15, 1904. While lying upon his death-bed in the Arlington Hotel, the President called to inquire after his condition and on February 5 received this pencilled note: "My dear Mr. President: You touched a tender spot, old man, when you called personally to inquire after [me] this A.M. I may be worse, before I can be better, but all the same such 'drops of kindness' are good for a fellow." To this Roosevelt replied: "Dear Senator: Indeed it is *your* letter from your sick bed which is touching, not my visit. May you soon be with us again, old fellow, as strong in body and as vigorous in your leadership as ever." [2]

His death was regarded as a calamity in Cleveland; and in his State of Ohio, it seemed as if a prop to the nation had been taken away. Roosevelt wrote to Root on the next day: "No man had larger traits than Hanna. He was a big man in every way and as forceful a personality as we have seen in public life in our generation." [3] The Chaplain of the Senate, Reverend Edward Everett Hale, spoke thus over his dead body: "This man had at

---

[1] Much Ado, iii. 5.   [2] Croly, 453, 454.
[3] Bishop, i. 315.

once as no other man had, the confidence of capital and labor. He could mediate between the men who provide the tools and the workmen who handle them." Later his senatorial associates paid him high tributes. Foraker said : "He was one of the really great men of his day and generation. . . . He had before him seven years of service." His personal friend, Senator Platt of Connecticut, declared, "that when Marcus A. Hanna died all the people mourned with a grief that was deep and unfeigned." Senator Fairbanks said truthfully, "He possessed in full degree the power of great initiative." Senator Beveridge said that, "He was the man of affairs in statesmanship . . .; he was the personification of our commercial age." [1] "*The New York Evening Post* crowd," as Roosevelt called them, could not join in these tributes. They may have taken their cue from their great progenitor who wrote, "I do not like the Western type of man." [2] In that they differed from Roosevelt who broke out, "I do like these Westerners."

Between these eulogists and detractors of Hanna it is pleasant to hear from a moderator, Edward D. White, who as Justice of the Supreme Court was well acquainted with Hanna, admired and loved him, who one night in December, 1920, long after he had been Chief Justice, could talk of naught else, testifying his high regard for the ability, honor and unselfishness of Hanna.

Hanna was now out of the way. No man in public life took his place in partial antagonism to Roosevelt. The coast was clear. He was nominated by acclamation at the Republican National Convention that assembled

---

[1] Memorial Addresses, pp. 15, 31, 49, 77, 110.
[2] Life of Godkin, Ogden, ii.

in Chicago, June 21, 1904.   Charles G. Washburn, later
Congressman from the Worcester district, a keen judge
of men, wrote in his book adding to what I have already
cited: "Of course Hanna would not have been nominated. . . . The old order which was incarnated in Hanna
had not then passed away but it was passing. . . . When
McKinley and Hanna died, the old dynasty fell." [1]

---

[1] Roosevelt, 54.

CHAPTER XII

IN accepting the nomination for the presidency Roosevelt showed that he was a true partisan Republican as, in his speech of acceptance, he dilated on the "Record of the Republican party," on the currency and the tariff. "We have placed the finances of the Nation upon a sound gold basis," he said. "We have enacted a tariff law under which during the past few years the country has attained a height of material well-being never before reached." In his letter he elaborated his position on the tariff taking the ground of the educated man who had been led to believe in the virtue of protection. "The question of what tariff is best for our people is primarily one of expediency, to be determined not on abstract academic grounds but in the light of experience. It is a matter of business"; and he repeated the Republican stock argument against the Democratic tariff of 1894.[1]

The Democrats had nominated Alton B. Parker, Chief Justice of the Court of Appeals of the State of New York, who, declining to run on a platform squinting in the direction of free silver, had eliminated from the contest the money question. Nor was the tariff an issue to be decided. The issue of the campaign was Roosevelt. "Your personality has been the Administration," wrote Elihu Root.[2] This meant largely what Roosevelt had done in attacking the great financial interests of the coun-

---

[1] The speech was July 27; the letter, September 12. *Current Lit.* Pub. Co., 198, 200, 213.　　　　[2] Bishop, i. 323.

try which, after much consideration, had selected Parker
as their candidate. They had coquetted with Grover
Cleveland. "It is evident," wrote Roosevelt to Senator
Lodge on May 4, 1903, "Cleveland has the presidential
bee in his bonnet, and it is equally evident that a large
number of people are desirous of running him again." [1]
Nevertheless his decision not to accept another nomination became "unalterable."

Toward its end Parker brought personalities into the
campaign which must be considered. Roosevelt had selected as chairman of the Republican National Committee George B. Cortelyou, after having vainly endeavored
to secure Elihu Root, W. Murray Crane and Cornelius N.
Bliss. Cortelyou had been Cleveland's executive clerk,
private secretary of McKinley and Roosevelt, and was
then Secretary of Commerce and Labor, appointed
by Roosevelt. A fair inference from Judge Parker's
speeches was that President Roosevelt and Cortelyou
had used their official positions to induce corporations to
contribute funds. Roosevelt, having a high regard for the
dignity of his office, had held aloof from a public participation in the campaign but these speeches of Parker gave him
a long-sought-for opportunity of taking a hand in the contest
as a fighter, and on November 4 [2] he made this statement:
"The assertion that Mr. Cortelyou had any knowledge
gained while in an official position, whereby he was enabled
to secure and did secure any contributions from any corporation is a falsehood. . . . The assertion that there
has been made in my behalf and by my authority, by

---

[1] Bishop, i. 241.
[2] The election was on November 8. Charles W. Fairbanks of Indiana
was chosen Vice-President.

Mr. Cortelyou or by anyone else, any pledge or promise, or that there has been any understanding as to future immunities or benefits, in recognition of any contributions from any source, is a wicked falsehood. . . . As Mr. Cortelyou has said to me more than once during the campaign, if elected I shall go into the Presidency unhampered by any pledge, promise or understanding of any kind, sort or description, save my promise made openly to the American people, that so far as in my power lies I shall see to it that every man has a square deal, no less and no more." [1]

The Nation, which was an enthusiastic supporter of Parker, maintained that the gravamen of Parker's charges was that the beneficiaries of the tariff policy of the Republican party were to be recouped for their contributions in the event of Republican success. But Roosevelt did not so interpret the charges. Indeed *The Nation* failed to iterate with its accustomed vigor Parker's charges against Roosevelt and Cortelyou, proposing apparently to shield him under the stock Democratic argument against the tariff and the Republican party.[2]

Of the same nature was the Harriman attack which was made public more than two years later and which was to the effect that Roosevelt had requested Harriman to raise $250,000 for the presidential campaign. Roosevelt denied this emphatically. "I never," he said, "requested Mr. Harriman to raise a dollar for the Presidential campaign of 1904. On the contrary, our communications as regards the campaign related exclusively to the fight being made against Mr. Higgins for Governor of

---

[1] *Current Lit.* Pub. Co., 222 *et seq.*   [2] *The Nation*, 1904, 24, 180, 250, 365.

New York. . . . He was concerned only in getting me
to tell Mr. Cortelyou to aid Mr. Higgins so far as he
could, which I gladly did." [1]   It was well known that at
Republican headquarters, New York State was considered in danger, not lest its electoral vote should fail Roosevelt, but whether the Republican candidate for governor
should be elected.

Roosevelt was triumphantly chosen. He was almost
the only one among his supporters who doubted the result [2] that went far ahead of his anticipations. "I am
stunned by the overwhelming victory we have won,"
he wrote to his son. "I have the greatest popular majority and the greatest electoral majority ever given to
a candidate for President." [3] He carried the border
slave States, of West Virginia and Missouri; while having
a popular plurality of 50 in Maryland, he received only one
of her electoral votes. As a result of this election when
Congress met December 4, 1905, there were in the Senate
57 Republicans to 32 Democrats; [4] in the House, 249 Republicans to 137 Democrats.

On the night of election after it was known that he
was triumphantly chosen, he gave out from the White
House this statement, "The wise custom which limits
the President to two terms regards the substance and
not the form, and under no circumstances will I be a candidate for or accept another nomination." [5]

---

[1] *Current Lit.* Pub. Co., 427.
[2] See My Brother T. Roosevelt, Mrs. Robinson, 217. But Roosevelt
was eager to be elected and anxious in regard to the result.
[3] Bishop, i. 335; see also letter to Henry White, 316, 332, and to Kipling, 332.
[4] There was one vacancy.
[5] Life of Roosevelt, Lewis, 234. Bishop has "A" instead of "The,"
334.

Roosevelt had now received a mandate from the people with the House and Senate largely Republican. Before proceeding to tell what he accomplished during his second administration it will be well to recount what he had done when as Vice-President he succeeded to the presidency, that in the course of the narrative has not been considered. What exasperated the large financial interests was his so-called attack on them; he was insistent on Federal regulation and did not believe that it could properly be left to the States. "The Sherman Anti-Trust Law [the Act of 1890. For Acts of 1887 and 1890 see my viii. 288, 358] was a dead letter," wrote Cullom, "until Roosevelt instructed the Attorney General to prosecute its violators, both great and small." [1] Roosevelt said with truth, "Publicity and not secrecy, will win hereafter." [2] He had a Congress fairly obedient to his wish. He wrote during August, 1906: "By the enactment of the Elkins law and by the creation of the Department of Commerce and Labor including the Bureau of Corporations, Congress enabled us to make great strides in advance along the path of thus bringing the use of wealth in business under the supervision and regulation of the National Government — for, in actual practice it has proved a sham and pretence to say that the several States can thus supervise and regulate it." [3] The Elkins law, passed February 19, 1903, forbade rebates. Congress passed on February 14, 1903, an act creating a Department of Commerce and Labor including a Bureau of Corporations. Such action was due to the warm

---

[1] Fifty Years of Public Service, 292.   [2] Message of December, 1904.
[3] Letter to James E. Watson. *Current Lit.* Pub. Co., 400.

recommendation of the President, who appointed as its
first Secretary George B. Cortelyou.

During March, 1904, the President established by executive order "a service pension for all veterans of the Civil
War" between 62 and 70.[1] This was called by his opponents an unconstitutional exercise of power and a bid
for the soldiers' vote as represented by the Grand Army
of the Republic. But supporters of Roosevelt will adopt
a defence of this action as exhibited in his private letters.
In one written during May he said that the feeling in
Congress "was overwhelmingly for a full service pension
— that is $12.00 a month beginning at the age of 62."
Such a measure would have cost the Government about
fifty millions annually, while his order would carry
only about five millions. "So much," he wrote, "for
the technical argument." But "I hold that the ruling
was absolutely right and proper. Most of our friends
who live softly do not understand that the great majority
of people who live by hard manual labor have begun to

---

[1] D. M. Matteson has prepared the following note : The order which
is signed by the Commissioner of Pensions is dated March 15, 1904. It
is based on the Act of June 27, 1890, which declared that the pension should
be from $6 to $12 according to the degree of inability to earn a support.
The order said, "old age is an infirmity the average nature and extent of
which the experience of the Pension Bureau has established with reasonable certainty." As the Act of 1887 established an old age pension for
Mexican War veterans 39 years after that war, and as 1904 is 39 years
after the Civil War, therefore it is ordered that all veterans of the Civil
War of 62 years or more shall be considered as "disabled one half in ability
to perform manual labor" and entitled to $6 a month; after 65 years,
to $8; after 68, to $10; and after 70, to $12.

President Cleveland had issued an order making 75 years a complete
disability and President McKinley one making 65 a half disability.

Congress on Feb. 6, 1907, established a regular old age pension for Mexican veterans of a minimum of 60 days' service and Civil War veterans
of a minimum of 90 days' service, giving $12 a month at 62 as the minimum
and $20 at 75 as the maximum.

find their wage-earning capacity seriously impaired by the
time they are sixty. . . . Now the average wage worker
does not lay by enough money to keep him in his old age,
and when he has fought in the Civil War I am entirely
willing that he shall be cared for to the extent indicated
in my order." [1]

The phrase "our friends who live softly" is a partial
keynote to Roosevelt's administrative career. Assuredly
he thought more highly of them if they were doing what
he considered good work than of men devoted to the
mere amassing of wealth, and he was willing to award
them full credit; but other letters written at about this
time show that he did not look to them for his main support. They were "the gentle folk," as he wrote to his
friend Owen Wister after the election of 1904, "the people
whom you and I meet at the houses of our friends and
at our clubs; the people who went to Harvard as we
did." But I owed my election "above all to Abraham
Lincoln's 'plain people,' to the folk who worked hard on
farm, in shop, or on the railroads, or owned little stores,
little businesses which they managed themselves." [2] In
the same vein he wrote to Sir George Otto Trevelyan
soon after his inauguration in 1905: "My supporters
are to be found in the overwhelming majority among
those whom Abraham Lincoln called the plain people.
. . . The farmers, lumbermen, mechanics, ranchmen,
miners of the North, East and West have felt that I was
just as much in sympathy with them, just as devoted
to their interests, and as proud of them and as representative
of them as if I had sprung from among their own ranks." [3]

---

[1] Bishop, i. 318 *et seq.*
[2] Bishop, i. 345.   [3] Ibid., 364.

Yet Roosevelt was far from being a demagogue. He upheld without ceasing the right of private property; he was bitterly opposed to socialism and he agreed in the main with those who held to individual ideas; he enjoyed the companionship of men who lived softly and he liked a good dinner party. To those who appreciated the innate refinement of John Hay, his words come with peculiar force. "It is a comfort to work for a President who . . . happened to be born a gentleman."[1] As the event has shown, the financial interests and many of the men who lived softly — perhaps a majority — committed an error when they did not at this time hold up the hands of Theodore Roosevelt. Publicity was important for the investor, which he had through the Fourth Estate; the prohibition of rebates was necessary for the small business men; the watering of stock was a menace to the sterling interest of the country; the wage earners had their journals which kept them informed of the doings of Big Business. To them it seemed easy work to cut off coupons, to draw dividends, to take the air by riding about in automobiles, and they looked upon Roosevelt as a champion who was going to insure them a better time, although they had leaders like John Mitchell who interpreted for them correctly what the Roosevelt good time meant. In the state of public sentiment succeeding the Cleveland-McKinley régime the financial interests should have looked upon Roosevelt as their best friend. It was true, as Elihu Root told many of the representatives of Big Business at the Union League Club during February, 1904: "You say Roosevelt is an un-

---

[1] Bishop, i. 263

safe man. I tell you he is a great conservator of property and rights." [1]

The year 1904 must not be passed by without a mention of the St. Louis World Fair which celebrated the Louisiana Purchase. John Hay "grumbled when the President made him go to St. Louis to address" the representatives of the press. "The years of my boyhood," he said, "were passed on the banks of the Mississippi, and the great river was the scene of my early dreams." [2] But Henry Adams remarked, "John Hay was as strange to the Mississippi River as though he had not been bred on its shores." Adams went with Hay and has thus described a part of their journey from Washington to St. Louis: "In this great region from Pittsburg through Ohio and Indiana, agriculture had made way for steam; tall chimneys reeked smoke on every horizon, and dirty suburbs filled with scrap-iron, scrap-paper and cinders formed the setting of every town."

Hay's address was a glorification of material progress, of the advance of America, of the great significance of the Louisiana Purchase, but the comment of his friend, Henry Adams, strikes more forcibly the student of affairs: "The St. Louis Exposition," he wrote, was the first creation of the new American "in the twentieth century and for that reason acutely interesting. One saw here a third rate town of half-a-million people without history, education, unity, or art and with little capital . . . doing what London or New York would have shrunk from attempting. This new social conglomerate, with no tie but its steam power and not much of that, threw away

---

[1] Washburn's Roosevelt, 67.   [2] Addresses, 244.

thirty or forty million dollars on a pageant as ephemeral as a stage flat." There were "long lines of white palaces exquisitely lighted by thousands on thousands of electric candles." [1]

But the correspondent of *The Nation* thought that in architectural beauty the St. Louis Exposition was inferior to that in Chicago and further said that in electrical display it had not the mighty Niagara for help.[2]

A feature was the "Congress of Arts and Science," the main purpose of which "was to place within reach of the investigator the objective thought of the world, so classified as to show its relations to all similar phases of human endeavor, and so arranged as to be practically available for reference and study." To the disinterested and valuable advice of President Nicholas Murray Butler and President William R. Harper the Congress was under heavy obligations. The teaching was in the form of lectures and the reading of papers and more than a hundred leading scholars of Europe assisted the American contributors "under conditions where academic fellowship on an equal footing was a necessary part of the work. . . . It was a real feast of international scholarship." [3]

---

[1] Henry Adams, Education, 466.   [2] *The Nation*, 1904.
[3] Congress of Arts and Science. Universal Exposition, St. Louis, 1904, i. 3, 133. H. J. Rogers, Hugo Münsterberg.

CHAPTER XIII

BEFORE Roosevelt was inaugurated and before he began therefore the term which was his own, he showed his power as diplomatist. War between Russia and Japan began on February 10, 1904, and had in him an attentive observer. In his own words he tells the story. "During the early part of the year 1905," he wrote in his Autobiography, "the strain on the civilized world caused by the Russo-Japanese War became serious. The losses of life and of treasure were frightful. . . . If the war went on I thought it on the whole likely that Russia would be driven" farther west. "But it was very far from certain. There is no certainty in such a war. Japan might have met defeat and defeat to her would have spelt overwhelming disaster; and even if she had continued to win, what she thus won would have been of no value to her, and the cost in blood and money would have left her drained white. I believed therefore that the time had come when it was greatly to the interest of both combatants to have peace, and when therefore it was possible to get both to agree to peace." [1] During January he "privately and unofficially advised the Russian Government, and afterward repeated the advice indirectly through the French Government, to make peace." "The European powers want peace." But "it looks as if the foreign powers did not want me to act as peacemaker," [2] he wrote to Secretary Hay, who was in Europe on account of his physical condition.

---

[1] P. 583.   [2] Bishop, i. 376, 377.

In the two chapters which Bishop has devoted to this subject one may well be amazed, from the confidential correspondence there disclosed, at Roosevelt's knowledge of European conditions and at his various characterizations of European powers and their rulers. Talleyrand said of Alexander Hamilton that he had divined Europe. We may well affirm that Theodore Roosevelt in the early part of the twentieth century had divined Europe. "The Kaiser," he wrote, "has had another fit and is now convinced that France is trying to engineer a congress of the nations in which Germany will be left out. What a jumpy creature he is anyhow!" [1] He is a "fuss-cat." He desired that peace should be made between the two warring powers but he wanted to have a hand in it and was willing to accept other people's ideas if he could call them his own. The Kaiser, he wrote to Hay on April 2, "sincerely believes that the English are planning to attack him and smash his fleet, and perhaps join with France in a war to the death against him. As a matter of fact the English harbor no such intentions, but are themselves in a condition of panic terror lest the Kaiser secretly intend to form an alliance against them with France or Russia, or both, to destroy their fleet and blot out the British Empire from the map! It is as funny a case as I have ever seen of mutual distrust and fear bringing two people to the verge of war." In the same letter to Hay he gave his opinion of the Russian Emperor. "Did you ever know anything more pitiable than the condition of the Russian despotism? The Czar is a preposterous little creature as the absolute autocrat of

---

[1] Bishop, i. 377.

150,000,000 people. He has been unable to make war and he is now unable to make peace." [1]

Roosevelt told the Japanese, "it was in my judgment wise to build a bridge of gold for the beaten enemy"; and they took his advice. On May 27 and 28, 1905, the Japanese annihilated the Russian fleet in the Sea of Japan. Roosevelt, who was an excellent judge of naval matters, thus characterized the engagement, "Neither Trafalgar nor the defeat of the Spanish Armada was as complete — as overwhelming." [2] With amazing wisdom, directly on the heels of this great naval victory, the Japanese made overtures in writing for peace. Roosevelt saw at once the Russian ambassador and "told him to say to the Czar that I believe the war absolutely hopeless for Russia." Now he had the help of the Kaiser.

Roosevelt wrote to Senator Lodge on June 16: "The more I see of the Czar, the Kaiser and the Mikado, the better I am content with democracy, even if we have to include the American newspaper as one of its assets — liability would be a better term. Russia is so corrupt, so treacherous and shifty, and so incompetent, that I am utterly unable to say whether or not it will make peace or break off the negotiations at any moment. Japan is, of course, entirely selfish, though with a veneer of courtesy and with infinitely more knowledge of what it wants and capacity to get it." He wrote in a letter later to Senator Lodge soon after the negotiations had begun: "The Russians are utterly insincere and treacherous; they have no conception of truth, no willingness to look facts in the face, no regard for others of any sort

---

[1] Bishop, i. 378, 379.   [2] Ibid., 351, 352.

or kind, no knowledge of their own strength or weakness ; and they are helplessly unable to meet emergencies." [1]

As related by Bishop the tactfulness and patience of Roosevelt were unsurpassed. With the main point settled many questions of detail arose. There was naturally a conflict as to the place where the plenipotentiaries should meet, and after much debate Washington was fixed upon ; then, after that was decided, Russia desired to change the place of meeting to The Hague. She now ran up against a stone wall. Roosevelt, disgusted with so much shilly-shallying, sent this word to George von L. Meyer, our ambassador in Russia, with instructions to impart it to the Foreign Minister and if necessary to the Czar himself. "I notified Japan that Washington would be the appointed place and so informed" the Russian ambassador. "I then gave the same announcement to the public. It is, of course, out of the question for me to consider any reversal of this action and I regard the incident as closed, so far as the place of meeting is concerned." [2] "Meyer," wrote Roosevelt, "who was, with the exception of Henry White, the most useful diplomat in the American service, rendered literally invaluable aid by insisting on his seeing the Czar at critical periods of the transaction when it was no longer possible for me to act successfully through the representatives of the Czar, who were often at cross purposes with one another." [3] Roosevelt said in a private letter to Senator Nelson of Minnesota, "I have led the horses to water, but Heaven

[1] Bishop, i. 394, 395.
[2] Bishop, i. 391.
[3] Autobiography, 587; Life of Meyer, M. A. de Wolfe Howe, 196 *et seq.*

only knows whether they will drink or start kicking one another beside the trough." [1]

As the conference was to function during the summer, it was recognized that Washington would be too hot, therefore the place of meeting was changed to the Portsmouth Navy Yard [2] near Portsmouth, New Hampshire. The plenipotentiaries were all men of distinguished capacity. Russia was represented by Witte, Secretary of State, and Baron Rosen, Russian ambassador to the United States; Japan by Baron Komura, Secretary of Foreign Affairs, and Takahira, Japanese minister in Washington. The reception of the envoys by Roosevelt showed him a thorough man of the world accustomed to do the proper thing at the proper time. They went separately on two war vessels from New York to Oyster Bay, the summer residence of the President, and were there received by him on board the United States steamer *Mayflower*. Nothing occurred to mar the meeting of the two hostile envoys. The President had a luncheon prepared but, as they all moved together into the saloon and as it was taken standing, no question of preference could be raised. At its end the President proposed this toast: "I drink to the welfare and prosperity of the sovereigns and peoples of the two great nations whose representatives have met one another on this ship. It is my most earnest hope and prayer, in the interest of not only these two great powers but of all mankind, that a just and lasting peace may speedily be concluded between them." [3]   The en-

---

[1] Bishop, i. 398.
[2] The Portsmouth Navy Yard was really in Kittery, Maine.
[3] Bishop, i. 405.

voys then went to Portsmouth and set about their important work.

The President needed all of his tact and influence to prevent the Conference from breaking up. By despatches to Japan and to Russia he was, as Bishop wrote, its "guiding and controlling force." Late in August the crisis occurred and it arose from the Japanese demand for an indemnity and the cession of the island of Saghalien. The President suggested, sending the suggestion at the same time to the Kaiser and the Mikado, that Russia should pay no indemnity whatever and should receive back the north half of Saghalien "for which it is to pay to Japan whatever amount a mixed commission may determine." This suggestion brought about the terms of peace. Japan with paramount wisdom accepted the suggestion. "The Emperor," so came the word to Roosevelt, "after presiding at a Cabinet Council, decided to withdraw the demand of money payment for the cost of war entirely, if Russia recognize the occupation of Saghalien Island by Japan, because the Emperor regards humanity and civilization far more than his nation's welfare." [1] "An agreement was reached on August 29, 1905, on the terms laid down by the President and on September 5, 1905, a treaty of peace embodying them was signed." [2]

The President received praise from all sides. Baron Kaneko wrote to him: "Your advice to us was very powerful and convincing by which the peace of Asia was secured. Both Russia and Japan owe to you this happy conclusion." The Kaiser, the King of England, the

---

[1] Bishop, i. 412 *et ante.*   [2] Ibid., 412.

Czar and the Mikado expressed their approval gracefully.[1] On September 6 the President wrote to the Mikado a letter in which, in giving him high praise, he reflected also his own ideas. "I express," he wrote, "as strongly as I can, my sense of the magnanimity, and above all of the cool-headed, far-sighted wisdom, you have shown in making peace as you did. . . . During the last eighteen months your generals and admirals, your soldiers and sailors, have won imperishable renown for Nippon. . . . You have crowned triumphant war by a peace in which every great object for which you fought is secured, and in so doing you have given to the world a signal and most striking example of how it is possible for a victorious nation to achieve victory over others without losing command over itself. . . . A continuance of the war, no matter how damaging to Japan's opponent, would also have been necessarily of damage to Japan far beyond what could have been offset by any resulting benefit. The greatness of a people, like the greatness of a man, is often attended quite as clearly by moderation and wisdom in using a triumph as by the triumph itself." [2]

Roosevelt was modest in regard to his part in the transaction. He wrote to his daughter: "I am credited with being extremely long-headed. As a matter of fact I took the position I finally did not of my own volition but because events so shaped themselves that I would have felt as if I were flinching from a plain duty if I had acted otherwise." Thus he wrote to Whitelaw Reid, our Ambassador in London, "The Kaiser stood by me like a trump"; but I got only "indirect assistance" from the English Government.[3]

---

[1] Bishop, i. 412 *et ante*.   [2] Bishop, i. 415.   [3] Bishop, i. 415.

Roosevelt's ideas of nations and of men are always valuable. He wrote to Sir George O. Trevelyan on September 12: "I am bound to say that the Japs have impressed me most favorably, not only during these three months but during the four years I have been President. They have always told me the truth. . . . I cannot say that I liked Witte, for I thought his bragging and bluster not only foolish but shockingly vulgar when compared with the gentlemanly self-respecting self-restraint of the Japanese."[1] Witte was much impressed with the great prosperity, wealth and industries of this country; the "barbaric strength" was what appealed to him. Why all this talk about corruption? he inquired. I ask what is this corruption and they tell me that Murphy, the boss of New York, helps great financiers and then accepts presents from them. Why shouldn't he? he asked. Witte, in Roosevelt's opinion, was thoroughly selfish; everything for himself, the country second; while the Japanese were patriotic, so much so that they desired to withdraw that part of the correspondence in which they had made overtures for peace. This request Roosevelt denied and then they were surprised that he was going to make no mention of the matter in his message.[2]

Witte said of Roosevelt: "When one speaks with President Roosevelt he charms through the elevation of his thoughts. . . . He has an ideal and strives for higher aims than a commonplace existence presents." Rosen wrote that Roosevelt "had the moral courage to undertake the delicate and risky task of mediation";

---

[1] Bishop, 418.
[2] In this account, I have been assisted by my conversation with the President on Nov. 16, 1905.

he brought about "the Portsmouth Conference and the subsequent termination of the war by a peace of justice and conciliation." Martens, who was an adviser of the Russians, wrote, "The man who had been represented to us as impetuous to the point of rudeness displayed a gentleness, a kindness and a tactfulness mixed with self-control that only a truly great man can command." [1]

For his services Roosevelt was awarded the Nobel Peace Prize amounting to $36,734.79. [2]

The negotiations were conducted entirely by the President. He did not have the aid of his official Secretary of State, John Hay, who was in Nauheim, Germany, seeking a restoration of his health that never came, as on July 1, 1905, he passed away. Roosevelt paid a sincere tribute to the memory of his friend and showed an attachment to the refined gentleman from the West. [3] He had, so Roosevelt wrote to Senator Lodge, a "great career in political life" and has "also left a deep mark in literature"; to Senator Beveridge, "Hay was a really great man." Hay wrote in his diary seventeen days before he died: "I say to myself that I should not rebel at the thought of my life ending at this time. . . . I have had many blessings, domestic happiness being the greatest of

---

[1] Bishop, i. 419 *et seq.*; see also Impressions of Theodore Roosevelt, Abbott, 131.

[2] For the disposition of the money see Bishop, i. 422; also Albert Shaw, *Review of Reviews*, 151, 152. The *Brooklyn Times* says under the cartoon, "'Teddy the Good' in a new rôle. It is a very laudable purpose but would anybody but Theodore Roosevelt ever think of dedicating a Christmas windfall of $40,000 for such a purpose?" [The cause of industrial peace.]

[3] It used to be said that Hay was a Western man with Eastern culture, Roosevelt an Eastern man with Western principles.

all. . . . I have had success beyond all the dreams of my boyhood. My name is printed in the journals of the world without descriptive qualification, which may, I suppose, be called fame. By mere length of service I shall occupy a modest place in the history of my time. . . . I know death is the common lot and what is universal ought not to be deemed a misfortune; and yet — instead of confronting it with dignity and philosophy, I cling instinctively to life and the things of life as eagerly as if I had not had my chance at happiness and gained nearly all the great prizes." [1]

Roosevelt appointed to the vacant position, Elihu Root. "I wished Root," he wrote to Senator Beveridge, " as Secretary of State partly because I am extremely fond of him and prize his companionship as well as his advice, but primarily because I think that in all the country he is the best man for the position, and that no minister of foreign affairs in any other country at this moment in any way compares with him." To Senator Lodge he wrote, "I hesitated a little between Root and Taft, for Taft, as you know, is very close to me." [2]

These expressions exhibit Roosevelt as a rare judge of men and how deeply he prized the counsel of his official advisers. With Root and Taft to be called on for advice, he felt that he could not go far wrong; they were both good lawyers and men of affairs.

An opinion prevails among diplomatists that President Roosevelt averted a war between France and Germany in 1905. The story is told in a modest letter of the Pres-

---

[1] Life of Hay, Thayer, ii. 408.
[2] Bishop, i. 369 *et seq.*

ident to Whitelaw Reid dated April 28, 1906, and first printed by Bishop in 1920. Included in this is Roosevelt's attitude at the outset, which may be seen in a letter to W. H. Taft of April 20, 1905, who, while Roosevelt was on a bear hunt and Hay seeking recuperation in Europe, was acting Secretary of State, touching which Roosevelt wrote to him, "Dear Will: I think you are keeping the lid on in great shape!" Roosevelt further said: "The Kaiser's pipe dream this week takes the form of Morocco. Speck [Baron Speck von Sternburg, German Ambassador to the United States] has written me an urgent appeal to sound the British Government and find out whether they intend to back up France in gobbling Morocco. . . . I do not feel that as a Government we should interfere in the Morocco matter. We have other fish to fry and we have no real interest in Morocco. I do not care to take sides between France and Germany in the matter. At the same time . . . I am sincerely anxious to bring about a better state of feeling between England and Germany. Each nation is working itself up to a condition of desperate hatred of the other; each from sheer fear of the other. The Kaiser is dead sure that England intends to attack him. The English Government and a large share of the English people are equally sure that Germany intends to attack England." On the same day he wrote to Sternburg, "Our interests in Morocco are not sufficiently great to make me feel justified in entangling our Government in the matter." It would (I think) have been better for Roosevelt to adhere to his first position and absolutely to refuse to interfere in a European dispute. "The Christian nations in Africa," wrote Herbert Spencer in 1905, are "like hungry dogs around a carcass; they tear out piece after piece, pausing only to snarl and snap at one another."[1]

As long as a different view obtained, however, Roosevelt's action was wise and just. When he returned to Washington at the end of May, 1905, he found Jusserand[2] and Sternberg "greatly concerned lest there should be a war between France and Germany." Therefore Roosevelt determined to do his best to avert so great a trouble. "It really did look," he wrote, "as if there might be a war and I felt in honor bound to try to prevent the war if I could, in the first place, because I should have felt such a war to be a real calamity to civilization; and in the next place, as I was already trying to bring about peace between Russia and Japan, I felt that a new conflict might result in what would literally be a world conflagration; and finally, for the sake of France."

To settle the Morocco difficulty, the Kaiser desired a Conference. He thought France's policy aggressive; that France and Spain were a "political unity" who wished to divide up Morocco between themselves; and he feared England's support of France. Therefore, he deemed war with France a possibility. France finally gave way and accepted "the idea of a Conference in spite of serious reasons," as her Minister of Foreign Affairs wrote, "we had to entertain objections to such a project."

---

[1] *Fortnightly*, June, 1895. "Apart from the satisfaction of a somewhat childish pride, what does it matter to either France or Germany which of them owns Morocco. . . . In order that the French might acquire Morocco, England and France in 1905 and again in 1911, were brought to the verge of war with Germany. . . . Viewed as a means of obtaining any tangible gain, a diplomatic contest, such as that waged over Morocco, is a childish absurdity." Bertrand Russell, *Atlantic Monthly*, March, 1915, 371.

[2] Jusserand had been French Ambassador to the United States since 1902.

Meanwhile in Washington Roosevelt's efforts were entirely directed to the maintenance of peace. He had the confidence of both nations whose ambassadors to the United States were wise and peace-loving men. "Jusserand," wrote Roosevelt, "is a man of such excellent judgment, so sound and cool-headed, and of so high a standard of personal and professional honor that I could trust him completely. Indeed it was only because both Jusserand and Sternberg were such excellent men that I was enabled to do anything at all in so difficult and delicate a matter."

The Conference was held at Algeciras, Spain, and began on January 16, 1906. After it opened, the Kaiser by rattling his sword in the scabbard desired to sway its conclusions. Nevertheless, they were on the whole against Germany although she accomplished all that she professed to want. The Kaiser was a sincere admirer of Roosevelt, who wrought earnestly for peace and who had as one of his representatives at Algeciras Henry White, then our Ambassador to Italy. White saw eye to eye with the President and operated at Algeciras as the other did in Washington with the view of preserving the peace. "Loyal though Sternberg was to his Government," Roosevelt wrote soon after the Conference opened, "both Root and I became convinced that down in his heart the honest, brave little gentleman did not really believe Germany was acting as she should act." Finally, however, a Treaty was accepted by the Kaiser and on April 6 was signed by all the powers represented.[1]

---

[1] The authority for this account and the citations made are from Roosevelt's letter to Whitelaw Reid printed by Bishop, i. 467 *et seq*. See also La Conférence d'Algeciras, André Tardieu. "No one can peruse

It will be germane to make a contrast between Theodore Roosevelt and the German Emperor who were not infrequently compared. At this time Roosevelt was an admirer of the Kaiser, writing to Sternberg on June 25, 1905, "I feel that His Majesty stands as the leader among the sovereigns of to-day who have their faces set towards the future, and that it is not only of the utmost importance for his own people but of the utmost importance for all mankind that his power and leadership for good should be unimpaired." [1] Lapse of time and a personal acquaintance during 1910 modified this view. The only man of real ability I saw, speaking of his trip through Europe, he said, among the crowned heads was the German Emperor and he is superficial in his intelligence but has real executive ability. He was eager to get my opinion of himself and at last I said, If you were an American and lived in America you would carry your own ward, which is more than I can say for any other of the crowned heads. The Kaiser understood perfectly the remark and knew that it was a compliment. And he treated all the other kings with disdain except the King of England. A year later Roosevelt expressed himself as not being friendly to Germany. I seem, he said, to feel less near to them than to any of the peoples I met while abroad. They are not capable of a broad humanitarian impulse like the English, Americans and French.

---

this correspondence without a wish that there were in the world more diplomatists of the Roosevelt type. Everything he wrote was clear and concise with none of the tedious formalisms and conventional phrases of the old fashioned diplomacy; and though it went straight to the point it was tactful and calculated to influence those for whom it was meant and whose idiosyncrasies he had considered and allowed for." James Bryce, *Lit. Rev.*, Feb. 19, 1921.

[1] Bishop, i. 485.

The German Emperor is a capable administrator of superficial knowledge, and a great bluffer; he is proud of the things in which he has a superficial knowledge and not very proud of the matters in which he excels.[1]

On Roosevelt's arrival in Berlin during May, 1910, he took luncheon with the Kaiser at Potsdam, who invited him next day to see some remarkable field manœuvres, of which Henry White gave to Abbott an account. The Emperor was dressed in the uniform of a general of the army while Roosevelt was in a simple riding suit of khaki and wore a black slouch hat. During the review the Emperor surrounded by his body-guard of officers in brilliant uniforms said in German, "Roosevelt, mein freund, I wish to welcome you in the presence of my guards; I ask you to remember that you are the only private citizen who has reviewed the troops of Germany." [2]

Punch, in a well known cartoon in 1904, pictured the two as talking to one another with defiant mien and labelled it "Kindred spirits of the strenuous life." The page containing this was confiscated by the Berlin police, whereupon the same artist drew one respectable Berlin citizen and three soldiers looking at a representation of the same cartoon with amused expressions of laughter as they seemed to be asking, What are the Berlin police afraid of? [3]

The Kaiser resembled Roosevelt in being a wonderful talker. Reverend Francis G. Peabody kindly has given me this exact account of what took place: "At the Centenary of the University of Berlin, the German Em-

---

[1] Conversations with Mr. Roosevelt in Dec. 1910 and Dec. 1911.
[2] Impressions of Roosevelt, Abbott, 248.
[3] Autobiography, 558, 562.

peror gave a state dinner to many delegates and after the
dinner received them in a 'Cercle,' passing from one
to another with a hospitable word. President Hadley
and I stood together as the Emperor approached and,
after a few formal words, Dr. Hadley delivered a message
of greeting which President Roosevelt had asked him
to convey. Thereupon I added, in a lighter vein, that
the question had been raised in America, in the light of
President Roosevelt's extraordinary conversational gift,
whether in the Emperor's interview with him there had
been much opportunity for His Majesty to speak. The
Emperor laughed heartily and replied, 'I'll tell you.
Some of my people looked over toward the corner where
we were talking and said it was like two windmills going
around like this,' emphasizing his remark with a violent
waving of his arm. The inference was that the conversational competition was practically a draw."

The Emperor gave Roosevelt a photograph of the two
on horseback talking one to the other with this inscription on the back, "The Colonel of the Rough Riders
lecturing the chief of the German Army." [1]

Many Americans who visited Berlin, struck with the
Emperor's "very marked attractiveness of personality
and manner," [2] scouted before the Great War the suggestion that Roosevelt was his equal in ability. An eminent diplomatist, who was well acquainted personally
with both, bore contrary witness; he had not the least
doubt that Roosevelt was a match for the other in intellectual power. Opinion in France at this time was
that the two attracted more attention in Europe than

[1] Bishop, ii. 252.
[2] Impressions of Roosevelt, Abbott, 248.

any other men, but Roosevelt was trusted and the Kaiser
was not. It is impossible to conceive of Roosevelt making such a shipwreck of his life and career as did the German Emperor when he precipitated or allowed to be
precipitated the Great War. The Kaiser respected and
partly feared Roosevelt, feeling that he had a great country at his back. It is the opinion of some very well informed persons that had Roosevelt been President the
Great War would not have occurred during his occupancy
of the White House.

Regarding San Domingo, Roosevelt acted simply as
a policeman. The story was the usual one of the bor-
rower getting more money than he could pay and of foreign powers threatening to interfere for the payment of
debts. Naturally Roosevelt's action convinced his opponents that he proposed following the example of Grant
thirty-five years previous, and that the result would be
the annexation of San Domingo. In regard to annexation, he was entirely sincere when he wrote to Bishop,
"As for annexing the island, I have about the same desire to annex it as a gorged boa constrictor might have
to swallow a porcupine wrong-end-to." [1]
At the request of the San Domingo government, the
President took charge of their custom-houses; he was
to turn over to them forty-five per cent of the receipts
and distribute the rest to foreign powers that had claims;
he made a Treaty embodying these provisions and on
February 15, 1905, submitted it to the Senate. The
Senate did not immediately ratify the Treaty but the
President administered San Domingo affairs by virtue

---

[1] Bishop, i. 431.

of it on the principle that the President might do, not
only what the Constitution authorized but what it did
not distinctly forbid.   Finally, during the spring of 1907,
the Senate ratified the Treaty.   In a speech to the Harvard Union Roosevelt gave a true tale of the affair : "The
arrangement has gone on for two years now, while the
coördinate branch of the Government discussed whether
or not I had usurped power in the matter, and finally
concluded I had not and ratified the Treaty.   Of the
fifty-five per cent we have been able to put two and a
half millions towards paying their debts ; and with the
forty-five per cent that we collected for them, they have
received more money than they ever got when they collected one hundred per cent themselves ; and the island
has prospered as never before." [1]

In diplomatic action, Roosevelt had an opportunity
to show the true magnanimity of his soul.   As a result
of the Boxer rebellion of 1900, China had agreed to pay
to the United States nearly 24 and a half million dollars
as an indemnity for this action endangering American
lives and property.   It occurred to Dr. Arthur H. Smith,
an American missionary residing in China, that the
United States might remit a portion of her claim with
the understanding that China should use the money,
or the income from it, for the purpose of educating young
Chinese in American institutions of learning, thereby
fostering a spirit which should bear good fruit.   Smith
came to see Lyman Abbott, who was an intimate friend
of the President, and who asked him to set a day for an
interview.   On the day appointed, early in March, 1906,

---

[1] Bishop, i, 435; Autobiography, 548; President's Messages to the
Senate, Feb. 4, 1905.   March 6, *Review of Reviews* Co., ed., iii. 241, 273.

Lyman Abbott was unable to keep the appointment, therefore at Roosevelt's suggestion, Lawrence F., his son, went in his place with Dr. Smith to plead for the remission of a part of the indemnity. Their visit was attended with success. This story is interestingly told by Lawrence F. Abbott who refers for its sequel to the official document.

By June 1, 1907, a little over six millions had been paid and on June 15 the Secretary of State, Elihu Root, wrote to the Chinese Minister that he was "authorized by the President to say that . . . at the next session of the Congress he will ask for authority to re-form the agreement with China under which the indemnity is fixed by remitting and cancelling the obligation of China for the payment of all that part of the stipulated indemnity, which is in excess of the sum of $11,655,492.69 and interest at the stipulated rate." [1] This the President did in his Message of December, 1907, and on May 25 following, Congress adopted a joint resolution providing "for the remission of a portion of the Chinese indemnity." While there is no specification in the joint resolution, it was a tacit agreement that the proceeds of the sum remitted were to be used in the education of Chinese in America. As one goes over diplomatic correspondence, in which so much of it seems a game of grab, it is agreeable to read the despatch of Prince Ch'ing to our Min-

---

[1] This is the amount as stated in Root's letter but as given in the joint resolution and in the President's executive order of Dec. 28, 1908, it is $13,655,492.69 and interest. The difference is explained in the resolution thus: "the sum of two million dollars be reserved from the Chinese indemnity . . . for the payment" of American claims upon the Chinese indemnity which, having been rejected by the U. S. commissioners may be submitted *de novo* to the court of claims and approved by it, the balance out of the $2,000,000 to be returned to China.

ister in Peking. "I was profoundly impressed," he wrote, "with the justice and great friendliness of the American Government, and wish to express our sincere thanks." At such small cost was the friendship of a great Asiatic country purchased.[1]

---

[1] Impressions of Roosevelt, Lawrence F. Abbott, 143 *et seq.;* Doc. 1275, House of Reps., 60th Cong. 2d Sess.

CHAPTER XIV

"AMERICA had reached the point," so wrote ex-Senator Albert J. Beveridge, "where a transition from an outworn to a modern economic and social order was indispensable. . . . For a long time there was no labor congestion — first, because there was so much work to be done and secondly, because free land constantly drew people away from industrial centers. . . . Finally this outlet was closed. Free land was all gone." Labor troubles came. There was a "general unrest among the masses of the people." Then Theodore Roosevelt became President, tackled the question and, according to Beveridge, constituted "The Roosevelt Period." [1]

Roosevelt appreciated fully the task. "At this moment," he said, "we are passing through a period of great unrest — social, political and industrial unrest." [2] The railroads were the largest aggregate of capital representing fourteen and a half billions of dollars, and were the most salient object of attack by the reformer. For on the old theory, they were built on the King's highway and were subject to the State. But admitting this, with a power of generalization the envy of all, Senator Lodge said, "It is the railroads which have made the rapid yet solid development of the United States possible"; they are a great "proof of the energy and intelligence of the Amer-

---

[1] *Sat. Eve. Post*, Apr. 5, 1919, 10.
[2] Apr. 14, *Review of Reviews*, ed., 718.

ican people." [1] The railroad rate legislation of 1905 and 1906 was "stimulated by the aggressiveness of the Executive," [2] and it is a proper classification to call it Roosevelt's work, although by the progress of events he was led to a more radical stand than he at first proposed. On December 6, 1904, in his Annual Message to Congress he said, "While I am of the opinion that at present it would be undesirable, if it were not impracticable, finally to clothe the Interstate Commerce Commission with general authority to fix railroad rates, I do believe that, as a fair security to shippers, the Commission should be vested with the power, where a given rate has been challenged and after full hearing found to be unreasonable, to decide, subject to judicial review, what shall be a reasonable rate to take its place; the ruling of the Commission to take effect immediately, and to obtain unless and until it is reversed by the court of review." [3]

But the House of Representatives was more radical than the President and by a very large majority passed a bill on the principle, "Resolved, That we don't like railroads and wish we knew some way to bang 'em good." [4] This is known as the Hepburn bill fathered by William P. Hepburn, a representative from Iowa, and passed the House on February 9, 1905. There the matter rested, as it was the short session of Congress, expiring March 4, 1905; therefore the Senate and the country had the opportunity to look at the question on all sides.

Roosevelt held to his original position. "My proposal," he wrote in his Message to Congress of December 5, 1905, "is not to give The Interstate Commerce Commission

---

[1] Feb. 12, 1906, Record, 2415.   [2] Washburn's Roosevelt, 129.
[3] *Review of Reviews*, ed., iii. 134.   [4] *The Nation*, Feb. 16, 1905, 126.

power to initiate or originate rates generally, but to regulate a rate already fixed or originated by the roads, upon
complaint and after investigation." [1]   Nevertheless, as
it was a new Congress, the House repassed the bill on
February 8, 1906, by a vote of 346:7. Three answered
"present," and twenty-nine did not vote.[2]

The discussion in the Senate was illuminating. Senator Philander C. Knox said, "The framers of this bill
have succeeded in producing a measure which permits an
administrative body to make orders affecting property
rights, gives no right to the owners of the property to
test their lawfulness in proceedings to enforce them and
penalizes the owner of the property in the sum of $5000
a day if it seeks a supposed remedy outside of the provisions of the bill by challenging either its constitutional-
ity or the lawfulness of the acts performed under its provisions." Knox referred to two United States Supreme
Court decisions, one of which was, "When we recall that
as estimated over ten thousand millions of dollars are
invested in railroad property, the proposition that such
a vast amount of property is beyond the protecting clauses
of the Constitution, that the owners may be deprived
of it by the arbitrary enactment of any legislature, State
or nation, without any right of appeal to the courts is
one which cannot for a moment be tolerated." [3]   Then
Senator Knox went on to say: "From the decisions of
the Supreme Court it will be seen that railroads have a
constitutional right to just compensation for services
rendered, and that by direct act of legislation or indirectly
through an administrative body, as through the Inter-

---

[1] *Review of Reviews*, ed., iv. 568.   [2] Record, 2303.
[3] 1900, 176 U. S. 167, 172.

state Commerce Commission, they cannot be deprived of this right. They are entitled to their day in court." [1] Senator John C. Spooner said on the day that the bill passed the Senate, "The bill as it came to us from the House failed to provide affirmatively for a judicial review of the order of the Commission fixing rates. That objection has been eliminated." [2] The Senate made such an amendment and by its other action improved the bill. It passed on May 18 by a vote of 71:3; not voting, 15. Among the yeas were Knox and Lodge. Foraker made one of the three nays. Aldrich and Burton were among the "not voting." [3] As the Senate and House disagreed, the bill went to a Committee of Conference and the report of the Committee was adopted by both houses. The bill was approved by the President on June 29, 1906, and therefore became a law.

The important difference between advocates and opponents of this legislation lay in the question : Should the Government have the right to fix rates through the Interstate Commerce Commission? Roosevelt who began with tentative recommendations was finally brought to the position that the Interstate Commerce Commission should have that power. It is a quality of great minds that when they set out on a reform the bent of their thinking runs to action in the same direction and carries them further than they at first intended. I would not venture

---

[1] March 28, 1906, Record, 4377, 4381.

[2] May 18, 1906, Record, 7065. In addition to other authorities cited see Foraker, Notes of a Busy Life, ii. 210 *et seq.*; Cullom, Fifty Years of Public Service, 330.

[3] Record, 7088. Aldrich was absent. The statement was made that he would have voted yea; his general pair, Teller, voted yea. Burton evidently had no pair; no statement was made in his behalf. Depew was silent. Tom Platt was "unavoidably absent"; he would have voted yea.

to differ with so great a man as Roosevelt were I not but-
tressed by the opinion of Henry Cabot Lodge, Roosevelt's
intimate and faithful personal and political friend. If
one will compare the German assertions favoring complete action by the State, freely indulged in before the
Great War of 1914, with Roosevelt's arguments in favor
of the Interstate Commerce Commission, one will be
struck by their similarity in their ascription of power
respectively to the State and a creation of the State. It
was asserted that the Hepburn Act led to socialism but
any such result was resisted by Roosevelt. "Public
ownership of railroads," he declared, "is highly undesirable and would probably in this country entail far-reach-
ing disaster." [1] As to this result the President and the
Senator were at one, the Senator referring to Government ownership as "the worst of all disasters." [2] Nor
did Roosevelt alter his conviction. In a speech delivered
on October 4, 1906, he spoke of Government ownership
of railroads as "a policy which would be evil in its results from every standpoint." "Great corporations,"
he said in his Message of 1904, "are necessary, and only
men of great and singular mental power can manage such
corporations successfully, and such men must have great
rewards." [3] "The corporation has come to stay just as
the trade union has come to stay," he said a year later.
"We must all go up or go down together." I have no
"hostility to the railroads. . . . On the whole our railroads have done well and not ill. . . . The question of
transportation lies at the root of all industrial success." [4]

---

[1] Message of Dec. 5, 1905, *Review of Reviews*, ed., iv. 576.
[2] Feb. 12, 1906, Record, 2422. [3] *Review of Reviews*, ed., iii. 128, v. 837.
[4] *Review of Reviews*, ed., iv. 562, 572, 573, 575.

Before dilating on the differences between Roosevelt and Lodge it will be well to have the President's opinion of the Senator which he wrote on February 23, 1906. "Lodge has violent enemies. But he is a boss or the head of a machine only in the sense that Henry Clay and Daniel Webster were bosses and heads of political machines; that is, it is a very great injustice to couple his name with the names of those commonly called bosses. . . . He and I differ radically on certain propositions, as for instance on the pending rate bill; . . . but I say deliberately that during the twenty years he has been in Washington he has been on the whole the best and most useful servant of the public to be found in either house of Congress. . . . Lodge is a man of very strong convictions. . . . He has a certain aloofness and coldness of manner that irritates people who don't live in New England. But he is an eminently fit successor of Webster and Sumner in the Senatorship of Massachusetts. He is a bigger man than Sumner." [1]

Eleven days previous to this letter Lodge had made a great speech in the Senate opposing in the main the rate-making power of the Interstate Commerce Commission. He began his speech by a citation from Coleridge's Table Talk in reference to a bill before Parliament: "I have heard but two arguments of any weight adduced in favor of passing this reform bill, and they are in substance these: 1. 'We will blow your brains out if you don't pass it. 2. We will drag you through a horsepond if you don't pass it'; and there is a good deal of force in both." Lodge in this citation undoubtedly

---

[1] Impressions of Theodore Roosevelt, Abbott, 97; Bishop, ii. 6; see Autobiography, 383.

referred to the public sentiment which demanded that in some way the railroads be shorn of the power which they possessed. Such a sentiment was powerful in the country. It was shared by most shippers who desired lower rates on their products and who were apprehensive lest large competitors had in some way intrigued for greater advantages. Farmers thought that their grain and meat were debarred from markets by a high railroad tariff. Small business men could see greater profits if a reduction of rates were secured. The proletariat looked upon Wall Street with suspicion and thought that a blow at the railroads was one at the evil centre that might insure them a greater share of the good things of life. All together it formed a potent sentiment that had great sway in the House of Representatives. And the President deemed it necessary to warn his followers that an act of Congress could not do everything. "The most perfect laws," he said, "that could be devised by the wit of man or the wit of angels would not amount to anything if the average man was not a pretty decent fellow. . . . Nothing can take the place of the individual factor, of the average man's quality and character, his industry, his energy, his thrift, his decency, his determination to be a good man in his own home, a good neighbor and a good citizen in his relations to the State." [1]

To return to Senator Lodge's speech. "I have the gravest doubts," he said, "as to the wisdom of government rate making even in the most limited form." "We should not go too far in rate making by the government. The lessons to be learned from the experience of other

---

[1] York, Pa.   Oct. 4, 1906.   *Review of Reviews*, ed., v. 843.

nations confirm this view and admonish us to proceed in this direction with the utmost caution." "In the desire to have rates fixed in some form by an executive commission, exercising powers delegated to it by Congress, we shall fail to give an effective remedy for the worst evil which has arisen, that known as 'personal discriminations.'" [1]

What was proposed by the President and by the House was to have rates determined and prescribed by seven men who should constitute the Interstate Commerce Commission and receive an annual salary of ten thousand dollars. They were to be appointed by the President who would naturally be governed by political considerations; and these seven men, so far as rate making was concerned, were to take the place of experts who were fitted by training and long experience to perform that duty. If it were true that he who makes the rate would own the road, these experts who had risen to their position by merit and advancement were to be displaced by appointees of the President. Among the ablest men in the country were those at the head of railroads and to secure the proper amount of traffic that should insure the payment of interest and dividends was work that demanded fitness. "Our railroad freight rates are the lowest in existence," declared Senator Lodge. "The prosperity of the country is knit up with the well-being of the railroads, but it is also to be remembered that the profitable existence of the railroads depends upon the prosperity of the country. There is no body of people — and they constitute one-seventh of our population —

---

[1] Feb. 12, 1906, Record, 2422, 2423.

so profoundly interested in the prosperity of the United States as the people, great and small, who own our railroads, who operate them, and who work for them. It is preposterous to suggest that the railroads of the country are hostile to its well-being and eaten up by a short-sighted selfishness which would lead them to destroy any industry or injure any locality." [1]

Railroad men and the financiers of Wall and State streets who wrought with them had been guilty of grave evils which were fully expanded by the press. These were due to their greed for money and power, or in short to selfishness. But selfishness is a common attitude of humanity, possessed by members of the Interstate Commerce Commission as well as by the managers of railroads and by those engaged in high finance. As it was finely put by Senator Lodge on the day that the vote was taken in the Senate: "The Interstate Commerce Commission desire power. They would like to take the powers of the legislature and of the courts alike. They would like to take all the power that is possible." [2]

The remedy for the evils was, under slight limitations, the natural working of economic forces. As Senator Lodge stated it, "My own belief is that the natural economic forces will settle rates so far as an excess is concerned by the competition of the markets, by the play of natural forces, and by the certainty that if rates are put up to a point where it would make it profitable for someone else to come in, he will come in." [3]

It is remarkable that at one as Roosevelt and Lodge seemed in their public utterances they should differ so

[1] February 12, 1906, 2417, 2421.
[2] May 18, 1906, Record, 7068.   [3] Record, Feb. 12, 1906, 2423.

widely when their professions came to be translated into
legislative action. Both were strongly opposed to government ownership; and they agreed also in Roosevelt's
statement, that this Government should not be one by
a plutocracy nor one by a mob. We must avoid, he
said "a contest between the brutal greed of the 'have-
nots' and the brutal greed of the 'haves.'" [1]

The President said that the small investors in railroads deserved consideration,[2] apparently ignoring that
to some extent their interests were bound up in Big Business, as their living expenses, their deeds, not infrequently
of benevolence, depended upon the interest and dividends
from the railroads that Roosevelt attacked. When he
made the comparison between members of the Interstate
Commerce Commission and those of the United States
Supreme Court,[3] he was not fair to the Supreme Court
whose members, although appointed by the President,
received their appointments largely through the influence
of the bar and formed a body of highly trained public
servants. The likeness to the National Bank Examiners
was more apposite, but the scope of the Interstate Commerce Commission was far greater than that of the Bank
Examiners. The work of the one was positive while
that of the other was negative, being largely the decision
whether certain banks were solvent, in which they were
directly or indirectly assisted by competing and far-
seeing bankers who had attested suspicions due to their
machinery of operations.

The President was severe on E. H. Harriman, who is
properly called by Thayer "the railroad czar of the United

---

[1] *Review of Reviews*, ed., 585, 719.   [2] Ibid., 572.   [3] Ibid., 406.

States," [1] and who was indignant at the railway rate
bill and the general course of the administration. This
came out when J. S. Sherman, a Republican member of
Congress from New York State, asked him for a contri-
bution to the autumn campaign, when in 1906 Charles
E. Hughes was running against Hearst for governor of
New York. I do not care in the least, said Harriman,
whether the Hearst crowd is triumphant or not; those
people are crooks and I can buy them. Whenever I
want legislation from a State legislature I can buy it.
I can buy Congress and if necessary I can buy the judi-
ciary.[2] "At the same time," so wrote Roosevelt in a
private letter, "the Standard Oil people informed Pen-
rose that they intend to support the Democratic party
unless I call a halt in the suits begun against the Standard
Oil people . . . ; and they gave the same reason as Harriman, namely, that rather than have an administration
such as the present they would prefer to have an administration of Bryans and Hearsts, because they could make
arrangements with them. But they did not use the
naked brutality of language which Harriman used." [3]
"The Standard Oil Company," the President asserted
in a Message to Congress on May 4, 1906, "has benefited
enormously up almost to the present moment by secret
rates, many of these secret rates being clearly unlawful.
. . . The Standard also profits immensely by open
rates. . . . It has, largely by unfair or unlawful methods,
crushed out home competition." [4] The President also
attacked the so-called sugar and tobacco trusts.

---

[1] P. 234. [2] *Review of Reviews*, ed., 857; Bishop, ii. 32.
[3] Bishop, ii. 33. [4] *Review of Reviews*, ed., 740, 741, 743, 745.

"There is plenty of iniquity in business, in politics, in our social life," he said. But that is no reason why we should follow the "wild apostles of unrest" in "their campaign of hysterical excitement and falsehood." Although "the reactionaries and the violent extremists show symptoms of joining hands against us," this legislation was enacted in no spirit of "hysteria and rancor." "Better no legislation at all than legislation couched in a vindictive spirit of hatred towards men of wealth." The Hepburn Act drew the line plainly between Big Business and Roosevelt. High Finance thought that he had inaugurated a campaign of hysteria, while he himself deemed that he had pursued a middle course between the reactionaries and those who looked with favor on socialism.[1] So might anyone be convinced who, affected by the magnetism of his presence, listened to his arguments in private conference, and so may anyone now think who bases his judgment on his messages to Congress and other public utterances. He had the country at his back; "the plain people who think — the mechanics, farmers, merchants, workers with head or hand." [2] Members of Congress, who while in Washington toward the end of the session swore that they would no longer be swayed or dictated to by Theodore Roosevelt, returned at the commencement of the next session ready to follow whither he led because meanwhile they had been in contact with their constituencies. Men west of the Missouri River said when we hear that a week has

---

[1] *Review of Reviews*, ed., 573, 794, 835, 837, 917, 931.
[2] *Review of Reviews*, ed., 919. The *Minneapolis Journal* gave the title to their cartoon: "The country is back of him. Go ahead, Teddy; whichever path you choose you have U. S. back of you." See also Autobiography, 383.

passed and that "Teddy" has smashed no evil we think he must be ill because, owing to his activity, he must be crushing something that bodes no good to the body politic. No wonder he said, I love those Westerners.[1] A veteran senator declared that he had only one objection to the President — with his restless mind he was always doing something.

"We passed a law," wrote Roosevelt speaking of the work of Congress and himself regarding the Hepburn Act, "giving vitality to the Interstate Commerce Commission, and for the first time providing some kind of efficient control by the National Government over the great railroads." [2]

President Roosevelt might have said to Senator Lodge, "The ill that's done ye can compute but never what's resisted"; and the Senator could have replied, "Nature's patient ways shame hasty little man."

Whatever criticism may be meted out to the President for his action giving the Interstate Commerce Commission the power to fix railroad rates cannot obtain as we consider the Meat Inspection Act and the Pure Food law.

By special message to Congress of June 4, 1906, he transmitted the report of a special committee and urged the "need of immediate action by the Congress in the direction of providing a drastic and thorough-going inspection by the Federal Government of all stock yards and packing houses and of their products, so far as the latter enter

---

[1] I have said this previously. The *Toledo Blade* has a cartoon entitled Roosevelt "is pretty good at 'winning the West' himself." Albert Shaw, *Review of Reviews*, 172.

[2] Bishop, ii. 131. See the cartoon "Then and Now. The Railroads and Roosevelt. (Before and after the long struggle for anti-rebate legislation)," Albert Shaw, *Review of Reviews*, 155.

into interstate or foreign commerce. The conditions shown," he added, "to exist in the Chicago stock yards are revolting. It is imperatively necessary in the interest of health and of decency that they should be radically changed. . . . The stock yards and packing houses are not kept even reasonably clean and the method of handling and preparing food products is uncleanly and dangerous to health." [1] Senator Albert J. Beveridge had offered an amendment to the appropriation act of the Department of Agriculture and the President urged that this be substantially enacted. It is a mark of Roosevelt that he never claimed credit unless it was his due and an evidence of this is seen in a letter to Beveridge on the day after he had signed the bill. "You were the man," he said, "who first called my attention to the abuses in the packing houses. You were the legislator who drafted the bill which in its substance now appears in the Amendment to the Agricultural bill and which will enable us to put a complete stop to the wrong-doing complained of." [2]

Senator Beveridge who had read much and travelled much and was yet to write his *magnus opus*, "The Life of Chief-Justice Marshall," which could have been written only by a man of letters and the law, was not outdone in generosity, declaring in open Senate that the act "we owe to the courage, determination and the absolutely unselfish devotion to the interest of the people of President Roosevelt." [3] Of the same mind when he penned his eulogy, he wrote, " that important reform never would

---

[1] *Review of Reviews*, ed., 772.
[2] July 1, 1906.   The *Sat. Eve. Post*, Apr. 5, 1919.
[3] June 20, Record, 8766.

have had the slightest chance of accomplishment had not President Roosevelt thrown himself into the fight with every ounce of his personal power and all the resources of the Administration." "The fight over that measure," he said, "was one of the most desperate in our legislative history." [1]

"The enactment of the pure food bill," so Roosevelt wrote to Congressman Watson on August 18, "and the passage of the bill which rendered effective the control of the Government over the meat packing industries are really along the same general line as the passage of the interstate commerce law and are second only to it in importance." [2] The title of the pure food law was, "An act for preventing the manufacture, sale or transportation of adulterated or misbranded or poisonous or deleterious foods, drugs, medicines and liquors and for regulating traffic therein." This applied of course only to foreign and interstate commerce and was approved by the President on June 30. The act defined precisely what should be understood by adulterated drugs, confectionery and food. In the case of food it forbade the addition of any poisonous or deleterious ingredient "which may render such article injurious to health." In brief the act was in the interest of the health of the community and was a protection to the purchaser of food and drugs.

"Partly by law and partly by executive order," Roosevelt wrote, "we have completely reorganized the consular service of the United States." [3] As President, he was as true to the cause of Civil Service Reform as he was as Civil

---

[1] The *Sat. Eve. Post*, Apr. 5, 1919.
[2] *Current Lit.* Pub. Co. 401.
[3] Bishop, ii. 131.

Service Commissioner. "In my opinion," wrote in 1919 William D. Foulke, a veteran in the cause, "Roosevelt was more consistent and energetic than any other President in advancing the reform." [1]

An employers' liability act for corporations engaged in interstate commerce was passed. Declared unconstitutional by the United States Supreme Court, a law which met the objections of the Court was enacted at a subsequent session of Congress. [2]

"Do come on and let me see you soon," Roosevelt wrote to Dooley on June 18. "I am by no means as much alone as in Cuba, because I have an ample surrounding of Senators and Congressmen, not to speak of railroad men, Standard Oil men, beef packers and venders of patent medicines, the depth of whose feelings for me cannot be expressed in words." [3]

Roosevelt's muckrake speech attracted much attention from the people and from the press. The verb to muckrake was speedily coined, obtained wide currency and finds a place in Webster's New International Dictionary published in 1909 with a direct reference to this very address. The speech was delivered at the laying of the corner-stone of the office building of the House of Representatives on April 14, 1906. "In Bunyan's 'Pilgrim's Progress,'" [4] he said, "you may recall the description

[1] Fighting the Spoilsmen, 257.

[2] Bishop, ii. 80, 131. The original act was passed June 11, 1906; it was declared unconstitutional on Jan. 6, 1908. The amended act was passed April 22, 1908, and upheld by the Court on Jan. 15, 1912. The objection to the original act was that it was not limited to injuries incurred in interstate commerce.

[3] Bishop, ii. 34.

[4] "Bunyan's 'Pilgrim's Progress' is to my mind one of the greatest books that was ever written." Roosevelt to Dr. Milner, Bishop, ii. 115.

of the Man with the Muckrake, the man who could look no way but downward with the muckrake in his hand; who was offered a celestial crown for his muckrake but who would neither look up nor regard the crown he was offered but continued to rake to himself the filth of the floor." Muckraking leads to slander that may untruthfully "attack an honest man or even assail a bad man with untruth. An epidemic of indiscriminate assault upon character does not good but very great harm," declared the President. He had found an important deterrent to the entrance to the public service of able men of normal sensitiveness, in the gross and reckless assaults on their character and capacity both without and within Congress. "Hysterical sensationalism is the very poorest weapon wherewith to fight for lasting righteousness," he said. "There is mighty little good in a mere spasm of reform." Sanity as well as honesty is needed. Mud slinging is as bad as whitewashing.[1]

That Roosevelt should know his Shakespeare and his Burke is not surprising; that this preachment should be on a text from Bunyan is more surprising; but it is really amazing that one of his illustrations should be from the "Ecclesiastical Policy" of "that fine old Elizabethan divine," Bishop Hooker, who, one might suppose, was read only by students of terse and expressive English.

The Constitution makes the President Commander-in-Chief of the Army of the United States and Roosevelt manifested that this was to him an earnest provision. Near midnight on August 13, 1906, the city of Brownsville, Texas, near Fort Brown, was shot up; one person

---

[1] For the muckrake speech, see *Review of Reviews*, ed., 712.

was killed, a number were assaulted with the intent to kill, women and children were fired at and nearly every one in the city was frightened. As Roosevelt said in his second Message to the Senate, "These crimes were certainly committed by somebody." [1] After making a thorough investigation of the subject through officers in whom he had confidence, he and the Secretary of War, William H. Taft, came to the conclusion that "from nine to fifteen or twenty of the colored soldiers" belonging to B. C. and D. colored of the 25th regular infantry took part in the attack. The "original crime," declared the President, was "supplemented by another . . . in the shape of a successful conspiracy of silence for the purpose of shielding those who took part in the original conspiracy of murder." [2] Therefore "I ordered the discharge of nearly all the members of Companies B. C. and D. of the 25th infantry by name in the exercise of my constitutional power as Commander-in-Chief of the United States Army." [3]

"It appears that in Brownsville," the President said, "the city immediately beside which Fort Brown is situated, there had been considerable feeling between the citizens and the colored troops of the garrison companies. Difficulties had occurred, there being a conflict of evidence as to whether the citizens or colored troops were to blame." But "any assertion that these men were dealt with harshly because they were colored men is utterly without foundation." "I condemned in unstinted terms the crime of lynching perpetrated by white men,

---

[1] Jan. 14, 1907, *Review of Reviews*, ed., 1097.
[2] Dec. 19, 1906, *Review of Reviews*, ed., 1065, 1070.
[3] Ibid., 1063.

and I should take the instant advantage of any opportunity whereby I could bring to justice a mob of lynchers.
In precisely the same spirit I have now acted with reference to these colored men who have been guilty of a black
and dastardly crime." [1] "The evidence shows beyond
any possibility of honest question that some individuals
among the colored troops whom I have dismissed committed the outrages mentioned."

Roosevelt's private letters support his public view.
"I have been amazed and indignant," he wrote, "at the
attitude of the negroes and of shortsighted white sentimentalists as to my action. . . . There has been great
pressure, not only by the sentimentalists but by the
Northern politicians who wish to keep the negro vote. . . .
I believe in practical politics . . . but in a case like this
where the issue is not merely one of naked right and
wrong but one of vital concern to the whole country, I
will not for one moment consider the political effect." [2]

Awarding equal sincerity to Senator Foraker, I have
read carefully the three chapters in his book which he
has devoted to the "Brownsville Affray"; but I am not
convinced that he has made out his case. The contest between him and the President had become embittered
from some other cause, and his sarcasm directed against
the President and the Secretary of War does not add to
the cogency of his case.[3] Military matters in any case
require prompt decision and the despotic quality naturally inheres in any executive action. But a calm review of the whole matter cannot fail to convince the im-

---

[1] *Review of Reviews*, 1065, 1073, 1079, 1097.
[2] Bishop, ii. 28.
[3] See Foraker's Notes of a Busy Life, ii.; also Fifty Years, Cullom, 356.

partial observer that the President was right and acted on the best evidence, both legal and human, that was obtainable.

The President's tribute to Japan in his Message to Congress of December 3, 1906, represented fully the sentiment of the American people as it was during the war between Japan and Russia, when public opinion was largely on the side of Japan. Since that time, however, an "attitude of hostility" has developed which though "limited to a very few places, is most discreditable to us as a people and may be fraught with the gravest consequences to the Nation. . . . Since Commodore Perry, by his expedition to Japan over half a century ago, first opened the islands to western civilization, the growth of Japan has been literally astounding." Then, "Japan's development was still that of the Middle Ages; now she stands as one of the greatest of civilized nations; great in the arts of war and in the arts of peace; great in military, in industrial, in artistic development and achievement. . . . We have as much to learn from Japan as Japan has to learn from us. . . . Throughout Japan Americans are well treated and any failure on the part of Americans at home to treat the Japanese with a like courtesy and consideration is just so much a confession of inferiority in our civilization. . . . I ask for fair treatment for the Japanese as I would ask fair treatment for Germans or Englishmen, Frenchmen, Russians or Italians. . . . I ask it as due to humanity and civilization. I ask it as due to ourselves because we must act uprightly toward all men." [1]

No lover of peace can feel otherwise than thrilled when

[1] *Review of Reviews*, ed., 957, 958, 960, 961.

he reads that part of the President's Message of December, 1906, which is devoted to Secretary Root's visit to
South America.   The third International Conference was
held at Rio Janeiro from July 23 to August 29 and the
Secretary of State was sent as our delegate.   It was considered a great honor by the South American republics
that we should send so high an official and one of such
distinction.   He was cordially received and made an
honorary President.   How well Roosevelt understood
the value of such a meeting is seen in the words of his
Message.   "The example," he wrote, "of the representatives of all the American nations engaging in harmonious
and kindly consideration and discussion of subjects of
common interest is itself of great and substantial value
for the promotion of reasonable and considerate treatment of all international questions."   After the Conference Root "visited Brazil, Uruguay, Argentina, Chile,
Peru, Panama and Colombia.   He refrained from visiting Paraguay, Bolivia and Ecuador only because the
distance of their capitals from the seaboard made it impracticable with the time at his disposal.   He carried
with him a message of peace and friendship, and of strong
desire for good understanding and mutual helpfulness ; and
he was everywhere received in the spirit of his message."

There was a misunderstanding in regard to the Monroe
Doctrine.   The prevalent idea was that it involved an
assumption of superiority and the right to exercise some
kind of protectorate by the United States over the
South American republics.   "That impression," said the
President, "continued to be a serious barrier to good
understanding, to friendly intercourse, to the introduction
of American capital and the extension of American trade."

"It was part of Secretary Root's mission to dispel this unfounded impression"; and he therefore made an address at Rio on July 31, in which he said: "We wish for no victories but those of peace; for no territory except our own; for no sovereignty except the sovereignty over ourselves. We deem the independence and equal rights of the smallest and weakest member of the family of nations entitled to as much respect as those of the greatest empire, and we deem the observance of that respect the chief guaranty of the weak against the oppression of the strong. We neither claim nor desire any rights or privileges or powers that we do not freely concede to every American Republic. . . . Let us preserve our free lands from the burden of such armaments as are massed behind the frontiers of Europe."

The arches which spanned the streets in the city of Buenos Ayres had the names inscribed on them of Washington, Jefferson and Marshall and also those of James Monroe, John Quincy Adams, Henry Clay and Richard Rush, a silent testimony to the friends of South America who had labored for them in the greater republic. It was a "graceful courtesy" on the part of the Government of Brazil that the building in which the Conference was held was labelled "Palacio Monroe."

The President said, "Our grateful acknowledgments are due to the Governments and the people of all the countries visited by the Secretary of State for the courtesy, the friendship and the honor shown to our country in their generous hospitality to him."[1]

In these words the President represented the sentiment of the American people.

---

[1] *Review of Reviews*, ed., 966, 967, 968, 969, 970.

CHAPTER XV

NINETEEN hundred seven may be called the Panic Year. In making a study of the panic of 1857 I wrote, "The reason of panics lies deep in the human heart." Passing through the panic of 1873 as a business man, those of 1893 and 1907 as an investor, I have seen no reason to change this opinion. Accepting the theory of periodicity of panics it is unnecessary to explain fully why the period is not always the same; sixteen years elapsed between 1857 and 1873, twenty between 1873 and 1893, and fourteen between 1893 and 1907. But the cause is always the same. If men were always wise, if they themselves or corporations in which they held stock never ran into debt, if there were never fluctuations in the prices of produce — in short if all business was done for cash, if men never incurred obligations which they could not at once meet, if they did not spread out with the idea that every extension, every conversion of liquid into fixed capital meant a larger income from their enterprise, financial panics would never occur. But a society of that kind would lack commercial energy, would cease its material progress and, in fact, would be impossible in one based on European civilization.

Taking into account the actual state of affairs debt seems a necessary adjunct. Certain men have more energy than money; others more money than energy. It was entirely natural then that out of this condition should be developed on the one side the manager and the promoter and on the other the investor.   Banks are the basis of all financial affairs and they are deeply in debt to their depositors.   It is a commonplace that the function of a bank is to lend money to borrowers at a higher rate of interest than it pays its depositors.   Financial panics mean a loss of confidence, and one of its marks is that Savings Banks depositors start a run on banks where their savings are placed.   This puts a strain on National Banks which have a large amount of Savings Bank money and besides have their own troubles to face in the vain endeavor to collect their loans and to meet the demands of their own depositors.   So far as I know such have been the characteristics of the panics of '57, '73 and '93.   Theodore Marburg in his business dissertation attempted to show that "each recurring panic has its own special causes" [1] but to my mind he in no way traverses the general law.   It is true enough that 1857 and 1873 were caused by the too rapid building of railroads, that the operation of the silver purchase provision of the Act of 1890 was a contributing cause to the panic of 1893, but if one needs one word to describe the cause of all these he finds it in "overtrading."

A Boston banker found in a printed description of the panic of 1857 substantially the same characteristics as were passing before his eyes in 1907.   A. Piatt Andrew, Assistant Professor of Economics at Harvard University, in an article printed in the New Year's number of the New York *Journal of Commerce* on January 2, 1907, found a close parallel between the situation at the beginning of the year 1907 with that of 1857, and wrote further

---

[1] Address before the American Academy of Political and Social Science, April 10, 1908.

that a financial panic might occur during the year as it had a half a century earlier.[1]

The devotees of high finance ascribed the panic wholly to the Roosevelt policies both "legislative and executive."[2] A cartoon in *Life* pictured Roosevelt emerging from a bear hunt in the South with the usual eyeglasses, showing his front teeth on the broad grin, dancing in high glee and shooting to the death "Big Game" labelled "prosperity."[3] The cartoon represented the general feeling among financial men as is shown in Roosevelt's speeches and messages, in his private letters and in varied recollections of the period. Everywhere that these men congregated, the conversation was Roosevelt and the financial ruin which he had brought upon the country.

A glance at Roosevelt's own description will be useful. "We have our ups and downs," he said on October 22, "no law and the administration of no law can save any body of people from their own folly. If a section of the business world goes a little crazy, it will have to pay for it; and being excessively human, when it does pay for it, it will want to blame someone else instead of itself. If at any time a portion of the business world loses its head, it has lost what no outside aid can supply. If there is reckless overspeculation or dishonest business management, just as sure as fate there will follow a partial collapse. There has been trouble in the stock market, in the high financial world during the past few months. The statement has frequently been made that the policies for which I stand, legislative and executive, are responsi-

---

[1] Letter of A. Piatt Andrew, Oct. 15, 1921; Boston *Daily Advertiser*, Nov. 2, 1907.

[2] Roosevelt, Speech, Oct. 22, 1907, *Review of Reviews*, ed., 1964.

[3] *Life*, Oct. 31.

ble for that trouble." [1] In another speech Roosevelt
admitted that his policies might have possibly been a
contributory cause to the panic; [2] but in a special Message to Congress of January 31, 1908, he said, "So far
as the business distress is due to local and not world wide
causes and to the actions of any particular individuals,
it is due to the speculative folly and flagrant dishonesty
of a few men of great wealth who seek to shield themselves from the effects of their own wrong-doing by ascrib-
ing its results to the actions of those who have sought to
put a stop to the wrong-doing."

The panic began with a "flurry in stocks" in March,
it gained new strength in August [3] and reached its height
during October and November. On the 22d of October
the Knickerbocker Trust Company failed; the Electric
and Manufacturing Company, of which George Westinghouse was President, applied for the appointment of
receivers. [4] General Electric stock which had sold at
162 during the year went to 90, and other shares suffered
a like decline. Banks in all of the large cities issued
clearing-house certificates of which 84 million dollars
were emitted in New York City alone. There were runs
on many of the banks and practically all of the banks
in large cities requested their customers to make their
cheques through the clearing house only and to draw
no currency unless absolutely needed. Currency went
to a premium of $4\frac{1}{2}$ per cent, which lasted from the first
day of November through the first half of December.
Money on call, if it could be had during the days before

---

[1] Oct. 22, *Review of Reviews*, ed., 1464.   [2] Oct. 1, ibid., 1377.
[3] Bishop, ii. 43; *Review of Reviews*, ed., 1358.
[4] Oct. 23, Life of George Westinghouse, Leupp, 208.

the banks issued clearing-house certificates, was lent at 125 per cent. Summoned from the General Episcopal Convention in Richmond, where he was a diligent reader of the newspapers, J. P. Morgan arrived on the scene and took command. Indeed the financiers desired a general and he was one in whom all had entire confidence. Back of Morgan were the old and experienced men of finance, who had regarded with no favor the operations of the new school of financiers who had been conspicuous in the overtrading that brought on the panic. They might have said with Prometheus, "Youthful pilots rule Olympus." [1] The new school had originated the system of "chain banking" which meant the buying up of the majority of shares of any one bank, then hypothecating these shares and with the proceeds purchasing the control of another bank which was dealt with in a similar manner and so on until a coterie controlled a number of banks which assisted them in their wild speculations that were those of "infatuated promoters and grumbling millionaires." [2]

Nightly meetings were held in Morgan's library and methods were devised to allay the panic. The Secretary of the Treasury, George B. Cortelyou, came to New York and gave his timely aid. The President took a hand in the same direction and acted with his usual promptness. One evening he was informed that two representatives of the United States Steel Corporation desired to see him early next morning, when in company with Secretary of State Root he saw them and gave this account of the interview dated November 4.

"Judge E. H. Gary and Mr. H. C. Frick, on behalf

---

[1] Lawton, *Atlantic Monthly*, 62, 215.
[2] Noyes, *Forum*, Jan. 1908, 313.

of the Steel Corporation, have just called upon me.   They
state that there is a certain business firm (the name of
which I have not been told but which is of real importance in New York business circles), which will undoubtedly fail this week if help is not given.   Among its assets
are a majority of the securities of the Tennessee Coal and
Iron Company.   Application has been urgently made to
the Steel Corporation to purchase this stock as the only
means of avoiding a failure.   Judge Gary and Mr. Frick
informed me that as a mere business transaction they do
not care to purchase the stock ; that under ordinary circumstances they would not consider purchasing the stock,
because but little benefit will come to the Steel Corporation
from the purchase ; that they are aware that the purchase
will be used as a handle for attack upon them on the ground
that they are striving to secure a monopoly of the business
and prevent competition — not that this would represent
what could honestly be said, but what might recklessly and
untruthfully be said.

"They further informed me that, as a matter of fact,
the policy of the company has been to decline to acquire
more than sixty per cent of the steel properties, and that
this purpose has been persevered in for several years past,
with the object of preventing these accusations, and, as
a matter of fact, their proportion of steel properties has
slightly decreased, so that it is below this sixty per cent,
and the acquisition of the property in question will not
raise it above sixty per cent.   But they feel that it is
immensely to their interest, as to the interest of every
responsible business man, to try to prevent a panic and
general industrial smash up at this time, and that they
are willing to go into this transaction, which they would

not otherwise go into, because it seems the opinion of those best fitted to express judgment in New York that it will be an important factor in preventing a break that might be ruinous; and that this has been urged upon them by the combination of the most responsible bankers in New York who are now thus engaged in endeavoring to save the situation. But they asserted that they did not wish to do this if I stated that it ought not to be done. I answered that, while of course I could not advise them to take the action proposed, I felt it no public duty of mine to interpose any objections." [1]

The President acted wisely, and was completely vindicated by the Courts; first by the United States District Court for the District of New Jersey and then by the United States Supreme Court.[2] Judge Gary and Frick had told the President the truth. Gary had then begun to gain the confidence of the newspaper reading community that with the years has been largely augmented. Henry Clay Frick had worked up from the bottom, was truthful, cool and shrewd. The action of the President which was announced on the Stock Exchange at its opening that morning did much toward allaying the disturbed confidence.

Notwithstanding the financial stress, the pressure of various kinds brought to bear upon him, Roosevelt proposed to pursue his policies. If they, he declared, have been a contributory cause to the panic they "must be accepted as a disagreeable but unavoidable feature in a course of policy which as long as I am President will not

---

[1] Autobiography, 478.
[2] The Supreme Court decision was in 1920 and it stood 4 to 3. The decision was delivered by Justice McKenna.

be changed." [1] "Everyone," he said in his special Message to Congress of January 31, 1908, "must feel the keenest sympathy for the large body of honest business men, of honest investors, of honest wage-workers who suffer because involved in a crash for which they are in no way responsible. At such a time there is a natural tendency on the part of many men to feel gloomy and frightened at the outlook." [2]   But he wrote in his Annual Message of December 3, 1907, "swindling in stocks, corrupting legislatures, making fortunes by the inflation of securities, by wrecking railroads, by destroying competitors through rebates — these forms of wrong-doing in the capitalist" must be stopped. [3] "If it were true," he said to Congress on January 31, 1908, "that to cut out rottenness from the body politic meant a momentary check to an unhealthy seeming prosperity, I should not for one moment hesitate to put the knife to the corruption." [4] "Our main quarrel," he said in the same Message, "is not with the representatives of the interests. They derive their chief power from the great sinister offenders who stand behind them. They are but puppets who move as the strings are pulled. It is not the puppets, but the strong cunning men and the mighty forces working for evil behind and through the puppets with whom we have to deal. We seek to control law-defying wealth." [5]

Roosevelt's own comment is highly interesting. Thus he wrote to his brother-in-law during November: "Of course I am gravely harassed and concerned over the

---

[1] Oct. 1, *Review of Reviews*, ed., 1377.
[2] *Review of Reviews*, ed., 1636.   [3] Ibid., 1528.   [4] Ibid., 1637.
[5] Ibid., 1619.

situation. . . . I am doing everything I have power to do; but the fundamental fact is that the public is suffering from a spasm of lack of confidence. Most of this lack of confidence is absolutely unreasonable and therefore we can do nothing with it. There is a part for which there is a substantial basis however. There has been so much trickery and dishonesty in high places; the exposures about Harriman, Rockefeller, Heinze, Barney, Morse, Ryan, the insurance men and others have caused such a genuine shock to people that they have begun to be afraid that every bank really has something rotten in it. In other words they have passed through the period of unreasoning trust and optimism into unreasoning distrust and pessimism. I shall do everything I can up to the very verge of my power to restore confidence, to give the banks a chance to get currency into circulation." [1]

Roosevelt was especially severe in his criticism of Rockefeller whom I have already considered; but Rockefeller would have been astonished to know that he was classed with men of evil intent; on the contrary he was at this time working at the back of Morgan and with the same purpose in view as that of the President "to restore confidence." It was, it is true, a selfish purpose, as to disturb the complex arrangements of business and of finance was worse, so far as the amount of loss is concerned, for the large financiers than for the wage-earner and small shop-keeper.

By February 1, 1908, confidence was practically restored. On the last day of 1907 the premium on cur-

---

[1] Bishop, ii. 48.

rency was only ¼ of one per cent. But the strain had
been great. One week during November the deficit in
the legal reserve was 54 millions; this was when the
weekly statements were made on the old basis before
the passing of the Federal Reserve Act. One hundred
million dollars of gold were imported from Europe. At
the close of the year the Bank of England rate was the
highest for thirty-four years. So far as New York City
was concerned the panic according to Alexander D. Noyes
was not approached in 1893 and hardly paralleled in
1873; although the remark would hardly hold true of
the West.[1]

In the West was a large amount of so-called desert
land. But "the very condition of aridity," wrote George
Wharton James in his useful book, "is an assurance of
great fertility when water is applied. . . . The most fertile countries are the arid ones, and not the humid and

----

[1] An excellent authority is Alex. D. Noyes whose articles in the *Forum*
for July, Oct. 1907, and Jan., April, 1908, give a true and exact account of
the panic. I have also consulted *The Nation* for Oct. and Nov. 1907, the
financial articles in which were probably written by Noyes; also the N. Y.
Tribune for Oct. 21, 22, 23, 24 and Nov. 5.
    "During the panic of 1893 no bank failure of any consequence occurred
in New York City. In October, 1907, one national bank, four trust companies and six state banks closed their doors in that locality and in the
closing week of January the suspension was announced of four banks doing business in Manhattan Island. These were not institutions of the
first importance but at the start they threatened complications to the
general situation. . . . All of these January bank failures represented
the cleaning up process which followed an experiment in reckless and unusual banking undertaken during the recent boom. These banks, directly
or indirectly, had been involved in the process known as 'chain banking.' " — Noyes. The *Forum*, April, 498.
    In July, 1893, in New York City only one national bank suspended with
assets of $800,000 and one state bank with assets $400,000. During
August, 1893, two more state banks and during December another state
bank closed their doors.

well watered ones." [1]   And water was plenty but it came
from the mountains, partly from the melting of snow,
and during the late winter and spring rushed down the
river-beds in torrents, frequently overflowing the plains
and sometimes carrying destruction to farms, villages and
towns.   The rain descended and the floods came and the
winds blew.   The problem was to chain this force, to
store the water when it was plenty and let it loose during
the intense heat of the summer and whenever wanted.
The method to be applied was well known; the money
and the ability properly to spend it were necessary factors.   Something had been done by private companies
and by State and other official organizations but they
could not furnish the means to operate irrigation on a
large scale.   Soon after Roosevelt became President,
Gifford Pinchot and Frederick H. Newell called upon
him and presented "their plans for National irrigation
of the arid lands of the West."   They found in Roosevelt
a ready listener and one thoroughly comprehending.   As
a young man he had passed much time on a ranch [2] and
understood the marvels of irrigation, so that no argument
was needed to convert him to the scheme which he advocated in his first Message to Congress.   "The forest
and water problems," he declared, "are perhaps the most
vital internal problems of the United States." [3]   On June
17, 1902, he had the satisfaction of signing the bill which
provided for the work being done by the Nation.   This is
known as the Newlands Act from its author, Senator Newlands, who had wrought strenuously to effect its passage.

---

[1] Reclaiming the Arid West, 25, 26.
[2] See My Brother, T. Roosevelt, Mrs. Robinson, chap. vi.
[3] Autobiography, 431.

Part of James's book reads like a magical romance. "For a life-time," he wrote, "I have sung the majestic chorus of Mendelssohn from Elijah, 'Thanks be to God; he laveth the thirsty land.' Again and again have I thrilled to its passionate power, but never did I dream of its full significance until I saw water pouring through the irrigation canals of our thirsty West; the gentle murmuring of the flowing waters suggesting the music made by the land as it soaked up, absorbed, drew into every thirsty pore, the life-giving, stimulating, seed-growing fluid."[1]

When one thinks that the United States is, according to European opinions, a loosely administered country, one reads with satisfaction James's tribute to the "knowledge, skill, ingenuity, tact, patience and equanimity of the officials, engineers and managers of the Reclamation Service";[2] and one cannot help thinking that nowhere else could so large an undertaking have been more efficiently conducted. James is not a Californian, possessed with the idea that his is the greatest country on earth and full of blind enthusiasm for the Western States, as he is fully conversant with the English work in Egypt and India and the irrigation system of Argentina.[3] Roosevelt, on the completion of the Roosevelt Dam in Arizona, thanked the engineers present "for their admirable work, as efficient as it was honest and conducted according to the highest standards of the public service. As I looked," he said, "at the fine, strong, eager faces of those of the

---

[1] Reclaiming the Arid West, 34.

[2] James dedicates his book to John W. Powell, Francis G. Newlands, Charles D. Walcott, Frederick H. Newell, William E. Smyth, George H. Maxwell, Arthur P. Davis, Franklin K. Lane.

[3] Reclaiming the Arid West, 11, 37, 390.

force who were present and thought of the similar men in the service, in the higher positions, who were absent and who were no less responsible for the work done, I felt a foreboding that they would never receive any real recognition for their achievement." [1]

Roosevelt had a clear comprehension of what was needed when he became President. "The idea that our natural resources were inexhaustible," he wrote, "still obtained, and there was as yet no real knowledge of their extent and condition. . . . Our magnificent river system with its superb possibilities for public usefulness was dealt with by the National Government not as a unit but as a disconnected series of pork-barrel problems. . . . On June 17, 1902, the Reclamation Act was passed. It set aside the proceeds of the disposal of public lands for the purpose of reclaiming the waste areas of the arid West by irrigating lands otherwise worthless and thus creating new homes upon the land. The money so appropriated was to be repaid to the Government by the settlers, and to be used again as a revolving fund continuously available for the work." [2]

The storage dam, called after Roosevelt, at the canyon of the Salt River — "a wild, ragged and picturesque spot," is an excellent example of irrigation. "To create a dam here of sufficient power to stop and tame the Salt River, especially at flood time, meant a gigantic piece of solid engineering." [3] Such a one was constructed and the result is best told by a citation by Charles G. Washburn

[1] Autobiography, 435. The men whom Roosevelt held up especially for honor were Gifford Pinchot, John W. Powell, F. H. Newell, Charles D. Walcott, Francis G. Newlands, G. H. Maxwell, Dr. J. W. McGee.

[2] Autobiography, 430, 431.

[3] Reclaiming the West, James, 71. See that book for a fine account.

from an Arizona newspaper printed probably about 1916 :
"Ten years ago farm land in the Salt River Valley was
worth from thirty-five to a hundred dollars per acre.   It is
now worth from seventy-five to five hundred dollars. . . .
What effected the change?   The credit should be given
to the Roosevelt Reservoir. . . .   The Roosevelt Reservoir right now has more water in it than it ever had before, giving positive insurance of crops in the Salt River
Valley for years to come.   It is three-fourths full and
will be entirely filled before the snow stops melting this
spring." [1] The Roosevelt Dam was nearly five years
in construction,[2] and was opened by ex-President Roosevelt in March, 1911.

The Colorado River is the Nile of America, only it is
not navigable; it was dammed at Yuma, 251 miles south-
east of Los Angeles.[3] The results were excellent and
made for civilization.   "Every item," wrote Roosevelt
in 1913, "of the whole great plan of reclamation now
in effect was undertaken between 1902 and 1906.   By
the spring of 1909 the work was an assured success and
the Government had become fully committed to its continuance." [4]

James, in his chapter entitled "A Vision of the Future,"
the last one of his book published in 1917, wrote, "Who
that is familiar with the destructive floods of, say, three
Western rivers alone, the Columbia, Colorado and Sac-
ramento, does not understand that the *real* conquest of
these rivers has not yet even begun."   There are 80

---

[1] Washburn's Roosevelt, 126.
[2] Sept. 20, 1906 to March, 1911, James, 80.
[3] For a full account, ibid., 97.
[4] Autobiography, 432.

million acres of swamp lands and 400 million acres of
deserts, mostly public domains, in the United States.
"Our swamp and overflow lands," he continued, "embrace
an area greater than the whole superficial area of the
Philippines. Their reclamation would give employment
for years to hundreds of thousands of laborers and later
would afford opportunities for the establishment of
approximately two and a half million families in homes
of their own. Two or three harvests from these lands
would suffice to pay the entire cost of reclamation. . . .
The Man of Destiny is the hydraulic engineer." [1]

Theodore Roosevelt was no engineer but he appreciated fully the material interests of his country. "A
primeval forest," he wrote while governor, "is a great
sponge which absorbs and distils the rain water. And
when it is destroyed the result is apt to be an alternation
of flood and drought. Forest fires ultimately make the
land a desert." "I was a warm believer in reclamation
and in forestry," he wrote while President.[2] Forestry
is the science of caring for and cultivating forests. "Concerned over the destruction of the forests," Roosevelt
as President did what he could for their preservation.
He was attracted to Gifford Pinchot to whom he paid a
warm tribute. "He led," so Roosevelt wrote, "and indeed during its most vital period embodied the fight for
the preservation through use of our forests." [3] The
enemies of the forest were fires, the sawmill and other
inventions for getting timber and wood-pulp. By legislation which he furthered and by executive action the
President had always in mind that a fight must be made

---

[1] Pp. 389, 390, 393.   [2] Autobiography, 339, 431.
[3] Autobiography, 429.

for the preservation of the forests. They are, he told the people of Memphis, on October 4, 1907, "the most effective preventers of floods; . . . the loss from soil wash is enormous. . . . It is computed . . . that one billion tons in weight of the richest soil matter of the United States is annually gathered in storm rivulets, washed into the rivers and borne into the sea. . . . We are consuming our forests three times faster than they are being reproduced. . . . Yet forests, unlike mines, can be so handled as to yield the best results of use, without exhaustion, just like green fields." [1]

The President's trip down the Mississippi River on a steamboat was a notable occurrence. At St. Louis on October 2, 1907, he said, "I am taking a trip on the great natural highway which runs past your very doors — a highway once important now almost abandoned." In other parts of the country the railroad development had been at the expense of the rivers and of canals, natural and artificial waterways. In mercantile traffic we must follow the prime example of the Great Lakes as "the commerce that passes through the Soo far surpasses in bulk and value that of the Suez Canal." [2] At Memphis during the speech from which I have already quoted, he said, "The Mississippi Valley is a magnificent empire in size and fertility." In it there are "12,000 miles of waterway now more or less fully navigable." "This vast stretch of country lying between the Alleghanies and the Rockies, the Great Lakes and the Gulf will largely fix the type of civilization for the whole Western Hemisphere." [3]

---

[1] *Review of Reviews*, ed., 1429 *et seq.*   [2] Ibid., 1390.
[3] Ibid., 1420.

An important incident on this voyage was that the Inland Waterways Commission, appointed by the President during March, 1907, asked him to call a conference on the conservation of natural resources in Washington. Roosevelt carried out their request and wrote to the governors of the several States and to prominent men summoning them to Washington to attend such a conference. "The conservation of our natural resources," he wrote in a special Message to Congress of March 25, 1908, "is literally vital for the future of the Nation." [1] To the imposing conference assembled in the East Room of the White House he said in his address of welcome: "So vital is this question that for the first time in our history the chief executive officers of the States separately, and of the States together forming the Nation, have met to consider it." Men, "chosen for their special acquaintance with the terms of the problem that is before us, the Senators and Representatives in Congress, the Supreme Court, the Cabinet and the Inland Waterways Commission have likewise been invited to the conference." [2] A friendly criticism was that such an assemblage was perfectly obvious. But no President had ever initiated it before and it remained for Roosevelt, in this case as in many others, to make the precedent.

The Convention of Governors as it was called was an interesting assembly. It was of course presided over by the President who, as he stepped into the East Room, took his place at the presiding officer's table and called the meeting to order by a rap of the gavel, could not help

---

[1] *Review of Reviews* ed., 1687.
[2] Ibid., 1739.

reminding one of the Homeric Council at which Agamemnon, King of men, was at the head.   Verily Roosevelt was in this assemblage "King of men."   It was notable to an onlooker from the East to see the representative men of the South and West gathered together.   After much discussion the Conference adopted a report and the debate on it was instructive.   The governors of the Southern States were well to the fore and seemed to enjoy speaking of the President as a man of large brain and great heart — a man of "inside" views and generous ideas.   He was always received with enthusiasm, and next to this, though below it in intensity, was that awarded to William J. Bryan, who came by invitation as one of the delegates.   The Southern governors referred often to the indissoluble union of indestructible States, and their discussion of centralization and State rights was significant.   Bryan read his paper and the onlooker thought he was a poor reader and was disappointed that he did not speak those words of silver eloquence, of which report was common.   Bryan said: "I am a strict constructionist, if that means to believe that the Federal Government is one of delegated power and that constitutional limitations should be carefully observed.   There is no twilight zone between the nation and the State in which exploiting interests can take refuge from both, and my observation is that most — not all but most — of the contentions over the line between nation and State are traceable to predatory corporations which are trying to shield themselves from deserved punishment or endeavoring to prevent needed restraining legislation.   The first point which I desire to make is that earnest men with an unselfish purpose and controlled only for the

public good will be able to agree upon legislation which
will not only preserve for the future the inheritance which
we have received from a bountiful Providence but preserve it in such a way as to avoid the dangers of centralization.''

Roosevelt made this impromptu reply: "Just a word
on what has been called the 'Twilight Land' between
the powers of the Federal and State governments. My
primary aim in the legislation that I have advocated
for the regulation of the great corporations has been to
provide some effective popular sovereign for each corporation. I do not wish to keep this twilight land one
of large and vague boundaries, by judicial decision that
in a given case the State cannot act and then a few years
later by other decisions that in practically similar cases
the nation cannot act either. I am trying to find out
where one or the other can act, so that there shall always
be some sovereign power that on behalf of the people
can hold every big corporation, every big individual to an
accountability. . . . Give an ample reward to the captain of industry; but not an indeterminate and infinite
reward. . . . It is eminently right that he should be allowed to make ample profit from his development of the
privilege; but make him pay something for it and make
the grant for a fixed period so that when the conditions
change, as in all probability they will change, our children, the Nation of the future, shall have the right to
determine the condition upon which that privilege shall
be enjoyed. In these cases the State has not acted or
cannot act; therefore I hold the Nation should act.
Where the policy I advocate can be carried out best by
the State, let it be carried out by the State; where it

can be carried out best by the Nation, let it be carried out by the Nation." [1]

"The conservation movement was a direct out-growth of the forest movement," wrote Roosevelt.[2] For the results of this Conference on the conservation of natural resources, the reader is referred to Roosevelt's Autobiography, to the chapter on Conservation in Lewis's Life, and to the public documents. The actual effect on public sentiment was great. It directed men's attention to the subject and made them feel that they had been wasting Nature's heritage and that henceforward economy and not waste should be the rule.

"The business management of the Forest Service became so excellent . . . that it was declared by a well-known firm of business organizers to compare favorably with the best managed of the great private corporations, an opinion which was confirmed by the report of a Congressional investigation and by the report of the Presidential Committee on Departmental method. The area of the National Forests had increased from 43 to 194 million acres; the force from about 500 to more than 3000. There was saved for public use in the National Forests more Government timberland during the seven and a half years prior to March 4, 1909, than during all previous and succeeding years put together." [3]

"The United States Supreme Court," wrote Lewis, "has upheld every single action of Roosevelt for conservation that has been brought before it. With one exception all these decisions were unanimous." [4]

---

[1] Washington *Post*, May 16, 1908; *Review of Reviews*, ed., 1754.
[2] Autobiography, 444.
[3] Ibid., 441.   [4] Life of Roosevelt, 299.

CHAPTER XVI

AT a luncheon given to Roosevelt, when he was still Vice-President, at the Algonquin Club in Boston, the President of the Club, Charles H. Taylor, who was likewise the presiding officer of the feast, said, that if by any chance Roosevelt became President, men would lie uneasy in their beds with sleepless nights finding it impossible to get it out of their heads that he was a Jingo and would involve us in trouble; if the opportunity did not come he would make it. Roosevelt became President and had an excellent chance to "gobble" Cuba when an insurrection broke out there during August, 1906. The story is best told in Roosevelt's own words: "For seven years Cuba has been in a condition of profound peace and of steadily growing prosperity. For four years this peace and prosperity have obtained under her own independent government. Her peace, prosperity and independence are now menaced; for of all possible evils that can befall Cuba the worst is the evil of anarchy, into which civil war and revolutionary disturbances will assuredly throw her." [1] When he met the Congress in December, 1906, he told the whole story. "Last August," he wrote, "an insurrection broke out in Cuba which it speedily grew evident that the existing Cuban government was powerless to quell. This Government was repeatedly asked by the then Cuban government to intervene, and finally was notified by the President of Cuba that he in-

---

[1] *Review of Reviews*, ed., 821.

tended to resign; that his decision was irrevocable; that none of the other constitutional officers would consent to carry on the government and that he was powerless to maintain order. It was evident that chaos was impending. . . . Thanks to the preparedness of our Navy, I was able immediately to send enough ships to Cuba to prevent the situation from becoming hopeless; and I furthermore despatched to Cuba the Secretary of War [William H. Taft] and the Assistant Secretary of State [Robert Bacon] in order that they might grapple with the situation on the ground. All efforts to secure an agreement between the contending factions by which they should themselves come to an amicable understanding and settle upon some *modus vivendi* — some provisional government of their own — failed. Finally the President of the Republic resigned. The quorum of Congress assembled failed by deliberate purpose of its members, so that there was no power to act on his resignation and the government came to a halt. In accordance with the so-called Platt amendment, which was embodied in the constitution of Cuba, I therefore proclaimed a provisional government for the island, the Secretary of War acting as provisional governor until he could be replaced by Mr. Magoon, the late minister to Panama and governor of the Canal Zone on the Isthmus; troops were sent to support them and to relieve the Navy, the expedition being handled with most satisfactory speed and efficiency. The insurgent chiefs immediately agreed that their troops should lay down their arms and disband and the agreement was carried out. The provisional government has left the personnel of the old government and the old laws, so far as might be, unchanged, and will thus

Cuba

ter the island for a few months until tranquillity
restored, a new election properly held and a new
goverment inaugurated. Peace has come in the island,
and the harvesting of the sugar-cane crop, the great crop
of the island, is about to proceed." [1]

"In Cuba," he told the Harvard Union in February,
1907, "I am doing my best to persuade the Cubans that
if only they will be good they will be happy; I am seeking
the very minimum of interference necessary to make
them good." [2]   During April, 1907, he wrote to Andrew
Carnegie, "The United States Army is at this moment
in Cuba, not as an act of war, but to restore Cuba to the
position of a self-governing republic." [3]   Roosevelt was
exactly right. He lived up fully to his promise. Cuba
was turned over again to its inhabitants in January, 1909,
the last months of his two administrations. [4]

Next to his fight against high finance and his work
for the conservation of resources, Roosevelt is associated
in the public mind with his attitude to the Navy.   "The
United States Navy," he wrote in his Message of December, 1906, "is the surest guarantor of peace which this
country possesses."   This declaration must be borne in
mind as we recount his constant urging, care and attention to this branch of the service. He would be a rare
man in the Navy, whether officer, midshipman, marine or
seaman, who did not regard Roosevelt with veneration and
was not willing to follow whither he led. Such unstinted
confidence in a civilian is remarkable and as the same
feeling was shared by the Army it is the sort of enthusi-

---

[1] *Review of Reviews*, ed., 962.   [2] Ibid., 1178.
[3] Ibid., 1193.   [4] Life of Roosevelt, Lewis, 244.

asm evoked by a great military leader. Roosevelt was a profound student of naval operations, writing his first book on the subject at twenty-four, so that his advice to study our failures was the result of scholastic inquiry as well as practical observation. There was only one way, he affirmed, in which the War of 1812 could have been avoided as is well shown in Captain Mahan's history. "If," Roosevelt wrote, "during the preceding twelve years, a navy, relatively as strong as that which the country now has, had been built up and an army provided relatively as good as that which the country now has, there never would have been the slightest necessity of fighting the war; and if the necessity had arisen, the war would under such circumstances have ended with our speedy and overwhelming triumph. But our people during those twelve years refused to make any preparations whatever regarding either the Army or the Navy. They saved a million or two of dollars by so doing; and in mere money paid a hundredfold for each million they thus saved during the three years of war which followed — a war which brought untold suffering upon our people, which at one time threatened the gravest national disaster, and which, in spite of the necessity of waging it, resulted merely in what was in effect a drawn battle, while the balance of defeat and triumph was almost even." [1]

In 1906 he asked Congress "for the building each year of at least one first-class battle-ship." [2] But one year later he had changed his opinion and asked for four battle-

---

[1] *Review of Reviews* ed., 983.
[2] Annual Message, ibid., 984. The American Navy at that time had nine battleships and eight more in course of construction. Life of Roosevelt, Lewis, 261.

ships. The second Hague Conference, that held from June to October, 1907, meanwhile had declined to limit naval armaments; therefore "it would be most unwise for us to stop the upbuilding of our Navy. To build one battle-ship of the best and most advanced type a year would barely keep our fleet up to its present force. This is not enough. . . . The only efficient use for the Navy is for offence. The only way in which it can efficiently protect our own coast against the possible action of a foreign navy is by destroying that foreign navy." [1]

"This is a very rough-and-tumble, workaday world," Roosevelt wrote in a private letter; [2] and we peace-lovers must admit that he comprehended Europe in 1907 better than we did. Nobody could assert that he foresaw the terrible conflict which began in 1914, but he believed in being ready for any emergency and was less trustful of our European contemporaries than were we who sat in comfortable libraries and constructed theories. [3] Therefore the years have demonstrated that he was supremely right when he asked for four battleships, and we were wrong when we cut him down to two. [4] "Our army and navy," he wrote, "and above all our people learned some lessons from the Spanish War and applied them to our own uses. During the following decade the improvement in our army and navy was very great; not in material but also in personnel, and, above all, in the ability to handle our forces in good-sized units. By 1908 . . . the navy had become in every respect as fit a fighting instru-

---

[1] Message of 1907, *Review of Reviews* ed., 1573.
[2] Bishop, ii. 23.
[3] Ibid.
[4] Act of May 13, 1908, "to cost, exclusive of armor and armament, not exceeding six million dollars each."

ment as any other navy in the world, fleet for fleet. Even in size there was but one nation, England, which was completely out of our class; and in view of our relations with England and all the English-speaking peoples, this was of no consequence."[1] For the efficient use of the money which Congress gave him Roosevelt could be thoroughly trusted when he comprehended matters — and it is amazing the number that he did comprehend — and in his work, as we look at it now, he was above criticism when it is understood with what materials he had to work.[2] But he always had at his back the rank and file of the Navy and Army whose attitude toward him was almost one of worship. He was now to give the greatest proof of the efficiency of the Navy in the voyage around the world.

This was so stupendous a feat that it is well that Roosevelt himself should tell the story. "In my own judgment," he wrote in his Autobiography, "the most important service that I rendered to peace was the voyage of the battle fleet round the world. I had become convinced that for many reasons it was essential that we should have it clearly understood, by our own people

---

[1] Autobiography, 276. On March 9, 1905, he wrote to General Leonard Wood: "When I became President three years ago I made up my mind that I should try for a fleet with a minimum strength of forty armor clads; and though the difficulty of getting what I wished has increased from year to year I have now reached my mark and we have built or provided for twenty-eight battle-ships and twelve armored cruisers. This navy puts us a good second to France and about on a par with Germany; and ahead of any other power in point of material, except, of course, England." Bishop, i. 366.

[2] "I have had on occasions to fight bosses and rings and machines; and have to get along as best I could with bosses and rings and machines when the conditions were different." And he wrote to Sir George Trevelyan on May 13, 1905, "In practical life we have to work with the instruments at hand." Bishop, ii. 13, 150.

especially, but also by other peoples that the Pacific was as much our home waters as the Atlantic and that our fleet could and would at will pass from one to the other of the two great oceans. It seemed to me evident that such a voyage would greatly benefit the navy itself; would arouse popular interest in and enthusiasm for the navy; and would make foreign nations accept as a matter of course that our fleet should from time to time be gathered in the Pacific just as from time to time it was gathered in the Atlantic, and that its presence in one ocean was no more to be accepted as a mark of hostility to any Asiatic power than its presence in the Atlantic was to be accepted as a mark of hostility to any European power." [1] On July 4 the Secretary of the Navy in a speech at Oakland, California, said the Pacific coast would shortly receive a visit from the Navy. [2] But a letter to Secretary Root from Oyster Bay nine days later showed a further reaching program in Roosevelt's busy brain and also the most important reason for his determination.

"I am more concerned," he wrote to Secretary Root, "over the Japanese situation than almost any other. Thank Heaven we have the Navy in good shape. It is high time however that it should go on a cruise around the world. In the first place I think it will have a pacific effect to show that it can be done; and in the next place, after talking thoroughly over the situation with the naval board I became convinced that it was absolutely necessary for us to try in time of peace to see just what we could do in the way of putting a big battle fleet in the

---

[1] P. 592.   [2] Life of Roosevelt, Lewis, 266.

Pacific and not make the experiment in time of war. Aoki and Admiral Yamamoto were out here yesterday at lunch. . . . Yamamoto, an ex-Cabinet Minister and a man of importance, evidently had completely misunderstood the situation here and what the possibilities were. I had a long talk with him through an interpreter. He kept insisting that the Japanese must not be kept out save as we keep out Europeans. I kept explaining to him that what we had to do was to face facts; that if American laboring men came in and cut down the wages of Japanese laboring men, they would be shut out of Japan in one moment; and that Japanese laborers must be excluded from the United States on economic grounds. I told him emphatically that it was not possible to admit Japanese laborers into the United States. . . . I pointed out that under our present treaty we had explicitly reserved the right to exclude Japanese laborers. I talked freely of the intended trip of the battle-ship fleet through the Pacific, mentioning that it would return home very shortly after it had been sent out there; at least in all probability. I also was most complimentary about Japan." [1]

The fleet of sixteen battleships, all of them commissioned since the Spanish-American War, sailed from Hampton Roads on December 16, 1907. Their officers and crews numbered about 12,000 men. They were reviewed before their departure by President Roosevelt, when it was generally supposed that they were going to San Francisco and possibly as far north as Seattle. But after Roosevelt had returned to the White House

---

[1] Bishop, ii. 64.

"it was announced that the fleet would continue on to our insular possessions and return home by the Suez Canal." [1]

"I determined on the move," wrote Roosevelt, "without consulting the Cabinet. . . .   A council of war never fights and in a crisis the duty of a leader is to lead and not take refuge behind the generally timid wisdom of a multitude of councillors. At that time as I happen to know, neither the English nor the German authorities believed it possible to take a fleet of great battle-ships round the world. They did not believe that their own fleets could perform the feat and still less did they believe that the American fleet could."   In 1910 he had a confirmation of this which he related in his celebrated letter to Sir George O. Trevelyan: "Von Tirpitz [Secretary of the Imperial Admiralty] was particularly interested in the voyage of the battle fleet round the world and he told me frankly that he had not believed we could do it successfully and added that the English Naval Office and Foreign Office had felt the same way. . . .   He then said that he expected that Japan would attack us while the fleet was on its way round and asked me if I had not also expected this. I told him that I had not expected such an attack but that I had thought it possible ; in other words that I thought the chances were against it, but there was a chance for it. . . .   I had been doing my best to be polite to the Japanese, and had finally become uncomfortably conscious of a very, very slight undertone of veiled truculence in their communications in connection with things that happened on the Pacific Slope ;

---

[1] Life of Roosevelt, Lewis, 268.

and I finally made up my mind that they thought I was afraid of them. . . . I found that the Japanese war party firmly believed that they could beat us, and, unlike the Elder Statesmen, thought I also believed this." [1]

During 1907 and possibly a part of 1908 the friction between California as the leader of the Pacific coast and Japan became acute. The question of excluding the Japanese from the public schools was to the fore and there was also a hostile feeling regarding the Japanese possession of land. The opposition to the immigration of the Japanese was not on account of their inferiority as being of the yellow race, but on account of their superiority. They could live for less, work for less than the Caucasian and did they become actual possessors of land could cultivate it better and get more from it. Anyone who will take the trouble to compare the square miles and population of Japan with the area of California, Oregon and Washington and their number of inhabitants [2] can see at once the reason of the covetousness of Japan and the resistance of the Caucasian. It was fortunate that in the presidential chair was a man of culture who appreciated the Japanese civilization and at the same time was a true American full of sympathy for the West and who understood the view of the Californians.

To continue the story from the Autobiography: "I made up my mind that it was time to have a show down in the matter; because if it was really true that our fleet could not get from the Atlantic to the Pacific it was much better to know it and be able to shape our policy

---

[1] Bishop, ii. 249.

[2] Japan, 148,000 square miles, population over 48 millions; California, Oregon and Washington, 318,000 square miles, estimated population in 1907, three millions.

in view of the knowledge. Many persons publicly and privately protested against the move on the ground that Japan would accept it as a threat. To this I answered nothing in public. In private I said that I did not believe Japan would so regard it because Japan knew my sincere friendship and admiration for her and realized that we could not as a Nation have any intention of attacking her. . . . When in the spring of 1910 I was in Europe I was interested to find that high naval authorities in both Germany and Italy had expected that war would come at the time of the voyage. They asked me if I had not been afraid of it, and if I had not expected that hostilities would begin at least by the time that the fleet reached the Straits of Magellan? I answered that I did not expect it; that I believed that Japan would feel as friendly in the matter as we did; but that if my expectations had proved mistaken, it would have been proof positive that we were going to be attacked anyhow and that in such event it would have been an enormous gain to have had the three months' preliminary preparation which enabled the fleet to start perfectly equipped. In a personal interview before they left, I had explained to the officers in command that I believed the trip would be one of absolute peace, but that they were to take exactly the same precautions against sudden attack of any kind as if we were at war with all the nations of the earth; and that no excuse of any kind would be accepted if there were a sudden attack of any kind and we were taken unawares. . . .

"The cruise did make a very deep impression abroad. . . . But the impression made on our own people was of far greater consequence. No single thing in the history of

the new United States Navy has done as much to stimu-
late popular interest and belief in it as the world cruise.

"I first directed the fleet of sixteen battle-ships to go
round through the Straits of Magellan to San Francisco.
From thence I ordered them to New Zealand and Australia, then to the Philippines, China and Japan and
home through Suez. . . . Admiral Evans commanded
the fleet to San Francisco; there Admiral Sperry took
it. . . . The coaling and other preparations were made
in such excellent shape by the Department that there
was never a hitch, not so much as the delay of an hour,
in keeping every appointment made. All the repairs
were made without difficulty, the ship concerned merely
falling out of the column for a few hours, and when the
job was done steaming at speed until she regained her
position. Not a ship was left in any port; and there
was hardly a desertion. As soon as it was known that
the voyage was to be undertaken men crowded to enlist,
just as freely from the Mississippi Valley as from the
seaboard, and for the first time since the Spanish War the
ships put to sea overmanned — and by as stalwart a
set of men-of-war's men as ever looked through a port-
hole, game for a fight or a frolic, but also self-respecting and with such a sense of responsibility that in all the
ports in which they landed their conduct was exemplary.
The fleet practised incessantly during the voyage both
with the guns and battle tactics and came home a much
more effective fighting instrument than when it started
sixteen months before. [1] . . .

"It was not originally my intention that the fleet should
visit Australia but the Australian Government sent a

[1] For the torpedo boat destroyers incident see Autobiography, 596.

most cordial invitation which I gladly accepted. . . . The reception accorded the fleet in Australia was wonderful and it showed the fundamental community of feeling between ourselves and the great commonwealth of the South Seas. The considerate, generous and open-handed hospitality with which the entire Australian people treated our officers and men could not have been surpassed had they been our own countrymen. . . .

"The most noteworthy incident of the cruise was the reception given to our fleet in Japan. In courtesy and good breeding, the Japanese can certainly teach much to the nations of the Western world. I had been very sure that the people of Japan would understand aright what the cruise meant and would accept the visit of our fleet as the signal honor which it was meant to be, a proof of the high regard and friendship I felt and which I was certain the American people felt for the great Island Empire. The event even surpassed my expectations. I cannot too strongly express my appreciation of the generous courtesy the Japanese showed the officers and crews of our fleet and I may add that every man of them came back a friend and admirer of the Japanese. On October 28, 1908, Admiral Sperry wrote me that in Yokohama as many as a thousand English-speaking Japanese college students acted as volunteer guides. . . . In Tokyo there were a great many excellent refreshment places, where the men got excellent meals and could rest, smoke and write letters and in none of these places would they allow the men to pay anything though they were more than ready to do so. The arrangements were marvellously perfect." [1]

---

[1] Autobiography, 592 *et seq.* This citation and the other citations which I have made from the Autobiography are from the Macmillan

On the return of the fleet from their voyage round the world President Roosevelt on February 22, 1909, ten days before he was to give up the cares and delights of office, reviewed the fleet, addressing the officers and men in fitting words.[1]

President Roosevelt was fully alive to the Japanese situation. We cannot let in the Japanese, he said in private conversation during May, 1908, while the fleet was on its way round the world but before it visited Japan. I once thought that we could but I have given up that idea. My efforts have been to get the Japanese to stop emigration. The agreement which I now have is working fairly well but not perfectly. An exclusion Act may have to come and that may cause trouble. One reason for my desire of the increase of the Navy was the Japanese situation. We know what the Japanese are saying in their cups and there is a desire on the part of a certain class in Japan to go to war with us. But the Elder Statesmen are opposed to it. The sending of the fleet to the Pacific stopped the Japanese talk of war.

Co. edition of 1913. George P. Brett wrote to me under date of Dec. 23, 1921, that the Macmillan Company parted with their publishing rights in the Roosevelt Autobiography some two years ago and the reference in my manuscript to that book should therefore credit its publication to the Messrs. Scribner instead of to the Macmillan Company.

[1] Autobiography, 602.

CHAPTER XVII

Nineteen hundred eight was the year for the election of a President and it seemed almost a foregone conclusion that the Republican candidate could be chosen, and he would be named by the Republican Convention which met in Chicago during June. No man stood so strong with the people as Theodore Roosevelt and no doubt remains that he could have been nominated and elected by an overwhelming majority. But he insisted publicly and privately that on no account whatever would he be a candidate. "There has never been a moment," he wrote to Lyman Abbott on May 29, "when I could not have had the Republican nomination with practical unanimity by simply raising one finger." [1] There can be no question that this statement was absolutely true. Roosevelt would not accept the presidency because he had a high regard for Washington's example which had dictated his pronouncement on election day, 1904, and for the further reason that, as he felt now that the people were back of him, they might say that he had prevailed upon their support in order to further his own ends should he now stand for a third term. But he was in no respect tired of his job. "I have had an exceedingly good time," he wrote to William Allen White; "I have been exceedingly well treated by the American people; and I have enjoyed the respect of those for whose respect I care most." [2] He would have liked to remain President. He loved

---

[1] Bishop, ii. 86.   [2] Nov. 26, 1907, Bishop, ii. 51.

power and place and was in no way ashamed to own it. "I have finished my career in public life," he wrote to E. S. Martin, the editor of *Life*. "I have enjoyed it to the full; I have achieved a large proportion of what I set out to achieve." [1]

Despite many and various influences that were brought to bear upon him he was inflexible and resisted every attempt to induce him to stand for a third term. But as he would not be a candidate himself he could within certain limits name his successor. He had an unbounded admiration for Elihu Root and thought he would be exactly the sort of man he would like to follow him. I have never been so impressed with the praise of one great man by another as when I have heard Roosevelt speak of Root and I may add that this praise was concurred in by the Ambassador of Great Britain to the United States, James Bryce. But as Roosevelt wrote to Lawrence F. Abbott in 1912, "I found that the Westerners would not stand Root." [2] It was exceedingly improbable that Root could be nominated and, were he placed before the people, his election against Bryan was doubtful. Therefore Roosevelt dropped Root. Two other men were prominent as candidates, William H. Taft and Charles E. Hughes. "I could not have nominated," wrote Roosevelt to Abbott in 1912, "an extreme progressive or an extreme conservative but I could by a turn of the hand have thrown the nomination to either Taft or Hughes. The only way to prevent my own nomination was for me actively to champion and to force the nomination of someone else; I chose Taft rather than

---

[1] Bishop, ii. 123.   [2] Impressions, 65.

Hughes," [1] with the result that there were only two candidates really at the Chicago convention, Taft and Roosevelt. "As a matter of fact," he wrote to Lyman Abbott on May 29, "I doubt if Taft himself could be more anxious than I am that Taft be nominated and that any stampede to me be prevented." [2]

The Convention was held in Chicago and was presided over with dignity and force during his chairmanship by Senator Henry Cabot Lodge. [3] Roosevelt wrote to Mrs. Lodge on June 19, after Taft's nomination was made : "In point of judgment, taste and power it would be literally impossible to better either Cabot's words or his actions. He was in a peculiar sense the guardian not only of the national interests but of my own personal honor ; and to do his full duty as guardian it was necessary for him effectively to thwart the movements not merely of my foes but of the multitude of well-meaning friends who did not think deeply or who were not of very sensitive fiber. It was absolutely necessary that any stampede should be prevented and that I should not be nominated." [4] Five days later he wrote to Senator Lodge himself, "On every side I hear of the great success you made as chairman. . . . You rendered a great public service and you rendered me a personal service." [5]

On June 19 he wrote a letter to Sir George O. Trevelyan, a copy of which he sent to me that shows his intimate thought at the time.

---

[1] Impressions, 66.   [2] Bishop, ii. 87.
[3] It met June 16.   Lodge was permanent chairman.
[4] Bishop, ii. 91.   James S. Sherman of New York was nominated for Vice-President.
[5] Ibid., 92.

feel that I was the man of all others whom they wished to see President. Yet such I think has been the case; and therefore, when I felt obliged to insist on retiring and abandoning the leadership, now and then I felt ugly qualms as to whether I was not refusing to do what I ought to do, and abandoning great work on a mere fantastic point of honor.

"These are strong reasons why my course should be condemned; yet I think that the countervailing reasons are still stronger. Of course when I spoke I had in view the precedent set by Washington and continued ever since, the precedent which recognizes the fact that, as there inheres in the Presidency more power than in any other office in any great republic or constitutional monarchy of modern times, it can only be saved from abuse by having the people as a whole accept as axiomatic the position that one man can hold it for no more than a limited time. I don't think that any harm comes from the concentration of power, in one man's hands, provided the holder does not keep it for more than a certain, definite time, and then returns to the people from whom he sprang. In the great days of the Roman Republic no harm whatever came from the dictatorship, because great as the power of the dictator was, after a comparatively short period he surrendered it back to those from whom he gained it. On the other hand, the history of the first and second French Republics, not to speak of the Spanish-American Republics, not to speak of the Commonwealth, in Seventeenth Century England, has shown that the strong man, and even the strong man who is good, may very readily subvert free institutions if he and the people at large grow to accept his continued possession of vast power as being necessary to good government. It is a very unhealthy thing that any man should be considered necessary to the people as a whole, save in the way of meeting some given crisis. Moreover, in a republic like ours the vital need is that there shall be a general recognition of the moral law, of the law which, as regards public men, means belief in efficient and disinterested service for the public rendered without thought of personal gain, and above all without the thought of self-perpetuation in office. I regard the memories of Washington and Lincoln as priceless heritages for our people, just because they are the memories of strong men, of men who cannot be accused of weakness or timidity, of men who I believe were quite as strong for instance as Cromwell or Bismarck, and very much stronger than the Louis Napoleon type, who, nevertheless, led careers marked by disinterestedness just as much as by strength; who, like Timoleon and Hampden, in very deed, and not as a mere matter of oratory or fine writing, put the public good, the good of the people as a whole, as the first of all considerations.

"Now, my ambition is that, in however small a way, the work I do shall be along the Washington and Lincoln lines. While President I have *been* President, emphatically; I have used every ounce of power there was in the office and I have not cared a rap for the criticisms of those who spoke of my 'usurpation of power'; for I knew that the talk was all nonsense and that there was no usurpation. I believe that the efficiency of this Government depends upon its possessing a strong central executive, and wherever I could establish a precedent for strength in the executive, as I did for instance as regards external affairs in the case of sending the fleet around the world, taking Panama, settling affairs of Santo Domingo and Cuba; or as I did in internal affairs in settling the anthracite coal strike, in keeping order in Nevada this year when the Federation of Miners threatened anarchy, or as I have done in bringing the big corporations to book — why, in all these cases I have felt not merely that my action was right in itself, but that in showing the strength of, or in giving strength to, the executive, I was establishing a precedent of value.   I believe in a strong executive; I believe in power; but I believe that responsibility should go with power, and that it is not well that the strong executive should be a perpetual executive.   Above all and beyond all I believe as I have said before that the salvation of this country depends upon Washington and Lincoln representing the type of leader to which we are true.   I hope that in my acts I have been a good President, a President who has deserved well of the Republic; but most of all, I believe that whatever value my service may have comes even more from what I *am* than from what I *do*.   I may be mistaken, but it is my belief that the bulk of my countrymen, the men whom Abraham Lincoln called 'the plain people' — the farmers, mechanics, small tradesmen, hard-working professional men — feel that I am in a peculiar sense their President, that I represent the democracy in somewhat the fashion that Lincoln did, that is, not in any demagogic way but with the sincere effort to stand for a government by the people and for the people.   Now the chief service I can render these plain people who believe in me is, not to destroy their ideal of me.   They have followed me for the past six or seven

years, indeed for some years previously, because they
thought they recognized in me certain qualities in which
they believed, because they regarded me as honest and
disinterested, as having courage and common sense.
Now I wouldn't for anything in the world shatter this
belief of theirs in me, unless it were necessary to do so
because they had embarked on a wrong course, and I
could only be really true to them by forfeiting their
good will. For instance, if they made up their minds
that they would repudiate their debts, or under a gust
of emotion decided to follow any course that was wrong,
I could show loyalty to them only by opposing them tooth
and nail, without the slightest regard to any amount of
unpopularity or obloquy. But this of course isn't what
I mean when I say I do not want to shatter their belief
in me. What I mean is that I do not want to make them
think that after all I am actuated by selfish motives,
by motives of self-interest, that my championship of
their cause, that my opposition to the plutocracy, is
simply due to the usual demagog's desire to pander to
the mob, or to the no more dangerous, but even more
sinister, desire to secure self-advancement under the
cloak of championship of popular rights. Of course I
may be wrong in my belief, but my belief is that a great
many honest people in this country who lead hard lives
are helped in their efforts to keep straight and avoid envy
and hatred and despair by their faith in me and in the
principles I preach and in my practice of these principles.
I would not for anything do the moral damage to these
people that might come from shattering their faith in
my personal disinterestedness. A few months ago three
old back-country farmers turned up in Washington and

after awhile managed to get in to see me. They were rugged old fellows, as hairy as Boers and a good deal of the Boer type. They hadn't a black coat among them, and two of them wore no cravats; that is, they just had on their working clothes, but all cleaned and brushed. When they finally got to see me they explained that they hadn't anything whatever to ask, but that they believed in me, believed that I stood for what they regarded as the American ideal, and as one rugged old fellow put it, 'We want to shake that honest hand.' Now this anecdote seems rather sentimental as I tell it, and I do not know that I can convey to you the effect the incident produced on me; but it was one of the very many incidents which have occurred, and they have made me feel that I am under a big debt of obligation to the good people of this country, and that I am bound not by any unnecessary action of mine to forfeit their respect, not to hurt them by taking away any part of what they have built up as their ideal of me. It is just as I would not be willing to hurt my soldiers, to destroy my influence among men who look up to me as leader, by needlessly doing anything in battle which would give the idea that I was not personally brave; even though some given risk might seem a little unnecessary to an outsider. However certain I might be that in seeking or accepting a third term I was actuated by a sincere desire to serve my fellow countrymen, I am very much afraid that multitudes of thoroughly honest men who have believed deeply in me (and some of them, by the way, until I consented to run might think that they wished me to run) would nevertheless have a feeling of disappointment if I did try to occupy the Presidency for three consecutive terms, to hold it longer than it was deemed wise that Washington should hold it.

"I would have felt very differently, and very much more doubtful about what to do, if my leaving the Presidency had meant that there was no chance to continue the work in which I am engaged and which I deem vital to the welfare of the people. But in Taft there was ready to hand a man whose theory of public and private duty is my own, and whose practice of this theory is what I hope mine is; and if we can elect him President we achieve all that could be achieved by continuing me in the office, and yet we avoid all the objections, all the risk of creating a bad precedent."

The President used the utmost exertion for Taft's election consistent with the dignity of his office. Taft's Democratic opponent was William J. Bryan. But he was elected receiving 321 electoral votes against 162 for Bryan and a plurality of over 1,269,000 in the popular vote.

"Toward the end of his term (the second) the relations between Roosevelt and Congress became somewhat strained," wrote Charles G. Washburn, a member of the House at this time and a devoted friend of Roosevelt's. "This was due to a variety of causes. The President was, very properly, constantly pressing an elaborate programme of legislation. Congress could never meet his expectations or the expectations of the people, and the legislative body came to feel that its efforts were not properly appreciated and that the Executive held a place in the confidence of the people that properly belonged to Congress. The President preferred pretty direct methods to the arts of diplomacy. I think that the country rather enjoyed his controversies with Congress and as a rule sided with him." [1]

Whoever writes the story of Roosevelt's seven and one-half years of administration must necessarily recount that part of his life, for he so pervaded the administration that the two are essentially one. At the outset we must bear in mind what William H. Taft wrote of him in 1919: Theodore Roosevelt was "the most commanding, the most original, the most interesting and the most brilliant personality in American public life since Lincoln." [2] He was all of that and a man also of signal ability. One gets an idea of a man from a long personal and friendly acquaintance and in bearing my testimony I represent simply that of a thousand others in writing that in all my life I have never met one personally with whose ability I have been so impressed.

Roosevelt was a loveable man. He loved children and children were at once attracted to him; he gained their confidence and made on them a lasting impression. His letters to his own children show the relation of a father that many would gladly imitate, but imitation of Theodore Roosevelt was impossible. The President playing bear with his youngest daughter in an upper hall of the White House surprised a martinet on a visit who could not comprehend how a man dealing with the most serious affairs of life could so unbend. Roosevelt could do it in the most natural manner but it is impossible to conceive any other President who occupied the White House indulging in such a playful episode.

---

[1] P. 138.
[2] Life of Roosevelt, Lewis, xxii.

Children are better than books, he said. He preached continually to women their duty of bearing children. In a noble tribute to the farm and farmer he pleaded that the life of the farmer should be made happier and so the drift to the city stopped; nevertheless he declared, "There is plenty that is hard and rough and disagreeable in the necessary work of actual life." He laid emphasis on the fact that the men who tilled the soil fed and clothed the towns and cities; but "the best crop is the crop of children." [1]

Roosevelt was, in the most appropriate sense of the word, a bookish man. "I find reading a great comfort," he wrote to Sir George O. Trevelyan. [2] The list of books that he had read within two years that he furnished Dr. Nicholas Murray Butler and his discussion with Sir George O. Trevelyan of Ferrero's "La Grandeur et Décadence de Rome" are amazing from a man in the presidential office. He joined in the present of a silver loving cup to Trevelyan inscribed, "To the Historian of the American Revolution from his friends — Theodore Roosevelt, Henry Cabot Lodge and Elihu Root." Trevelyan's History struck him as one of the very few histories that can be called great and after a re-reading of it he came to the conclusion that the historian "had painted us a little too favorably." [3] Roosevelt, wrote Lawrence F. Abbott, who knew him intimately, "was a voracious and omniverous reader." [4] He was likewise

---

[1] *Review of Reviews* ed., 1291 *et ante;* also 1531.
[2] Bishop, ii. 142.
[3] Bishop, i. 265, ii. 144, 163, 166.
[4] Impressions, 183. He published at least 30 books. His life of Gouverneur Morris contains about 60,000 words; his African Game Trails, about 200,000. Making an average of 75,000 words, he wrote 2,250,000

a rapid one but his quick perusal did not prevent his seizing upon the salient points of any book. He discussed Henry Osborne Taylor's "Mediæval Mind" with a scholar in terms common to them both. He desired to read all that was written about the Mongols. He was a great admirer of Morley's "Gladstone."[1] He was fond of Milton, being especially attracted to his prose. He told Sir George Trevelyan that he had been reading Tacitus and further said, "You who are so blessed as to read all the best of the Greeks or Latins in the original must not look down too scornfully upon us who have to make believe that we are contented with Emerson's view of translations." Apparently he knew well Greek life, as he was disposed to agree with Galton in placing the average Athenian in point of intellect "above the average civilized man of our countries."[2] An author knows his own book best and I confess my delight at his knowledge of my fifth volume which I knew he had thoroughly read amid many distractions.[3] His reference to Martin Chuzzlewit in a speech at Cairo, Illinois, on October 3, 1907 exhibited the fullness of the presidential mind. The region where we are now standing, he said, was the seat of Dickens's forlorn "Eden." "It would be simply silly to be angry over 'Martin Chuzzlewit,' on the contrary, read it, be amused by it, profit by it; and don't be misled by it." I was surprised at his knowledge of a recent "Life of Fessenden" whence he derived an animated and full account of the Cabinet crisis of 1862.

---

words in permanent literary form. It is estimated that during his governorship and Presidency he wrote 150,000 letters; on an average of 100 words to the letter this amounts to 15 million words. Ibid., 169.

[1] Bishop, i. 268.   [2] Bishop, ii. 154, 160.   [3] See Mrs. Robinson, 219.

This was in 1908 when I was invited to make him a
visit to hear his criticism of my vi and vii volumes.
After luncheon at the White House he asked his cousin
W. Emlen Roosevelt, Francis D. Millet, Clifford Richardson and myself to accompany him on the rear veranda
of the White House.   In your last work, he said, you have
stepped down from your impartial judgment seat of
the earlier volumes and become something of an advocate.
During the Civil War you held the scales even, and while
you have perhaps properly criticised the North for her
Reconstruction policy you have not blamed the South
for the course she took that made radical measures possible.   Her conduct prevented any proper policy.   I am
inclined to think that the XIV amendment plan was
the best proposed.

It was a fine day and stimulated by the air and the
success of his Conservation Conference, which was just
ending, he talked freely and well.   I blame E. L. Godkin
and Carl Schurz, he declared, because after having supported the negro suffrage policy, they condemned the
results of it.   It was all right if they had avowed their
mistake but that they did not do.   They still held to
the negro suffrage policy as being the best.   Even now
the *Evening Post* condemns the President's action in the
Brownsville, Texas matter from purely sentimental reasons.   The negro has been hurt, therefore the President
is wrong.   But Carl Schurz and *The Nation* never stimulated the best young men to go into politics and they
never had any influence with the crowd.

It was perhaps all right, he continued, for you to say
that Carl Schurz was almost an ideal senator, but on that
level you failed to do justice to Oliver P. Morton.   Roose-

velt then told with great spirit and enthusiasm Morton's course during the Civil War, speaking of the Copperheads as bitterly as if he had been their personal antagonist. It was the appreciation of one fighter by another. The men at the East, he said, have books written about them in good literary style; they receive the adulation of writers and so get a larger share of commendation than they are entitled to. When talking of Morton the President said to his cousin, Because Winslow, Lanier & Co. advanced money to Morton in his time of trouble I am disposed to forgive a member of their firm for saying that I am crazy, indulge immoderately in drink and further-more that I am an opium fiend.

There is no foundation whatever for any of the finan-cier's alleged charges; that of immoderate indulgence in drink has lasted the longest but has finally been set to rest. The truth is that he rarely drank at luncheon and that when he drank wine at dinner, he drank with the moderation of a gentleman and never to excess.[1]

Next morning the President continued his talk: I have not gained the support of the cultivated class and there are points where I should have done so. But I have received the support of the plain people, of the "one suspender men." And yet I have done things that might have aroused a demagogic feeling. I have shut the people out from the White House grounds in the rear; I have stopped the public receptions and have done a great deal in the limitation of others.

The relations of some of the cultivated class with men of wealth were close and it may be regretted that so much

---

[1] See Bishop, ii. 118.

acerbity developed in the conflict which Roosevelt had
with high finance. He came at them, they thought,
"with axe and crowbar." [1] But the fault was more with
the financial interests than with the President. They
should have coöperated with him to a certain extent and,
when expediency would not permit them to go further
they might have managed matters so that the fighting
instinct would not have developed in Roosevelt. They
opposed his re-nomination and re-election in a manner
irritating and yet the results were abortive. For they
accomplished naught but an increase of the bitterness,
as Roosevelt was human and did not love his personal
opponents. And, on the other hand, it did not contribute to the amenity of the discussion for the rich men to
be told that they were corrupt and if they did not behave
they would be sent to jail. Nor were they pleased with
his invention of the Ananias Club in which he put all men
who, according to him, did not tell the truth. It was
abundantly easy in the way of retort to point out the
inconsistencies of Roosevelt himself. No man could
speak as often and as much as he did covering a series
of years and be absolutely consistent; but he was always
truthful and sincere and the discovery of his inconsistencies did not in any way affect his hold upon the mass.

Elihu Root was a good medium between the President
and the financial interests. Devoted to Roosevelt he
could at the same time see the point of view of high finance and when he said to a wealthy crowd in New York
City that the President was "really the great conservator of property and rights," [2] he spoke with a wise fore-

---

[1] Emerson, Representative Men, Lecture iv.
[2] I am aware that this is a quasi-repetition.

sight of the future. No stronger statement of the right of private property can be found than in Roosevelt's public and private utterances. He thoroughly believed that the protection of private property and the family were the bases of civilization. Thoroughly opposed to socialism, the difference between him and the financial men was that they believed in a more intense form of individualism than he did. He thought that the State had certain powers which they denied. He also believed that the President did not require a specific authorization of the Constitution to act in a manner that he conceived to be the welfare of the public. When he talked of bad corporations and good corporations, of good men of wealth and bad men, the question who should decide between the two arose. Roosevelt arrogated to himself the decision but at the same time he said, "Our judges, as a whole, are brave and upright men." [1] He believed that the reason of the failure of the Grecian, Roman, and Italian republics was that when the rich got the power, they exploited the poor, and when the poor got the power they plundered the rich. He was to stand midway between the two and prevent excess. A favorite expression of his was he desired to give everybody a square deal. He quoted from Burke with the assurance that such was his policy: "If I cannot reform with equity, I will not reform at all. . . . There is a state to preserve as well as a state to reform." Roosevelt added, "The bulk of our business is honestly done; . . . the great mass of railroad securities rest upon safe and solid

---

[1] Special Message to Congress, Jan. 31, 1908. *Review of Reviews* ed., 628.

foundations." [1]   As high finance and Roosevelt agreed
upon these general propositions they ought to have made
a basis for a certain coöperation. Of course it is difficult
to say how far men will coöperate when they apply
general truths to concrete cases. The President was
thoroughly satisfied with the Speaker, Joseph Cannon,
for his work in the Congress that adjourned in 1906, writing, "With Mr. Cannon as Speaker the House has accomplished a literally phenomenal amount of good work" [2];
but two years later he was far from being content with
the Speaker.

So far as I know his liking for Andrew Jackson first became public during his trip down the Mississippi River in
the autumn of 1907, but at the Hermitage where Jackson
lived and died it became enthusiasm. "Andrew Jackson
was an American," he said.   "I draw a sharp distinction
between Old Hickory and a great many other Presidents.
The Hermitage was the home of one of the three or
four greatest Presidents this Union has ever had. . . .
Andrew Jackson was a mighty National figure." [3] From
this time on Roosevelt was possessed with this admiration that he many times set forth. Before 1907 he con-
trasted the Washington-Lincoln theory of the presidential powers with the Jefferson-Buchanan; but afterwards
it became the Jackson-Lincoln example to justify his
use of the office. He may have been attracted to Jackson on account of his war against the financial magnates
of the country, and through his forceful personality, [4]

---

[1] May 30, 1907, *Review of Reviews* ed., 1255, 1263.
[2] Aug. 18, 1906, ibid., 801.
[3] *Review of Reviews* ed., 1458.
[4] See Life of Jackson, Bassett, chap. xxvii; Channing, History of the
United States, v. 356, 379, 388, 401.

but it was inconsistent with his admiration for Jackson
to remark, "I think the worship of Jefferson a discredit
to my country," as in my opinion he was, "not even excepting Buchanan, the most incompetent chief executive
we ever had." But Roosevelt always stuck to Lincoln.
"I like to see in my mind's eye," he said in the White
House, "the gaunt form of Lincoln stalking through these
halls." [1]

Roosevelt was a broad-minded man. Intensely devoted to the Northern cause he could see the other side.
Of Lee he said, "General Lee has left us the memory not
merely of his extraordinary skill as a general, his daunt-
less courage and high leadership in campaign and battle,
but also of that sound greatness of soul characteristic
of those who most readily recognize the obligations of
civic duty." [2] Many would have joined him in this tribute to Lee but it was noteworthy that a Republican
President should speak of Jefferson Davis as the favorite
son of the South, and should add, "The whole country
grows to feel the same stern pride in the deeds alike of
those who fought so valiantly for what they believed to
be right and triumphed, and of those who fought so valiantly for what they, with equal sincerity, believed to
be right, and lost." [3]

John Morley, who spent a number of days with Roosevelt at the White House, said of him, "He has many of
Napoleon's qualities — indomitable courage, tireless per-
severance, great capacity for leadership — and one thing

---

[1] Historical Essays, 235; Life of Roosevelt, Thayer, 273. Regarding Jefferson see Channing, History of the United States, iv, 248; v. 453;
John T. Morse, Jefferson, 215, 264, 302.
[2] Bishop, ii, 69.
[3] Vicksburg, Oct. 21, 1907, *Review of Reviews* ed., 1442.

that Napoleon never had — high moral purpose!"
James Bryce said that he had "never in any country
seen a more eager, high-minded and efficient set of public
servants, men more useful and creditable to their country
than the men then doing the work of the American Government in Washington and in the field." [1]

Roosevelt was rarely, if ever, impulsive in action. Senator Eugene Hale, who was generally among the Republican opposition, said that "in all his very long experience
in public life he had never known a man who sought counsel so much as did President Roosevelt. And yet,"
he added, "most people think he is impulsive and won't
even listen to advice, much less take it." [2]

He was a lover of beauty as his association with Saint
Gaudens, Francis D. Millet and Charles McKim abundantly shows.

Albert J. Beveridge, who knew Roosevelt intimately
said, "Had he lived in the age of chivalry he would have
been called Great Heart." [3] More than ten years previously Roosevelt himself had written, "Abraham Lincoln is the ideal Great Heart of public life." [4]

Taking him by and large Roosevelt was a great man.
He would have made an ideal war President. But as
he himself wrote: "When I left the Presidency I finished
seven and a half years of administration, during which
not one shot had been fired against a foreign foe. We
were at absolute peace and there was no nation in the
world with whom a war-cloud threatened, no nation in

---

[1] Life of Roosevelt, Lewis, 258.
[2] A. J. Beveridge's Eulogy, *Sat. Eve. Post*, Apr. 5, 1919; see Henry
Cabot Lodge's address, Feb. 9, 1919, 47.
[3] Feb. 10, 1919, Boston *Evening Transcript*.   [4] Bishop, ii. 115.

the world whom we had wronged, or from whom we had anything to fear." His carrying out of "the homely old adage," "Speak softly and carry a big stick: you will go far" had proved effective during his administration.[1]

Roosevelt had a wonderful brain; an indomitable capacity for work. His mistakes were few; his accomplishments many. Rudyard Kipling wrote thus to Brander Matthews in 1910: "I saw him for a hectic half hour in London and a little at Oxford. Take care of him. He is scarce and valuable."[2]

---

[1] The first mention that Bishop found was while he was governor, i. 240.

[2] Bishop, ii. 259.

I am much indebted to Edward L. Burlingame, Charles Scribner's Sons, Joseph B. Bishop and William R. Thayer.

D. M. Matteson has rendered me valuable assistance in historical research. I acknowledge the aid of my secretary, Miss Wyman, that of Charles K. Bolton, librarian, Miss Wildman, Miss Fowle and Miss Gerald, assistants of the Boston Athenæum. I am indebted to George A. Myers, of Cleveland for useful suggestions.

INDEX

401

tions, Roosevelt's influence, 307; credit to Roosevelt, 307, 308; Roosevelt on envoys, 309.

Ryan, T. F., and panic of 1907, 352.

SAGASTA, P. M., and Cuba, character, 47.

Saint Gaudens, Augustus, and Roosevelt, 398.

St. Louis World Fair, 300, 301; Congress of Arts and Science, 301.

Salvation Army, support of Hanna, 281.

Sampson, W. E., *Maine* inquiry, 50; war command, 81; and Shafter, absence at battle of Santiago, 89, 90; blockade, 90; and the victory, 92, 93 n.; on rescue of prisoners, 94; on the *Oregon's* voyage, 98 n.

San Domingo, Roosevelt and financial administration, 318.

San Juan Hill, battle, 85–87.

Sanitation, in Cuba, 178; at Canal Zone, 278.

Santiago, Cuba, Cervera at, 82; American military expedition, mismanagement, 82–87; battle of El Caney and San Juan Hill, 85–87; demoralization of American commander, 87; sortie of Spanish fleet, 88, 89; friction between American naval and military forces, 89, 90; American blockade and naval orders, 90; naval battle, 91, 92; credit for naval victory, 92, 93; decisiveness of naval victory, results, 93, 95; American humanity, 94; surrender of city, 95.

Schofield, J. M., and coal strike, 242.

Schurman, J. G., Philippine Commission, 190, 193.

Schurz, Carl, in campaign of 1896, 24; of 1900, 142; as anti-Imperialist, 188, 190, 194; and Reconstruction, 392.

Schurz nuggets, 24.

Schwab, C. M., on American steel rails, 117; and steel merger, 151; and Carnegie, 152 n.

Scott, T. A., and Carnegie, 146.

Sectionalism, disappearance, 169.

Shafter, W. R., expedition command, unfitness, 85; demoralized, 87, 90 n.; and Sampson, 89.

Sherman, J. S., and Harriman, 332; nomination for Vice-President, 380 n.

Sherman, John, Hanna's support (1884, 1888), 4; appointment as Secretary of State, unfitness, 31, 41; candor of appointment, 32–34; appointment and Spanish War, 35; relegation, resignation, 41, 42.

Sherman Anti-Trust Act. *See* Northern Securities; Trusts.

Silver, question in Republican Convention (1896), 13–16; Democratic plank for free, 17, 18; as issue in campaign, 18–20; Bryan's campaign presentation, 20–22, 28; Democratic campaign literature, 22, 23; Republican literature, 24-26; Senate resolution for payment of bonds in, 36; failure of international bimetallism, 37; in campaign of 1900, 132, 136; eliminated as issue (1904), 292. *See also* Gold standard.

Skagway, as port for Klondike, 255.

Smith, A. H., and Boxer indemnity fund, 319.

Smith, C. E., retirement from Cabinet, 219 n.

Smith, Goldwin, on Bryan, 22, 28.

Smyth, W. E., and reclamation, 355 n.

South, and Booker Washington incident, 229, 230; Roosevelt's attitude, 232, 361, 397.

South America, Root's tour, 342, 343.

South Carolina Interstate and West Indian Exposition, 231.

South Improvement Company, 160 n.

Spalding, J. L., Anthracite Coal Commission, 243, 244, 246.

Spanish War, and appointment of Sherman, 35; McKinley and Cuban problem, 41; appointment of minister to Spain, 42; Cuban Insurrection, Weyler's reconcentration policy, 44; Cleveland and Cuban belligerency, 44, 45; Congress and belligerency (1907), conduct of insurgents, 46; McKinley's waiting policy, 46, 48; Sagasta's reform measures, 47; disturbances in Havana, sending of the *Maine*, 47, 48; de Lôme's indiscretion, 48; destruction of the *Maine*, cause, influence, 49–51, 55–58, 65; Proctor's speech on Cuban conditions, 51–53; Day's dispatch on reconcentration,

This Index was made for me by D. M. Matteson.

Date Due